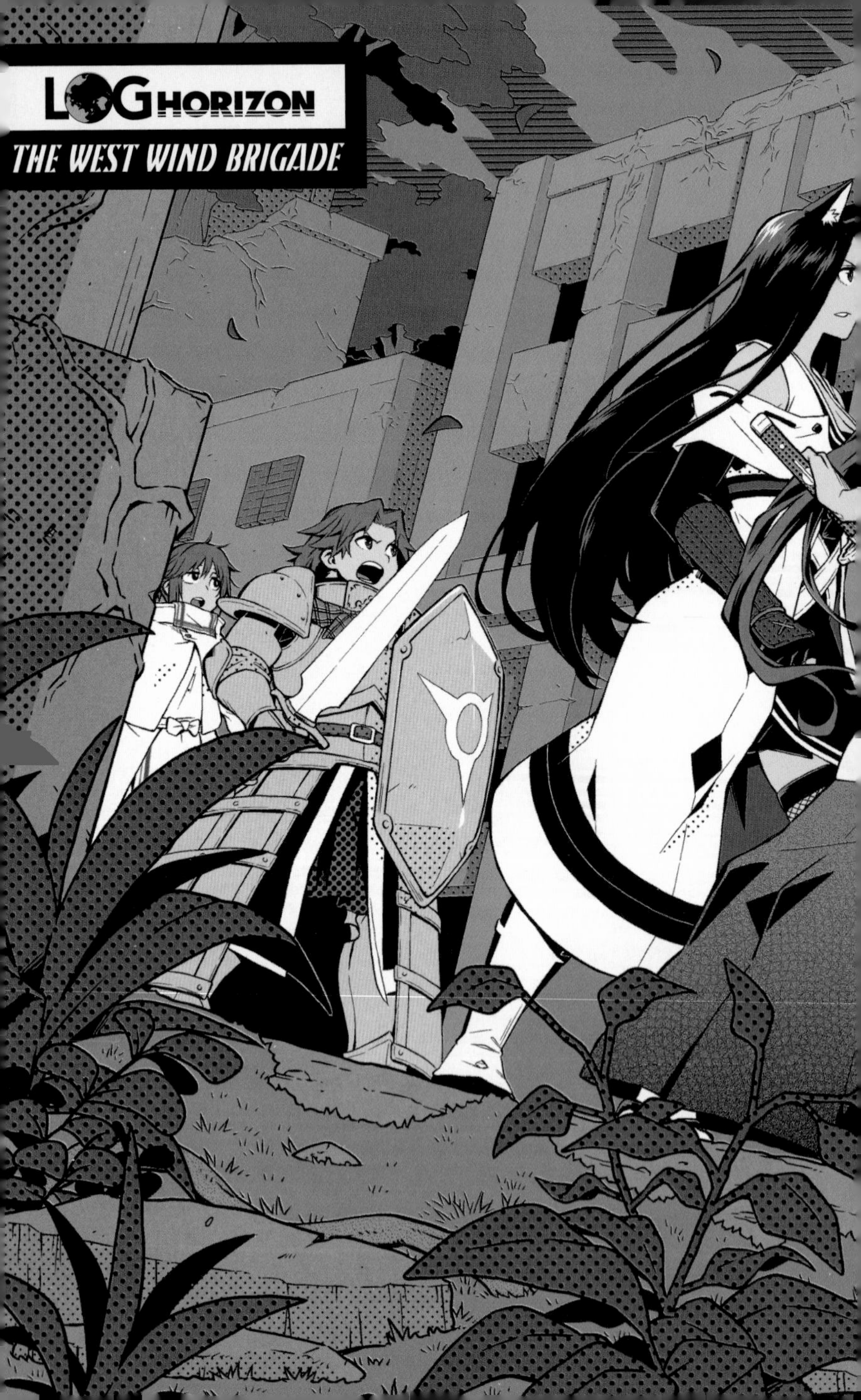
LOG HORIZON
THE WEST WIND BRIGADE

[CONTENTS]

LOG HORIZON **THE WEST WIND BRIGADE**

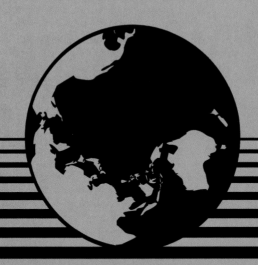

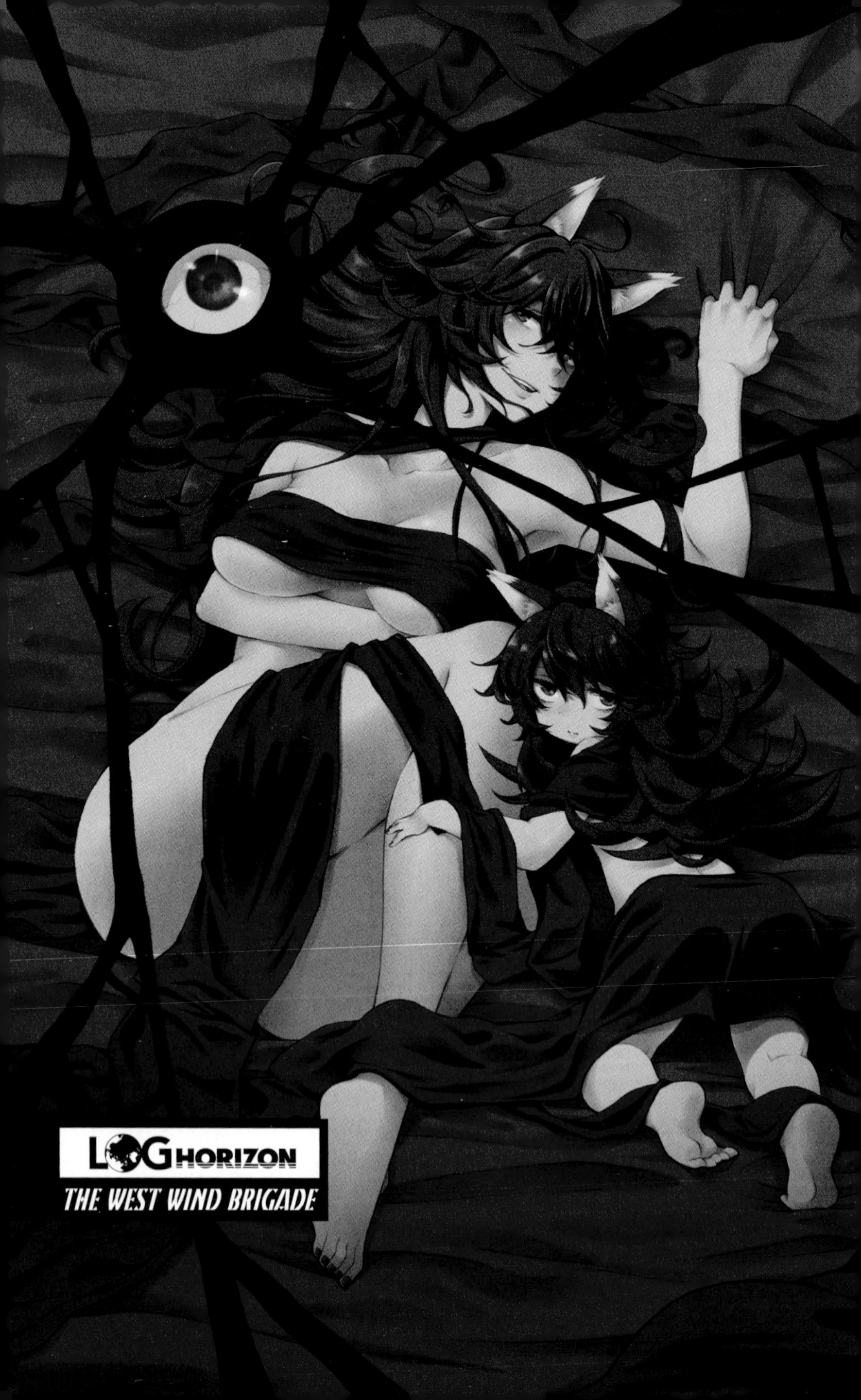
LOG HORIZON
THE WEST WIND BRIGADE

CHAPTER : 48 Equipment Hunter

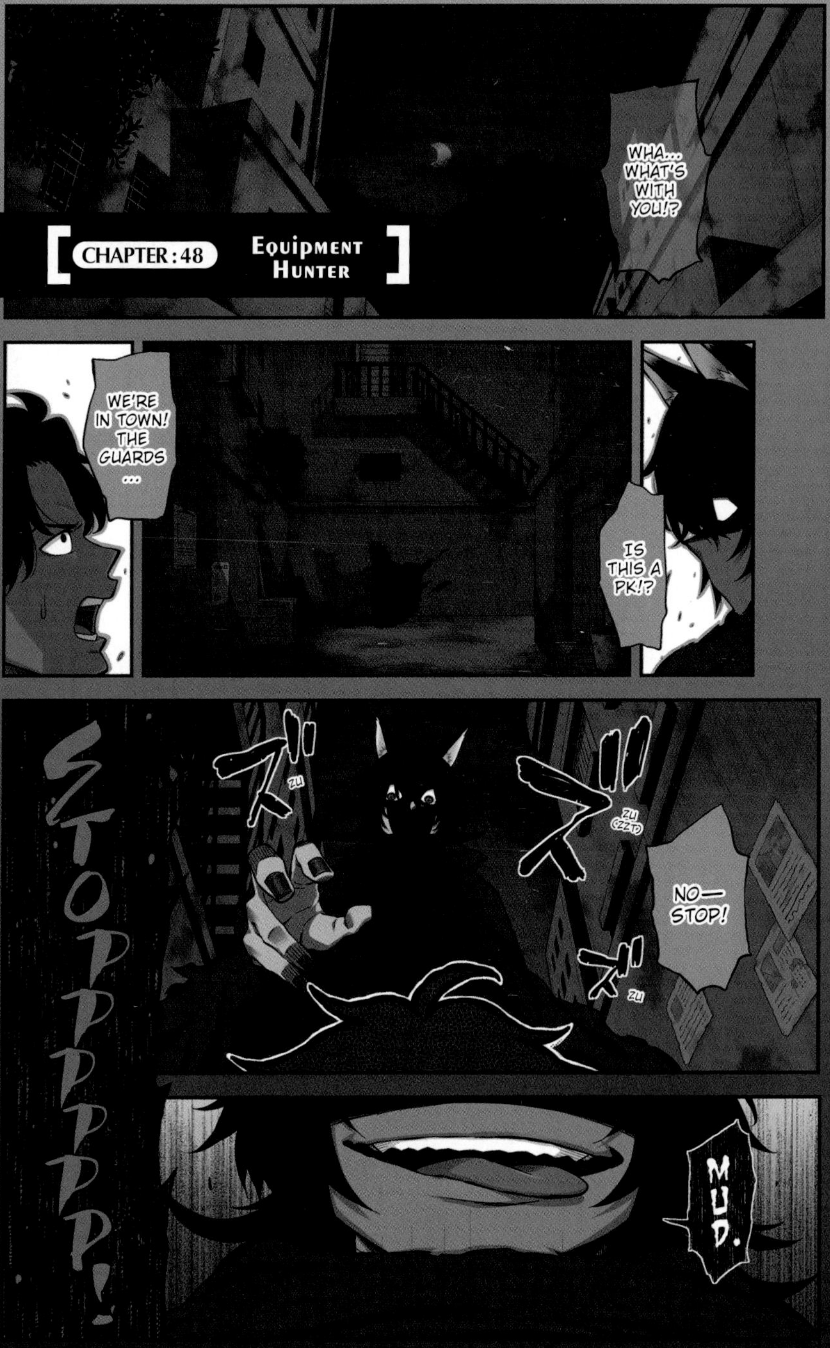
WHA... WHAT'S WITH YOU!?
IS THIS A PK!?
WE'RE IN TOWN! THE GUARDS ...
ZU (ZZT)
ZU
NO— STOP!
ZU
MUD.
STOPPPPPPP!

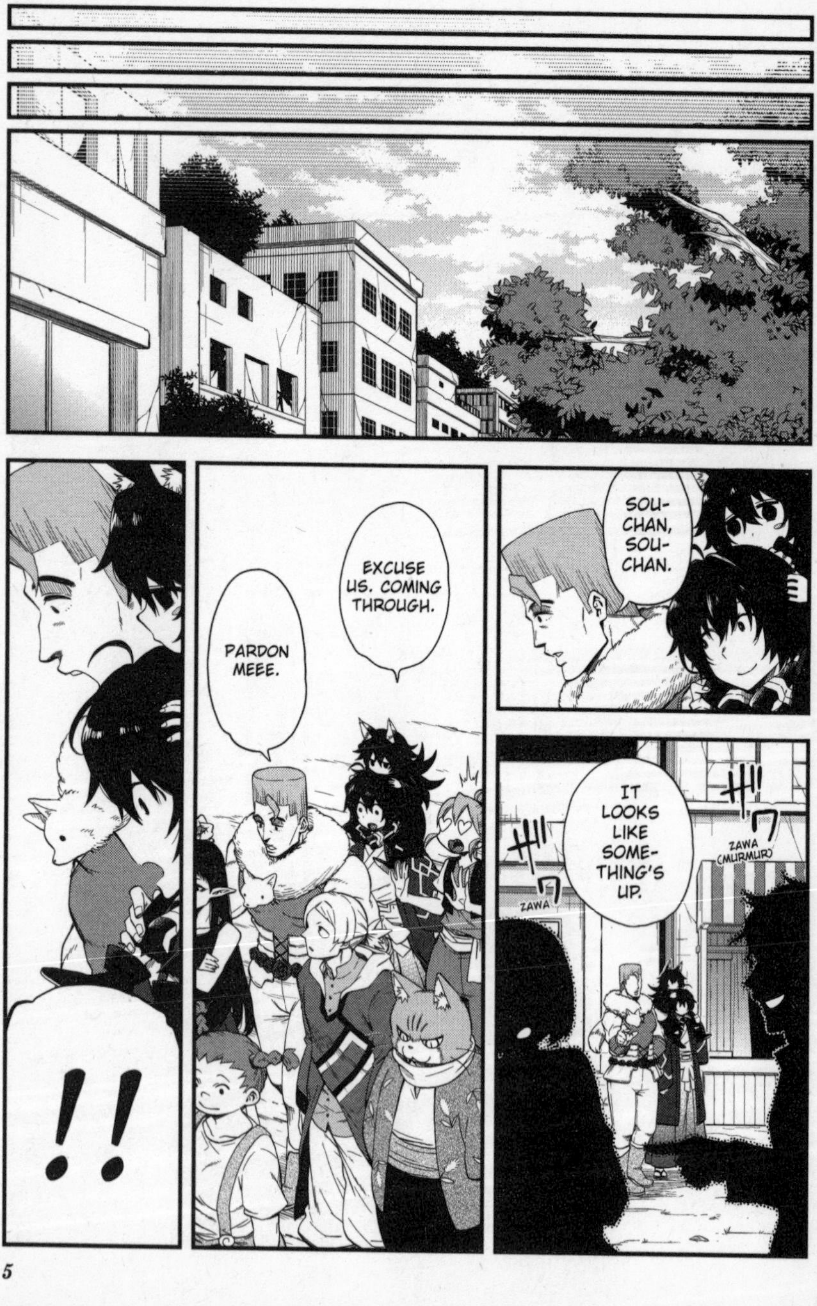
SOU-CHAN, SOU-CHAN.
ZAWA (MURMUR)
IT LOOKS LIKE SOME-THING'S UP.
ZAWA
EXCUSE US. COMING THROUGH.
PARDON MEEE.
!!

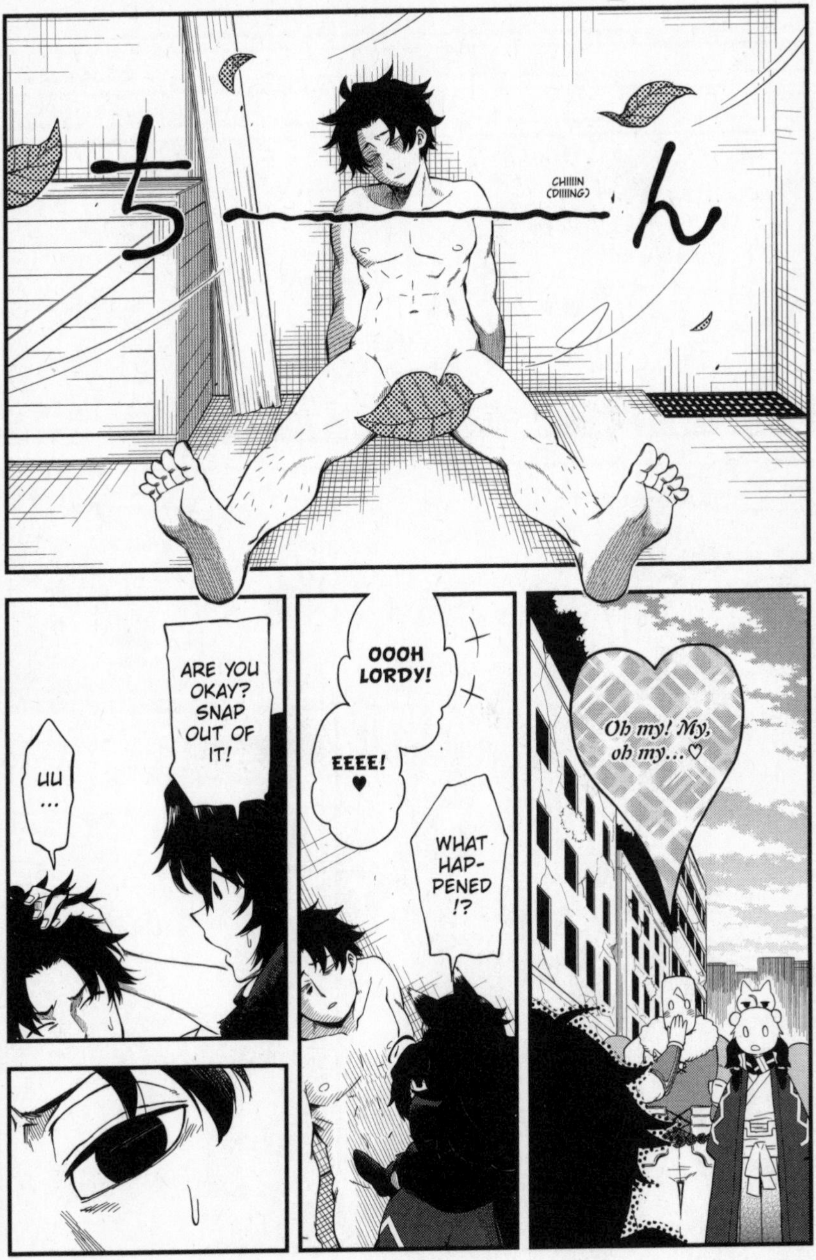
ち——ん
CHIIIIN (DIIIING)
Oh my! My, oh my...♡
OOOH LORDY!
EEEE! ♥
WHAT HAP-PENED !?
ARE YOU OKAY? SNAP OUT OF IT!
UU ...

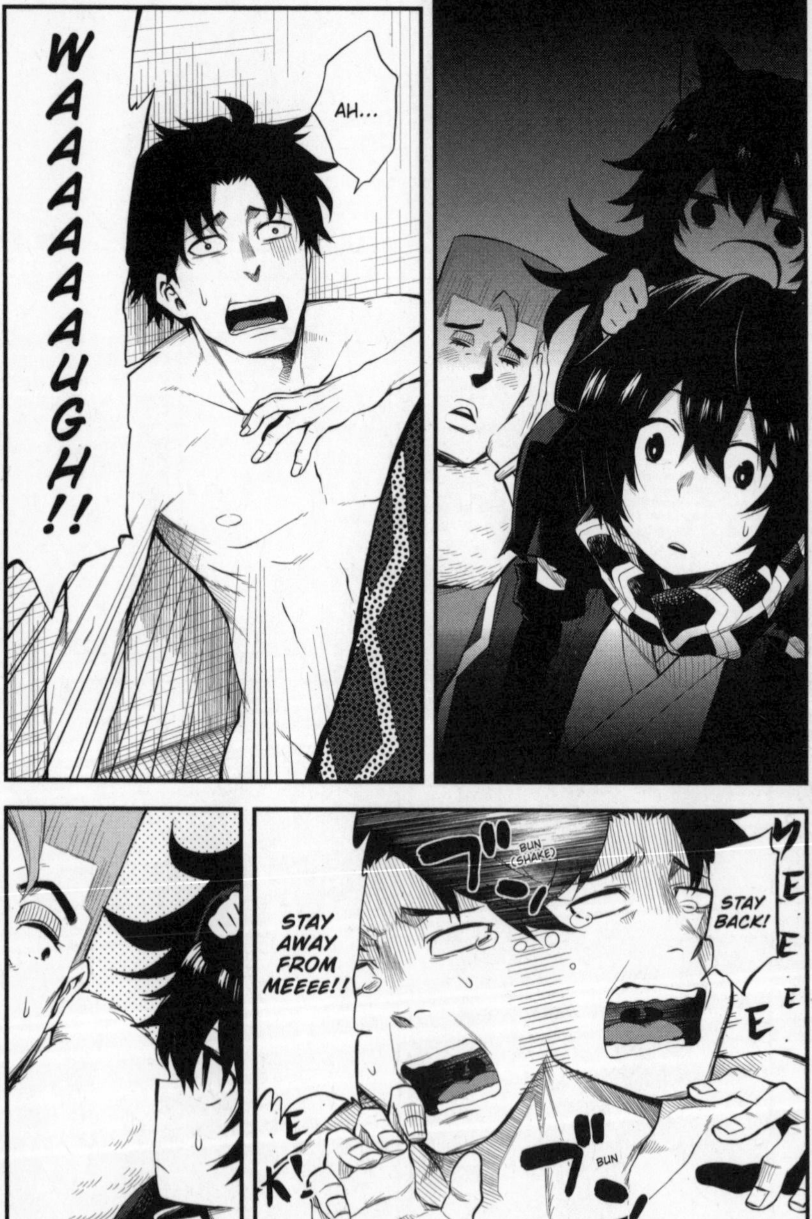

AH...
WAAAAAAUGH!!
STAY BACK!
EEEEE
BUN (SHAKE)
STAY AWAY FROM MEEEE!!
BUN
EEK!

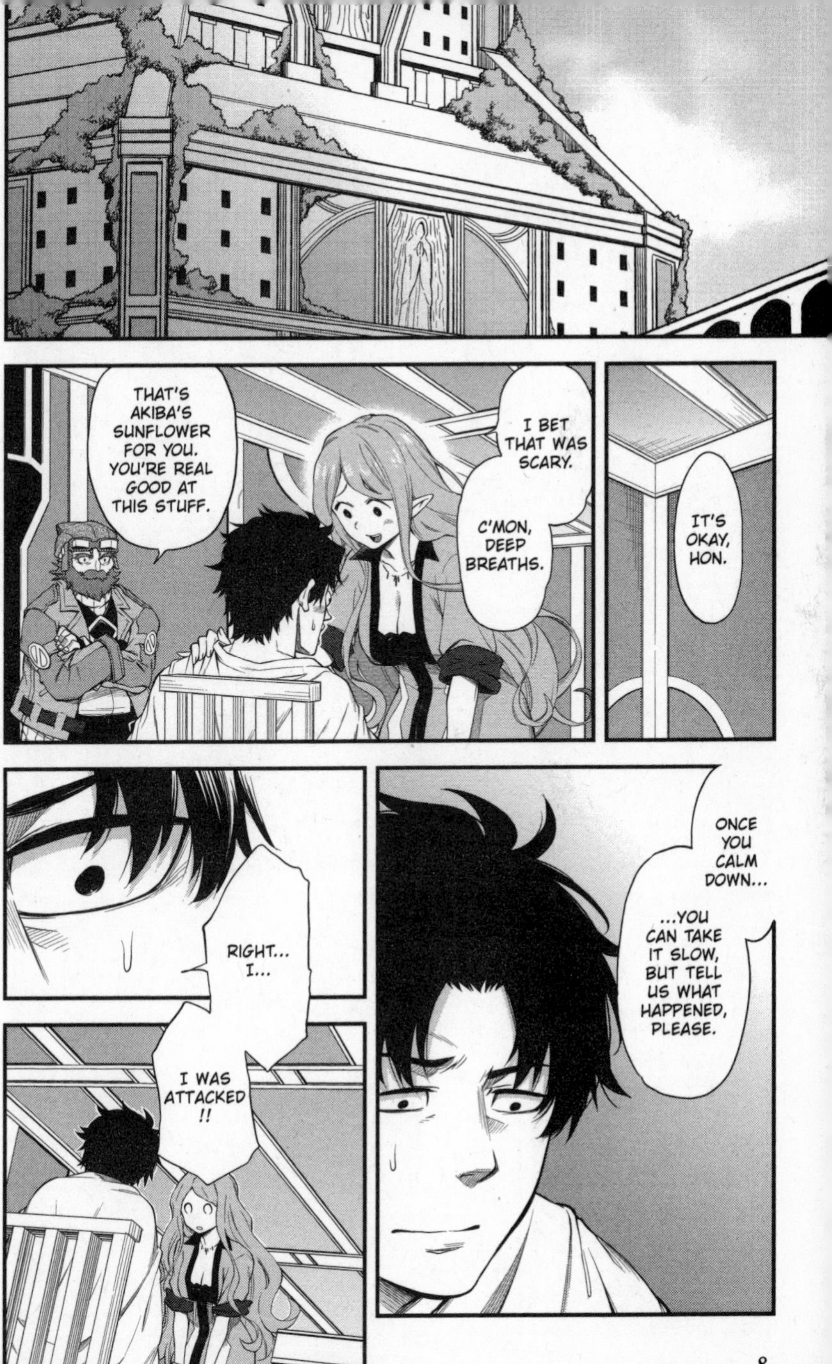
IT'S OKAY, HON.
I BET THAT WAS SCARY.
C'MON, DEEP BREATHS.
THAT'S AKIBA'S SUNFLOWER FOR YOU. YOU'RE REAL GOOD AT THIS STUFF.
ONCE YOU CALM DOWN...
...YOU CAN TAKE IT SLOW, BUT TELL US WHAT HAPPENED, PLEASE.
RIGHT... I...
I WAS ATTACKED!!

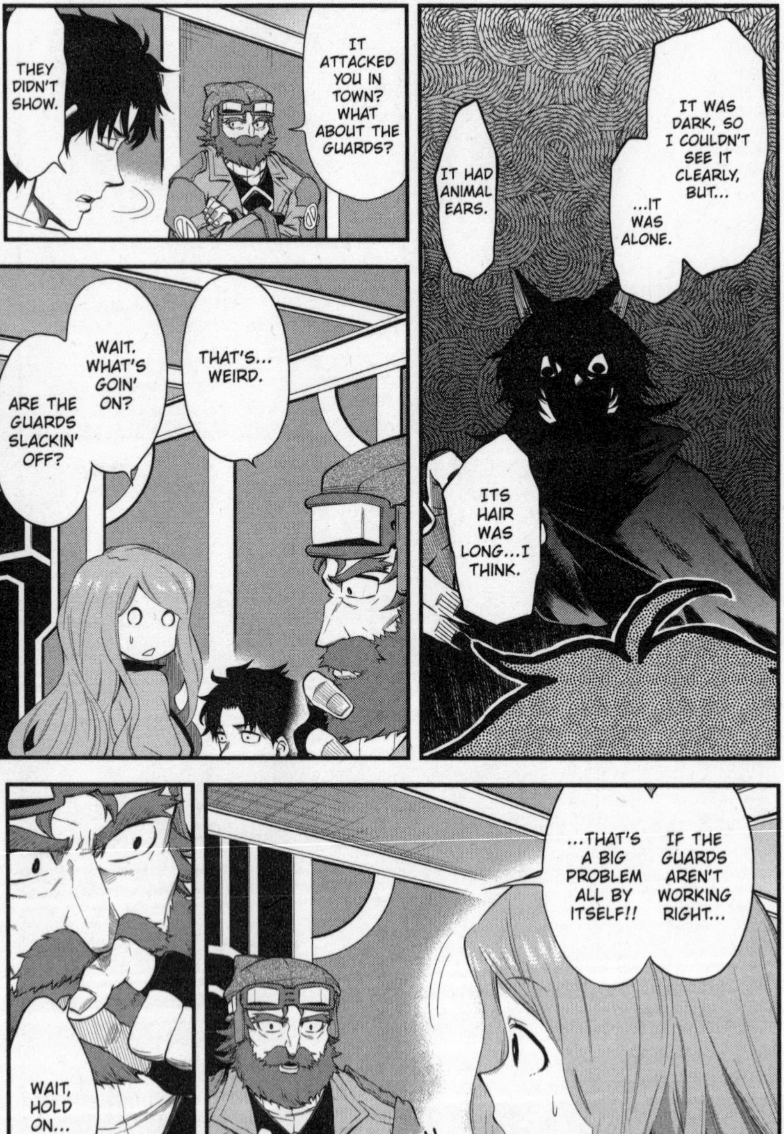
IT WAS DARK, SO I COULDN'T SEE IT CLEARLY, BUT...
...IT WAS ALONE.
IT HAD ANIMAL EARS.
ITS HAIR WAS LONG...I THINK.
IT ATTACKED YOU IN TOWN? WHAT ABOUT THE GUARDS?
THEY DIDN'T SHOW.
THAT'S... WEIRD.
WAIT. WHAT'S GOIN' ON?
ARE THE GUARDS SLACKIN' OFF?
IF THE GUARDS AREN'T WORKING RIGHT...
...THAT'S A BIG PROBLEM ALL BY ITSELF!!
UH-HUH.
WAIT, HOLD ON...

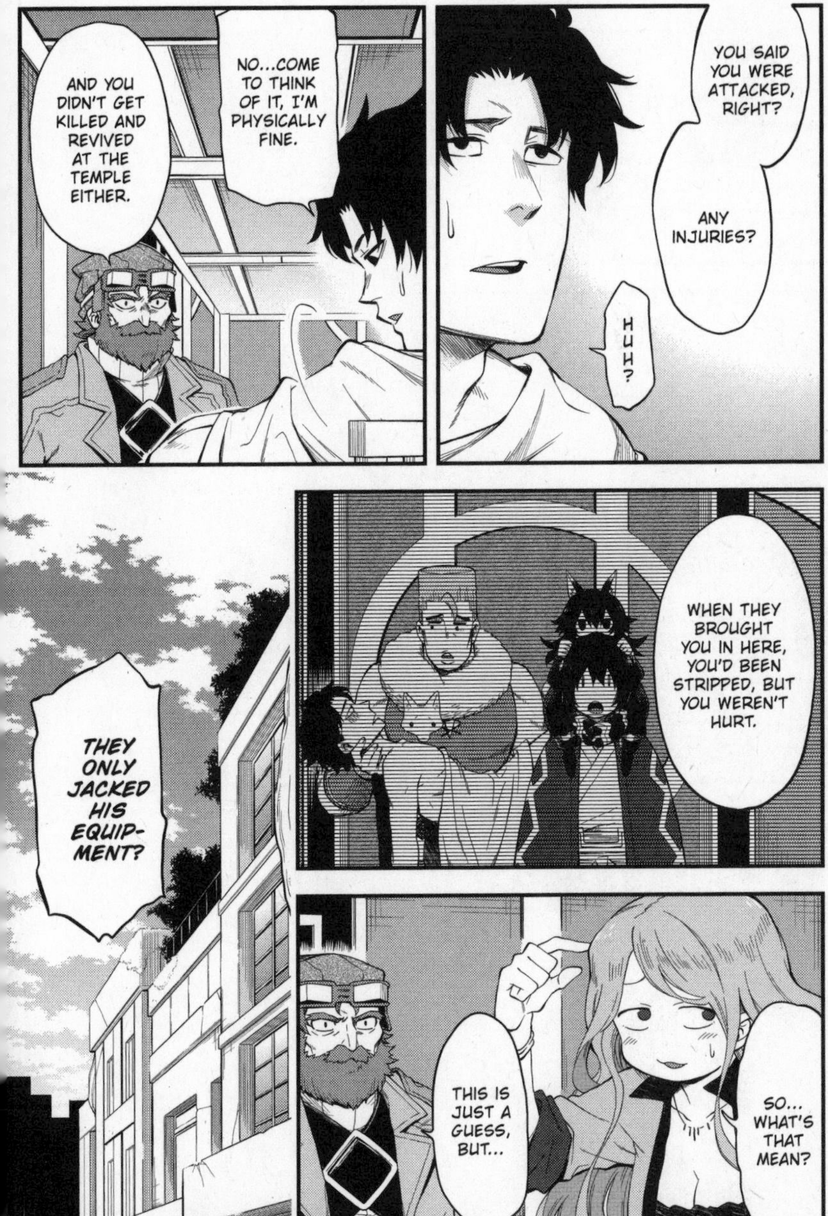
YOU SAID YOU WERE ATTACKED, RIGHT?
ANY INJURIES?
HUH?
NO...COME TO THINK OF IT, I'M PHYSICALLY FINE.
AND YOU DIDN'T GET KILLED AND REVIVED AT THE TEMPLE EITHER.
WHEN THEY BROUGHT YOU IN HERE, YOU'D BEEN STRIPPED, BUT YOU WEREN'T HURT.
SO... WHAT'S THAT MEAN?
THIS IS JUST A GUESS, BUT...
THEY ONLY JACKED HIS EQUIPMENT?

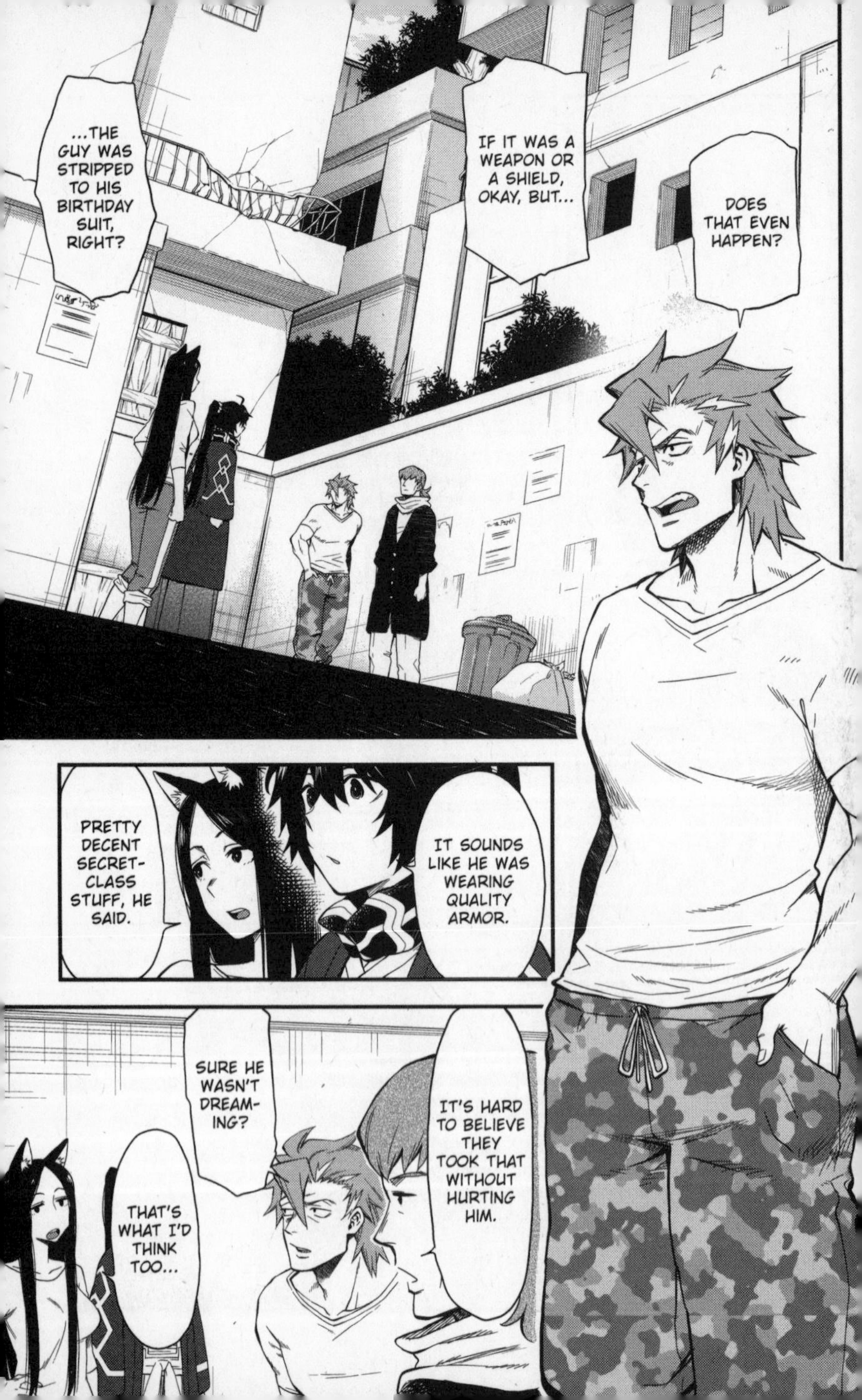
DOES THAT EVEN HAPPEN?
IF IT WAS A WEAPON OR A SHIELD, OKAY, BUT...
...THE GUY WAS STRIPPED TO HIS BIRTHDAY SUIT, RIGHT?
IT SOUNDS LIKE HE WAS WEARING QUALITY ARMOR.
PRETTY DECENT SECRET-CLASS STUFF, HE SAID.
IT'S HARD TO BELIEVE THEY TOOK THAT WITHOUT HURTING HIM.
SURE HE WASN'T DREAM-ING?
THAT'S WHAT I'D THINK TOO...

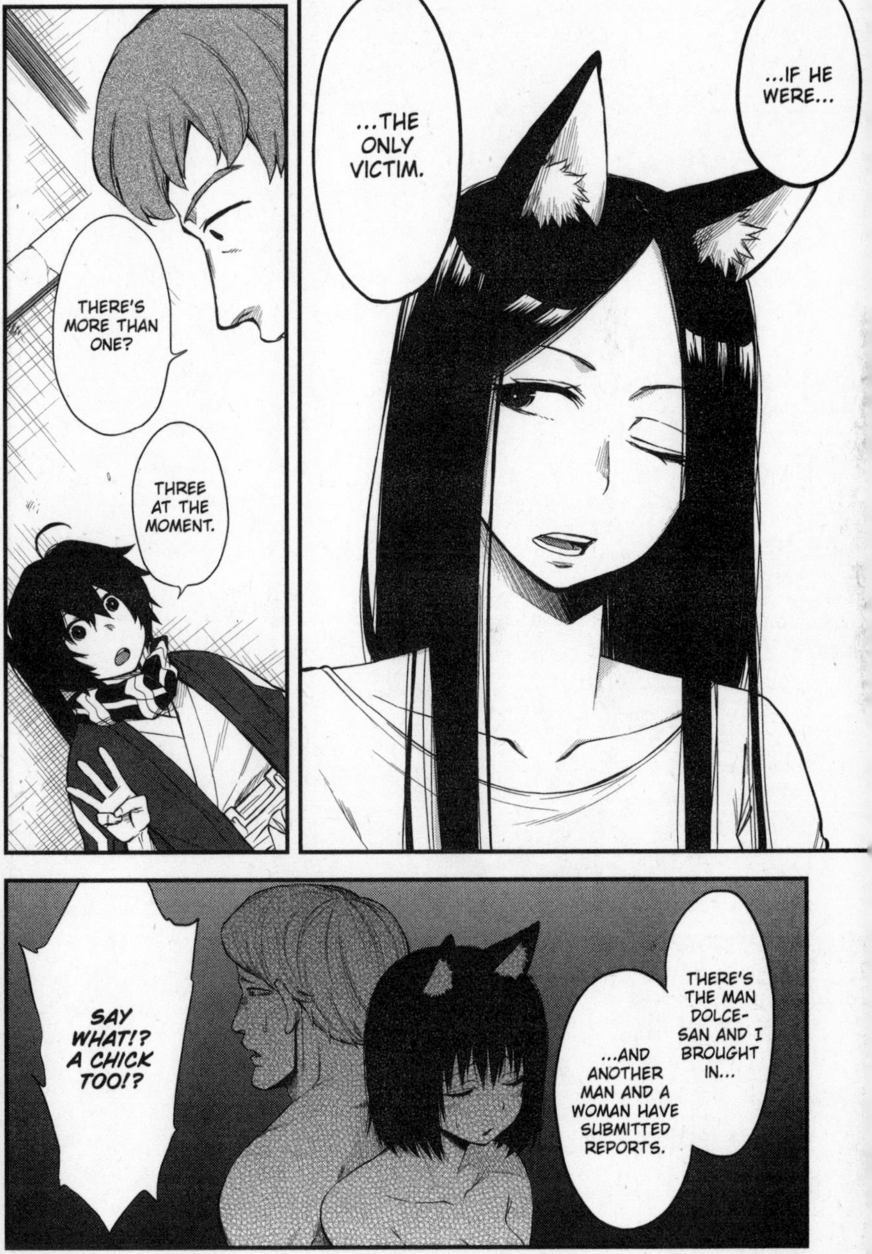
...IF HE WERE...
...THE ONLY VICTIM.
THERE'S MORE THAN ONE?
THREE AT THE MOMENT.
THERE'S THE MAN DOLCE-SAN AND I BROUGHT IN...
...AND ANOTHER MAN AND A WOMAN HAVE SUBMITTED REPORTS.
SAY WHAT!? A CHICK TOO!?

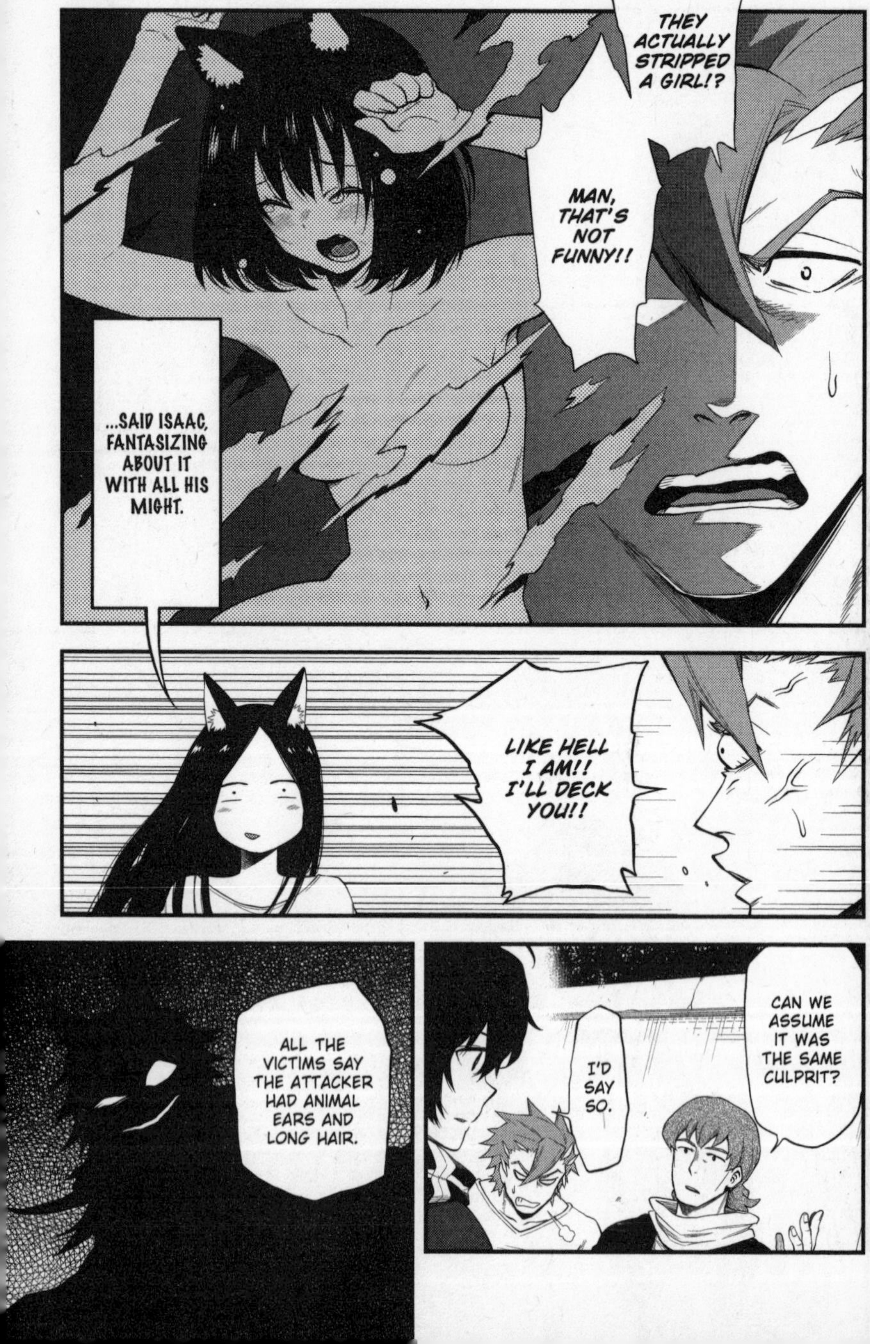
THEY ACTUALLY STRIPPED A GIRL!?
MAN, THAT'S NOT FUNNY!!
...SAID ISAAC, FANTASIZING ABOUT IT WITH ALL HIS MIGHT.
LIKE HELL I AM!! I'LL DECK YOU!!
CAN WE ASSUME IT WAS THE SAME CULPRIT?
I'D SAY SO.
ALL THE VICTIMS SAY THE ATTACKER HAD ANIMAL EARS AND LONG HAIR.

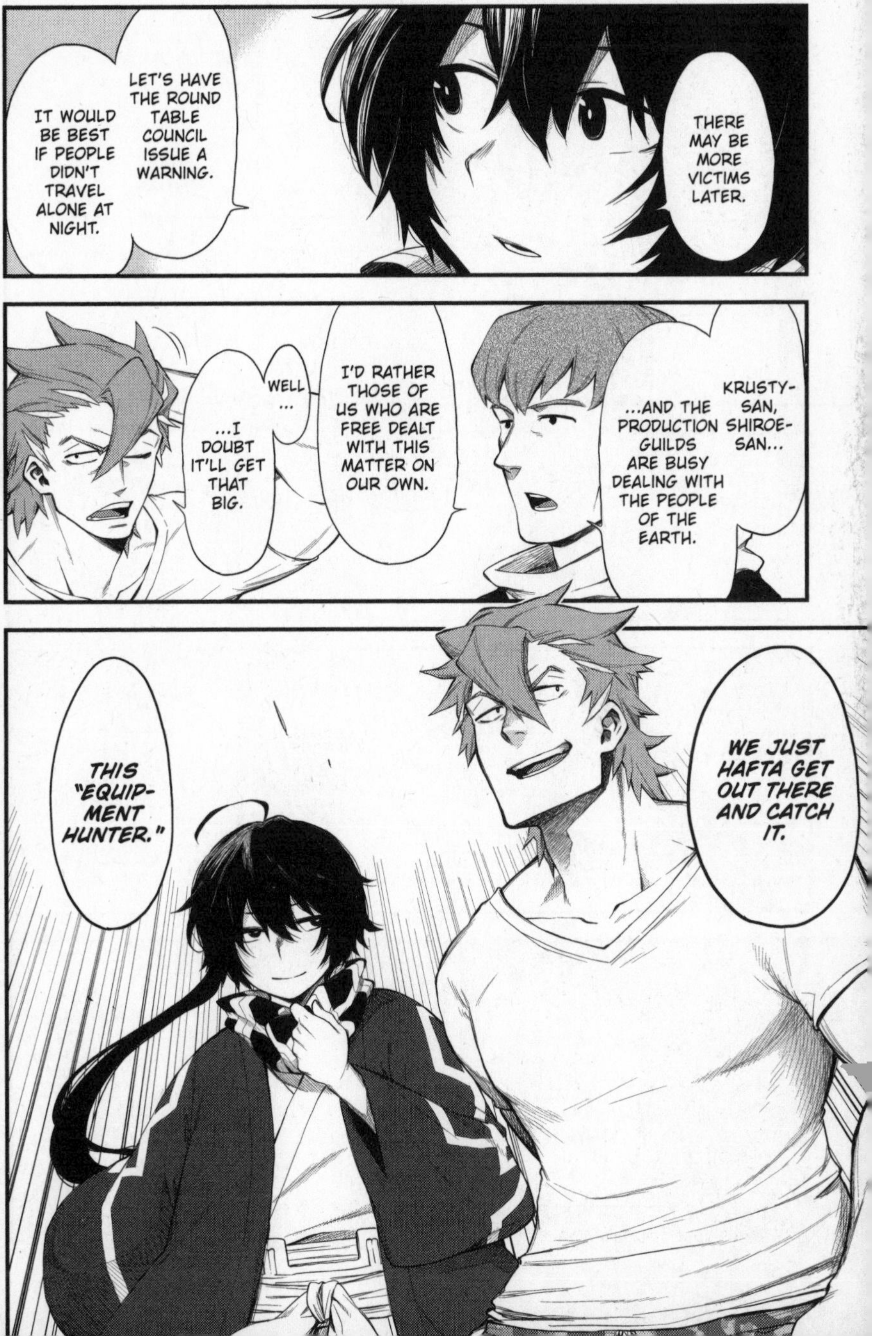
THERE MAY BE MORE VICTIMS LATER.
LET'S HAVE THE ROUND TABLE COUNCIL ISSUE A WARNING.
IT WOULD BE BEST IF PEOPLE DIDN'T TRAVEL ALONE AT NIGHT.
KRUSTY-SAN, SHIROE-SAN...
...AND THE PRODUCTION GUILDS ARE BUSY DEALING WITH THE PEOPLE OF THE EARTH.
I'D RATHER THOSE OF US WHO ARE FREE DEALT WITH THIS MATTER ON OUR OWN.
WELL...
...I DOUBT IT'LL GET THAT BIG.
WE JUST HAFTA GET OUT THERE AND CATCH IT.
THIS "EQUIP-MENT HUNTER."

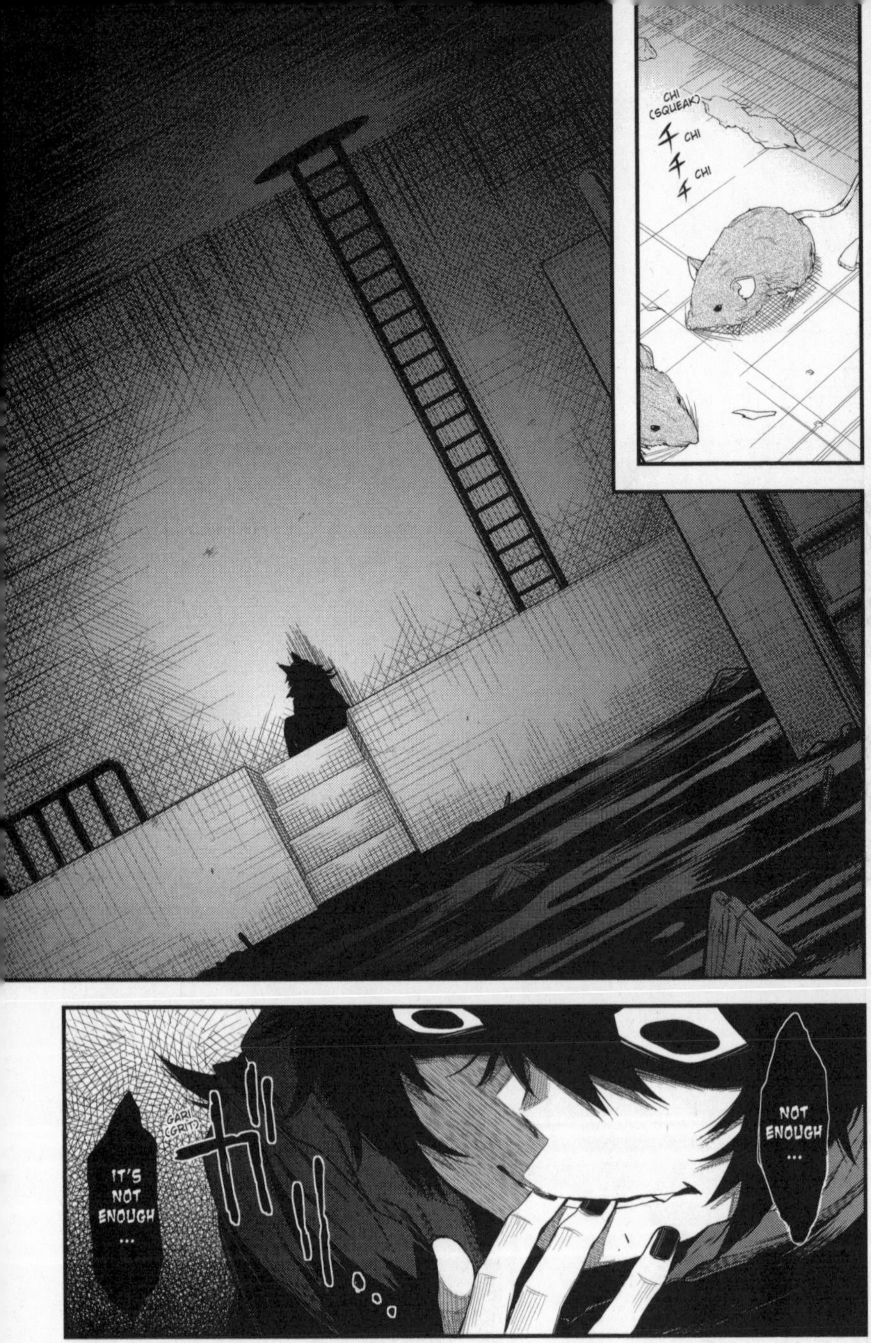
CHI (SQUEAK)
チ
CHI
チ
CHI
チ
NOT ENOUGH ...
GARI (GRIP)
IT'S NOT ENOUGH ...

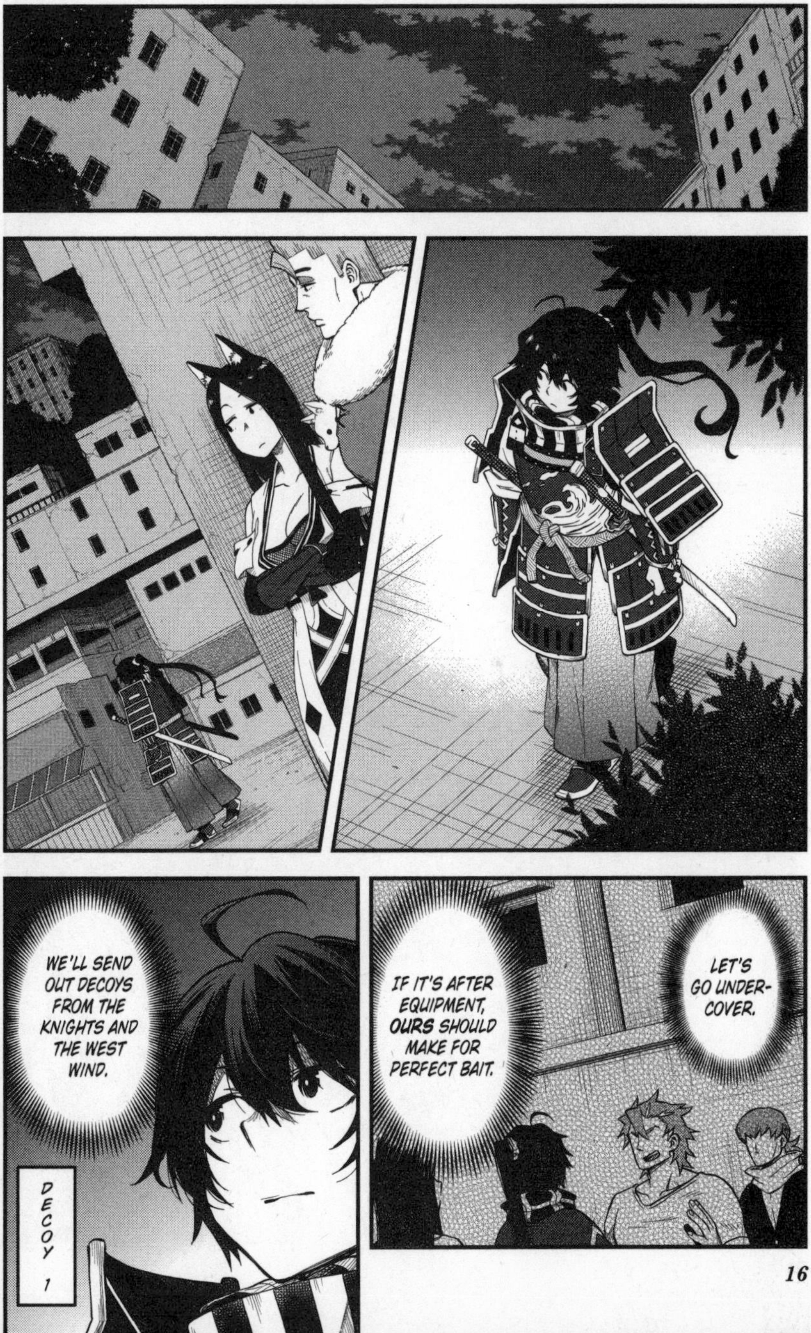
LET'S GO UNDER-COVER.
IF IT'S AFTER EQUIPMENT, **OURS** SHOULD MAKE FOR PERFECT BAIT.
WE'LL SEND OUT DECOYS FROM THE KNIGHTS AND THE WEST WIND.
DECOY 1

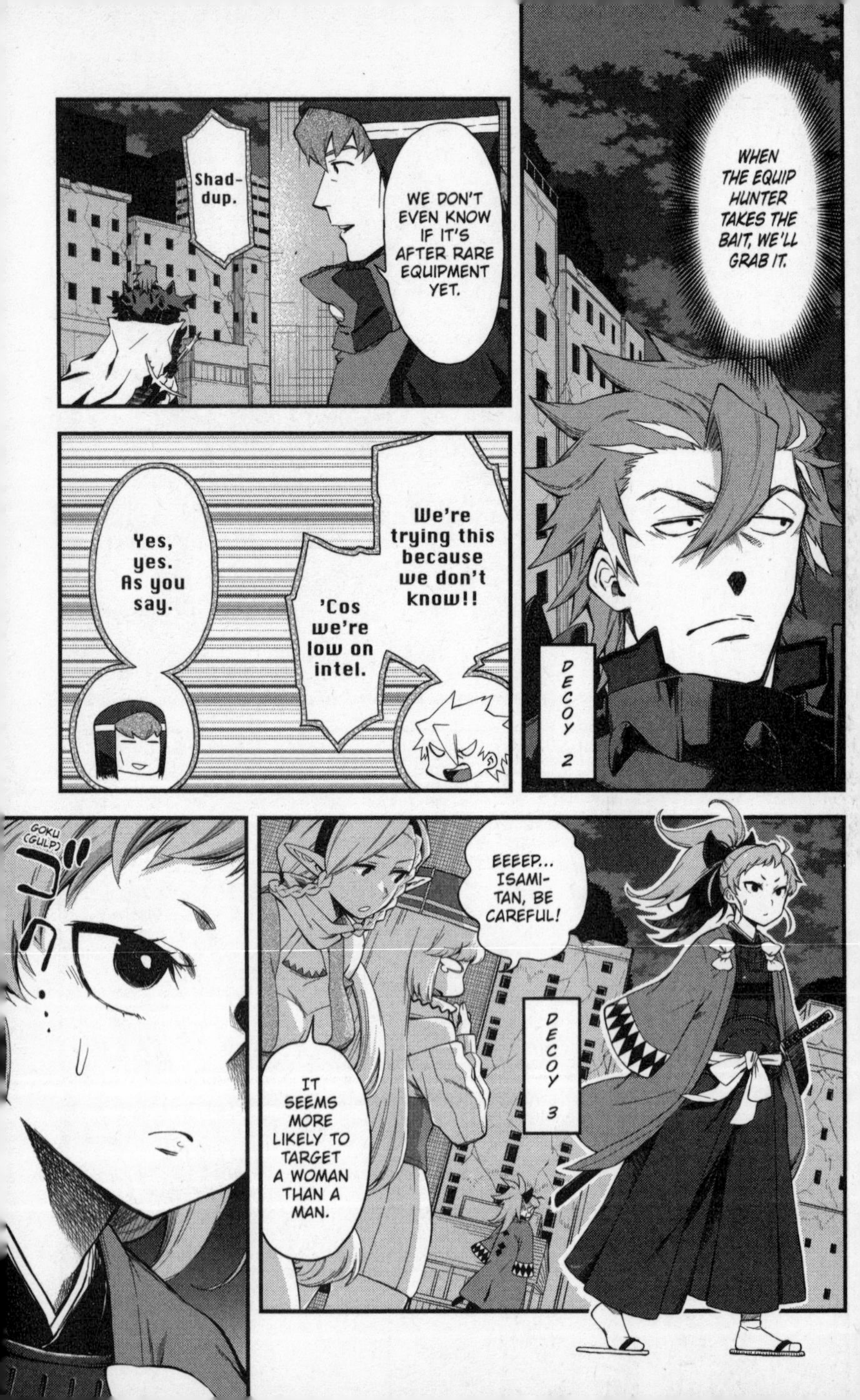
WHEN THE EQUIP HUNTER TAKES THE BAIT, WE'LL GRAB IT.
DECOY 2
WE DON'T EVEN KNOW IF IT'S AFTER RARE EQUIPMENT YET.
Shad-dup.
We're trying this because we don't know!!
'Cos we're low on intel.
Yes, yes. As you say.
EEEEP... ISAMI-TAN, BE CAREFUL!
DECOY 3
IT SEEMS MORE LIKELY TO TARGET A WOMAN THAN A MAN.
GOKU (GULP)

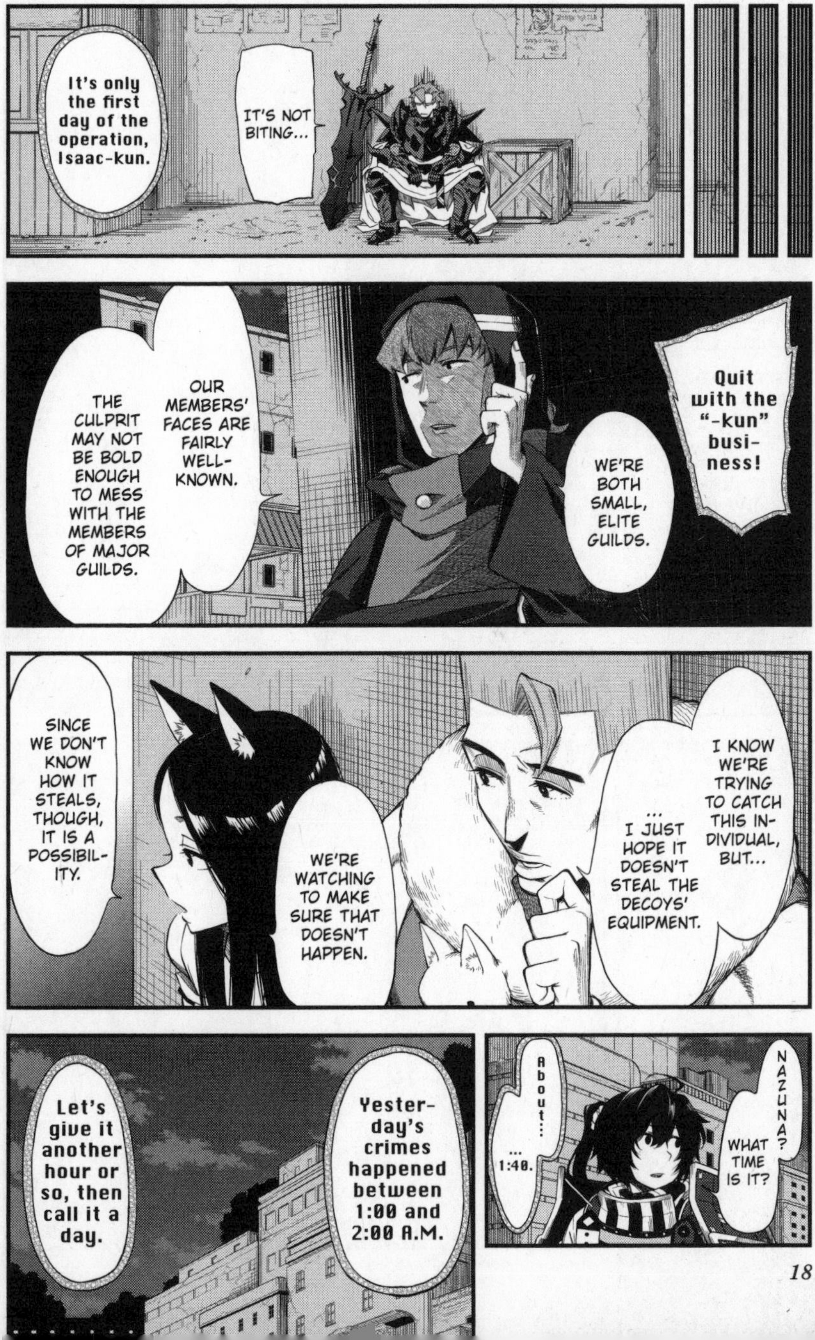
IT'S NOT BITING...
It's only the first day of the operation, Isaac-kun.
Quit with the "-kun" business!
WE'RE BOTH SMALL, ELITE GUILDS.
OUR MEMBERS' FACES ARE FAIRLY WELL-KNOWN.
THE CULPRIT MAY NOT BE BOLD ENOUGH TO MESS WITH THE MEMBERS OF MAJOR GUILDS.
I KNOW WE'RE TRYING TO CATCH THIS INDIVIDUAL, BUT...
... I JUST HOPE IT DOESN'T STEAL THE DECOYS' EQUIPMENT.
WE'RE WATCHING TO MAKE SURE THAT DOESN'T HAPPEN.
SINCE WE DON'T KNOW HOW IT STEALS, THOUGH, IT IS A POSSIBILITY.
NAZUNA? WHAT TIME IS IT?
About...
... 1:40.
Yesterday's crimes happened between 1:00 and 2:00 A.M.
Let's give it another hour or so, then call it a day.

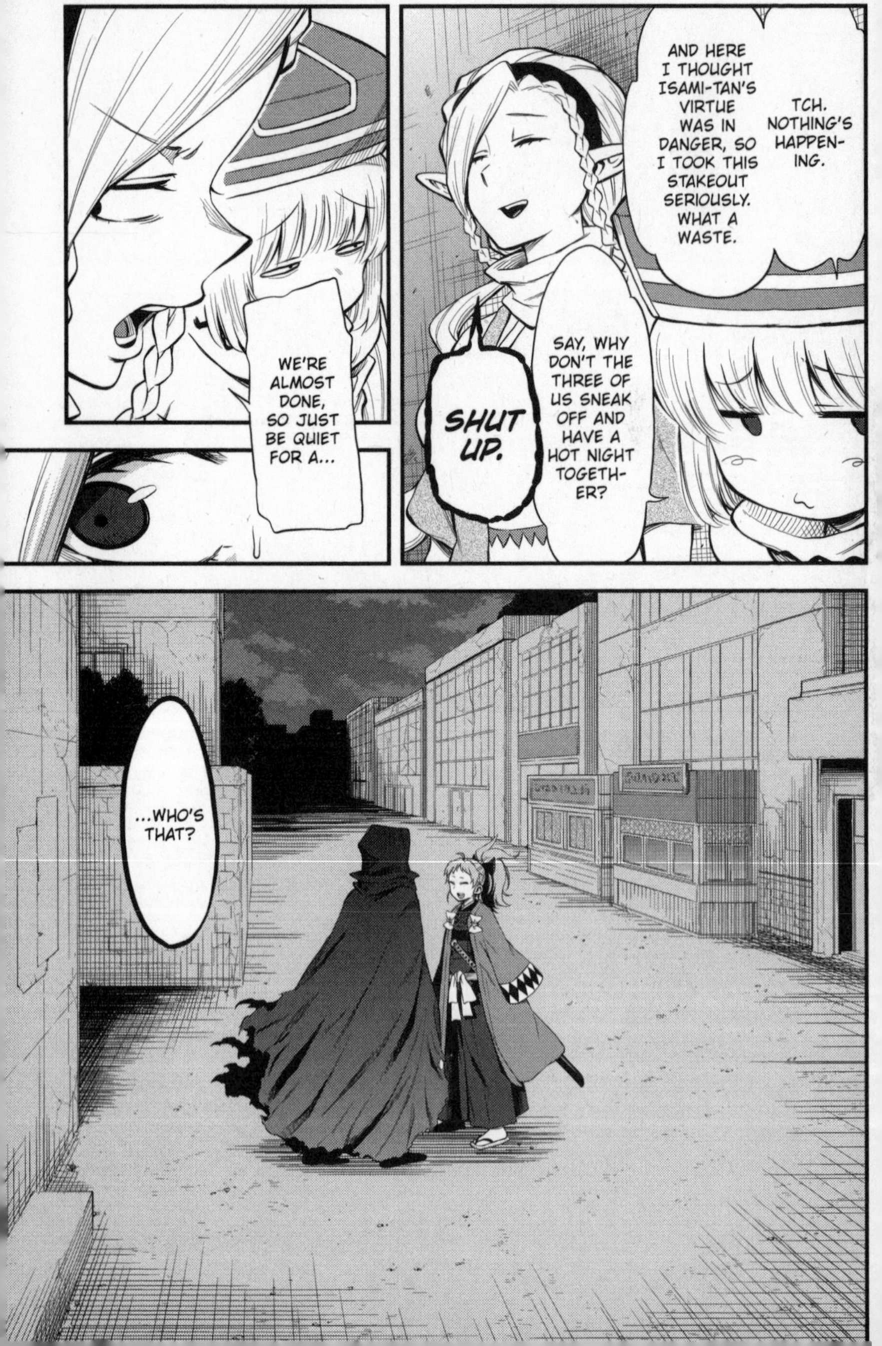
TCH. NOTHING'S HAPPEN-ING.
AND HERE I THOUGHT ISAMI-TAN'S VIRTUE WAS IN DANGER, SO I TOOK THIS STAKEOUT SERIOUSLY. WHAT A WASTE.
SAY, WHY DON'T THE THREE OF US SNEAK OFF AND HAVE A HOT NIGHT TOGETH-ER?
SHUT UP.
WE'RE ALMOST DONE, SO JUST BE QUIET FOR A...
...WHO'S THAT?

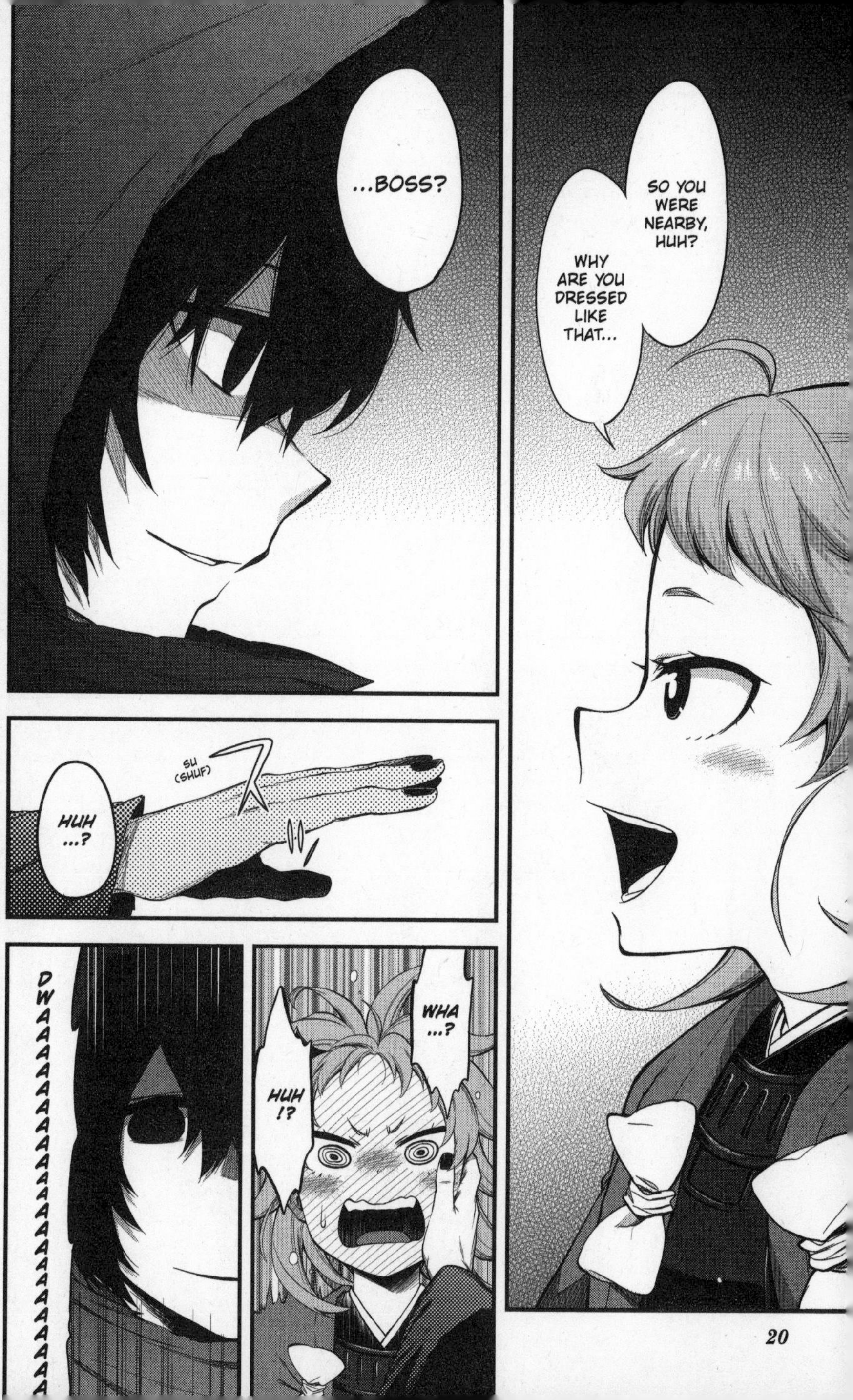
SO YOU WERE NEARBY, HUH?
WHY ARE YOU DRESSED LIKE THAT...
...BOSS?
SU (SHUF)
HUH ...?
WHA ...?
HUH !?
DWAAAAAAAAAAAAAAAAAAAA

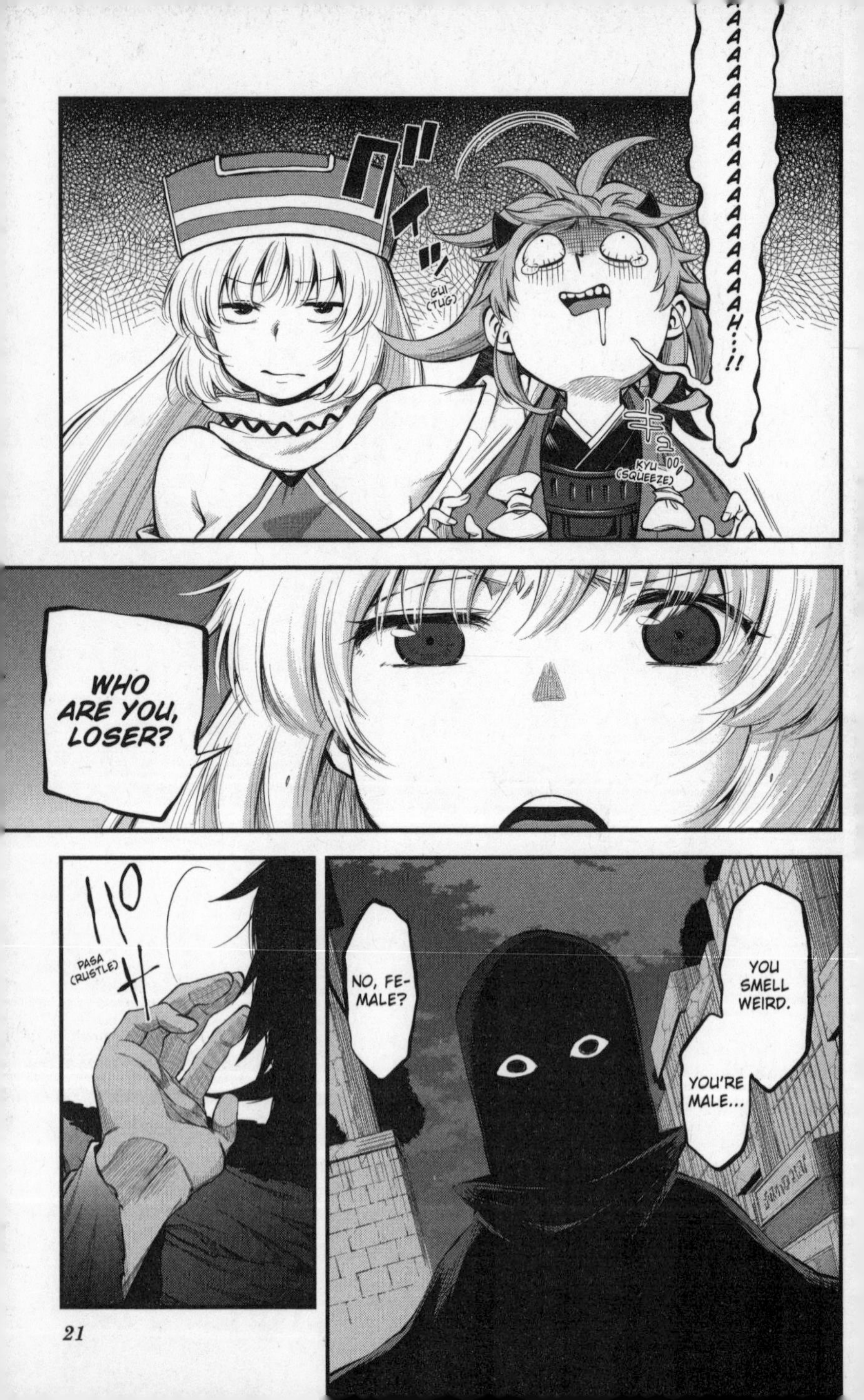

AAAAAAAAAAAAAAAAAAH...!!
GUI (TUG)
KYU (SQUEEZE)
WHO ARE YOU, LOSER?
YOU SMELL WEIRD.
YOU'RE MALE...
NO, FE-MALE?
PASA (RUSTLE)

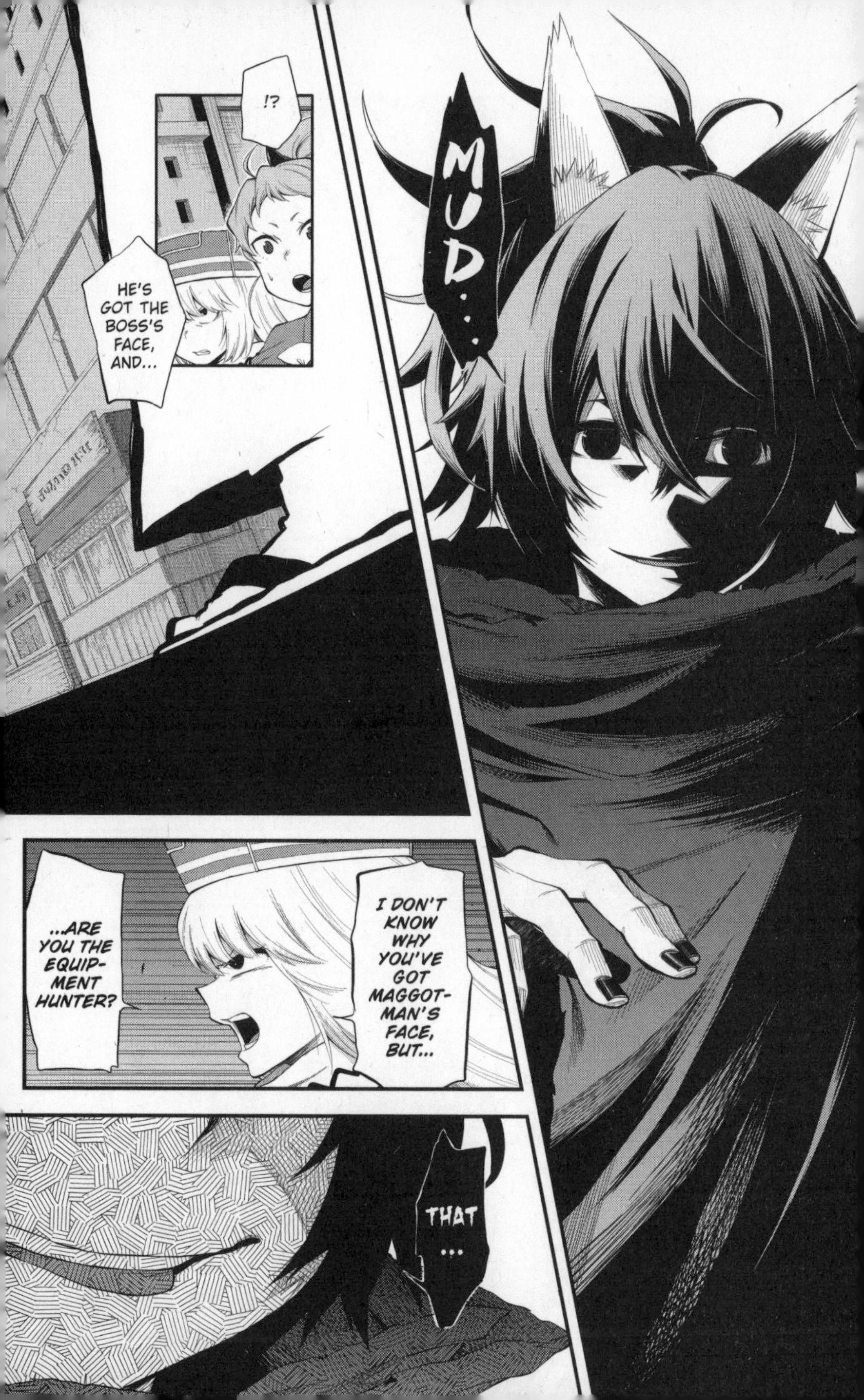
MUD...
!?
HE'S GOT THE BOSS'S FACE, AND...
I DON'T KNOW WHY YOU'VE GOT MAGGOT-MAN'S FACE, BUT...
...ARE YOU THE EQUIPMENT HUNTER?
THAT...

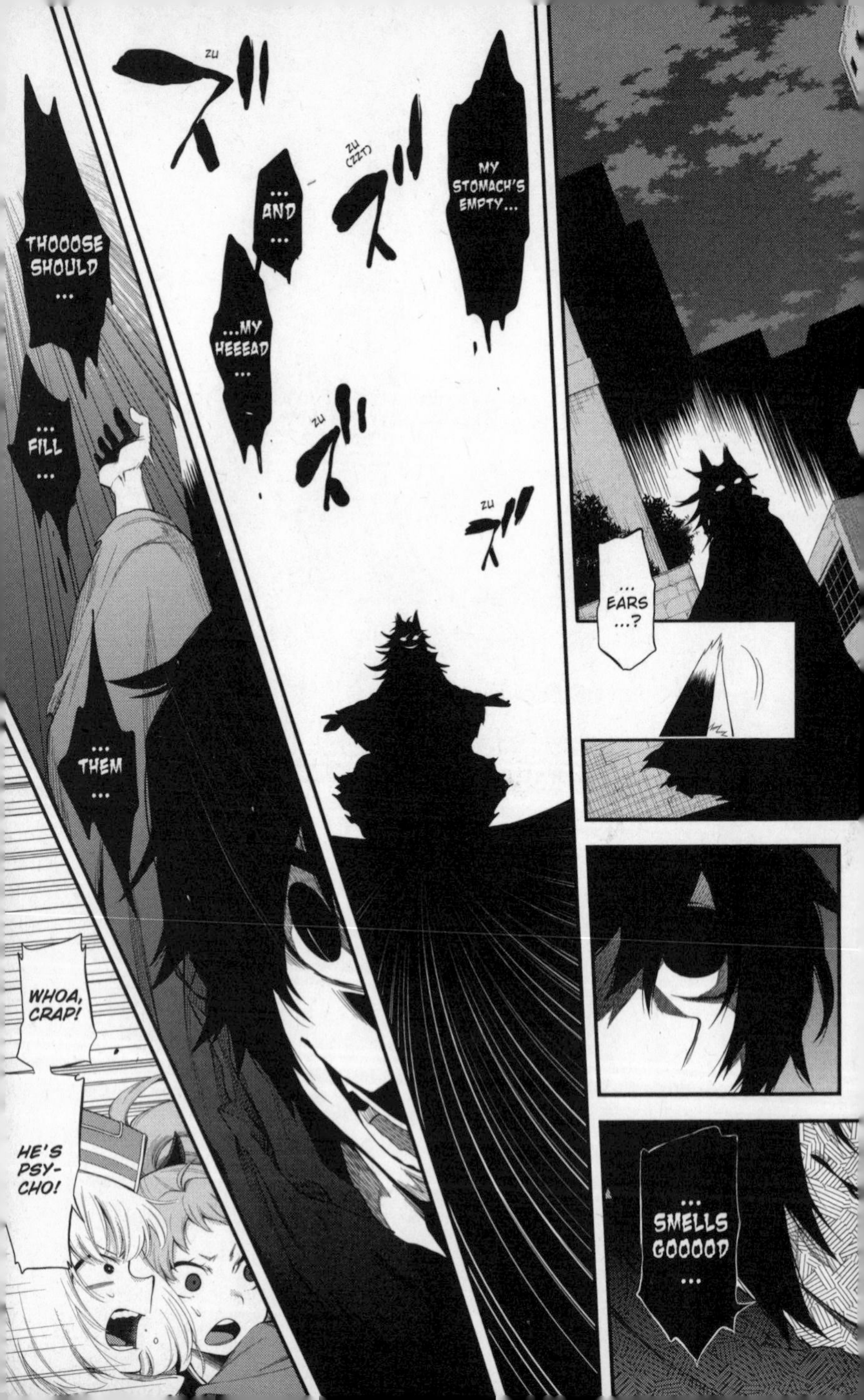
...EARS...?
...SMELLS GOOOOD...
MY STOMACH'S EMPTY...
ZU (ZZT)
...AND...
ZU
...MY HEEEAD...
ZU
ZU
THOOOSE SHOULD...
...FILL...
...THEM...
WHOA, CRAP!
HE'S PSY-CHO!

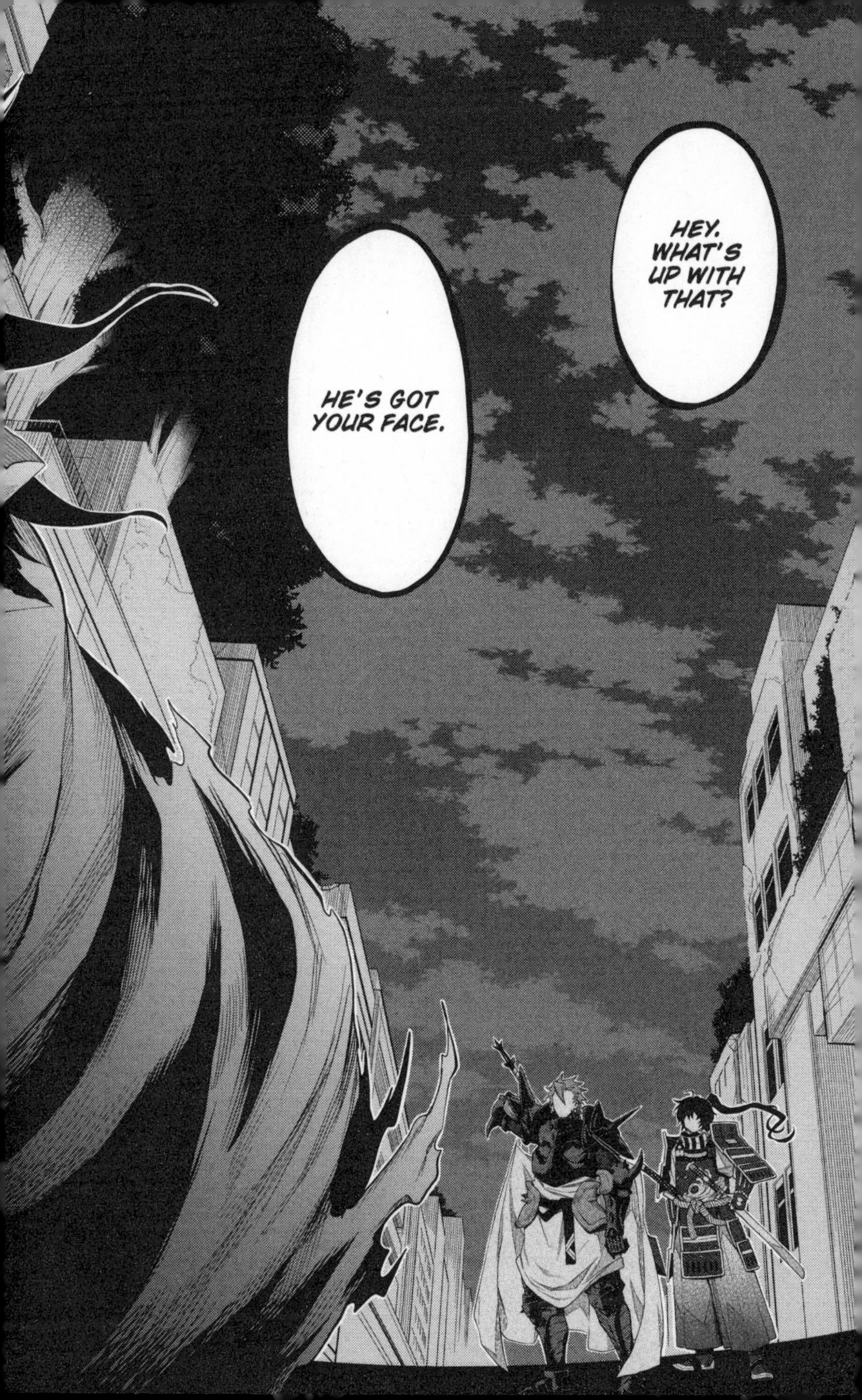
HEY. WHAT'S UP WITH THAT?
HE'S GOT YOUR FACE.

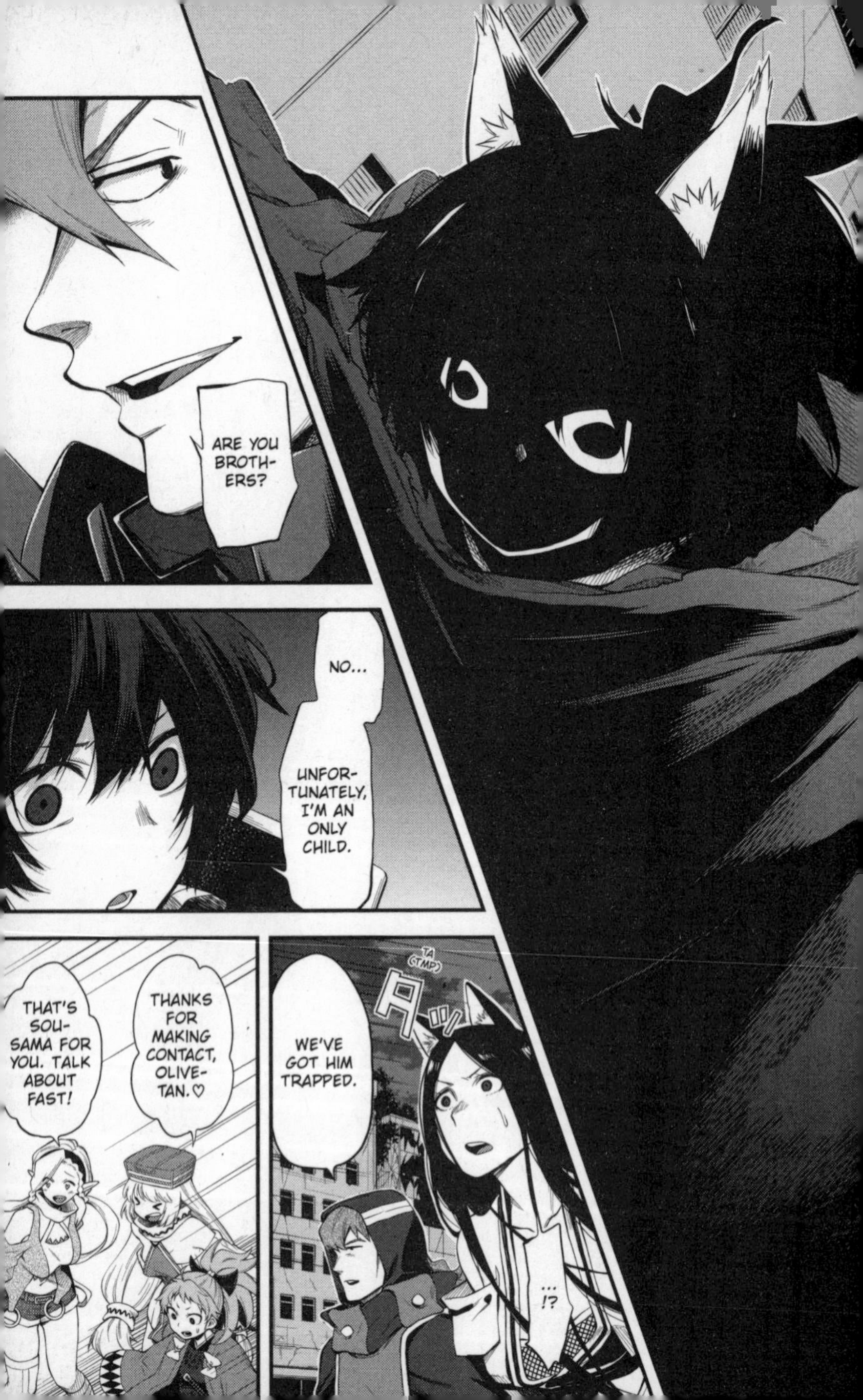
ARE YOU BROTH-ERS?
NO...
UNFOR-TUNATELY, I'M AN ONLY CHILD.
TA (TMP)
WE'VE GOT HIM TRAPPED.
...!?
THANKS FOR MAKING CONTACT, OLIVE-TAN.♡
THAT'S SOU-SAMA FOR YOU. TALK ABOUT FAST!

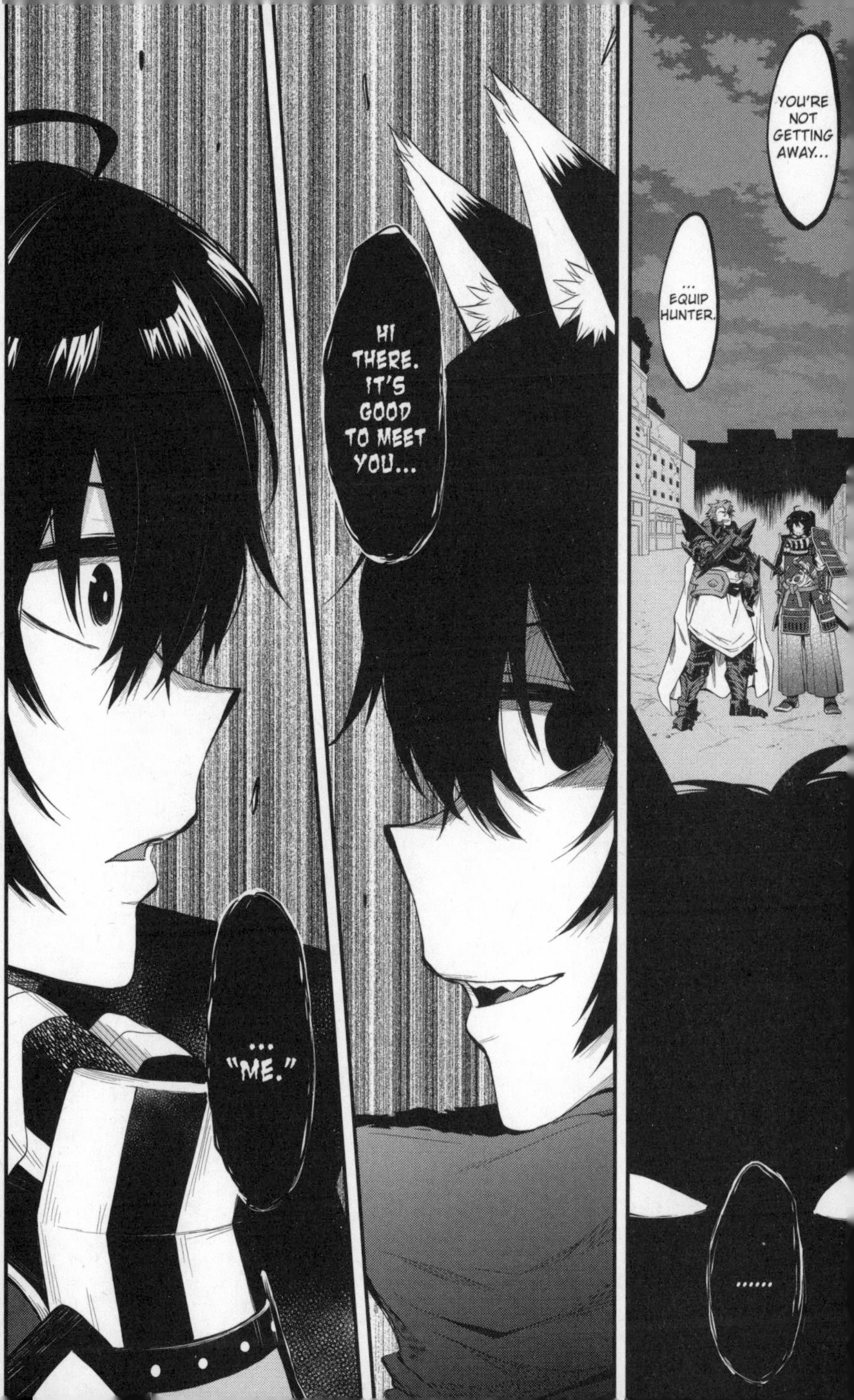
YOU'RE NOT GETTING AWAY...
... EQUIP HUNTER.
......
HI THERE. IT'S GOOD TO MEET YOU...
... "ME."

LOG HORIZON

THE WEST WIND BRIGADE

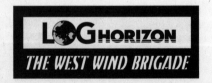

LOG HORIZON

THE WEST WIND BRIGADE

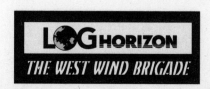

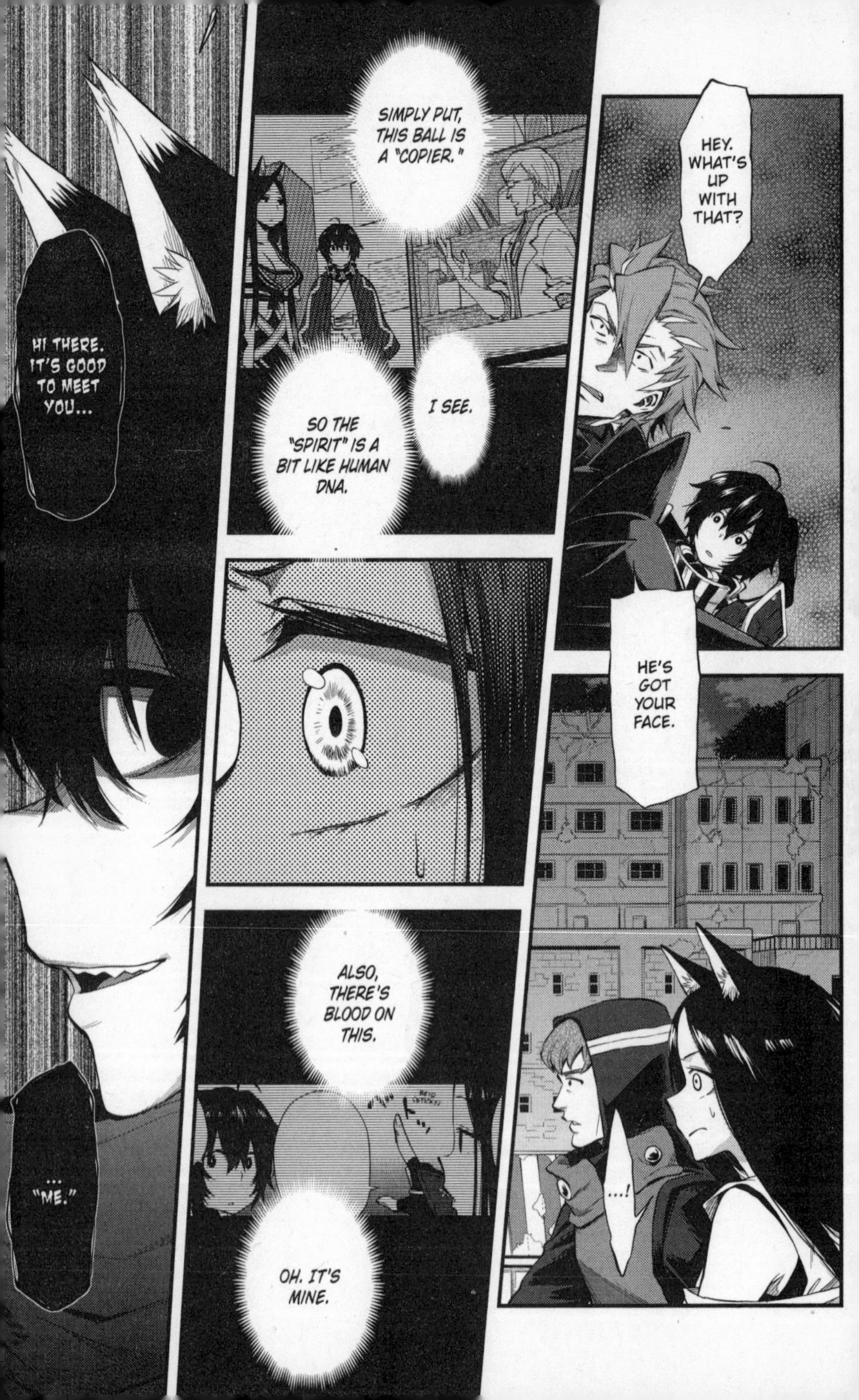
HEY. WHAT'S UP WITH THAT?
HE'S GOT YOUR FACE.
...!
SIMPLY PUT, THIS BALL IS A "COPIER."
I SEE.
SO THE "SPIRIT" IS A BIT LIKE HUMAN DNA.
ALSO, THERE'S BLOOD ON THIS.
OH. IT'S MINE.
HI THERE. IT'S GOOD TO MEET YOU...
... "ME."

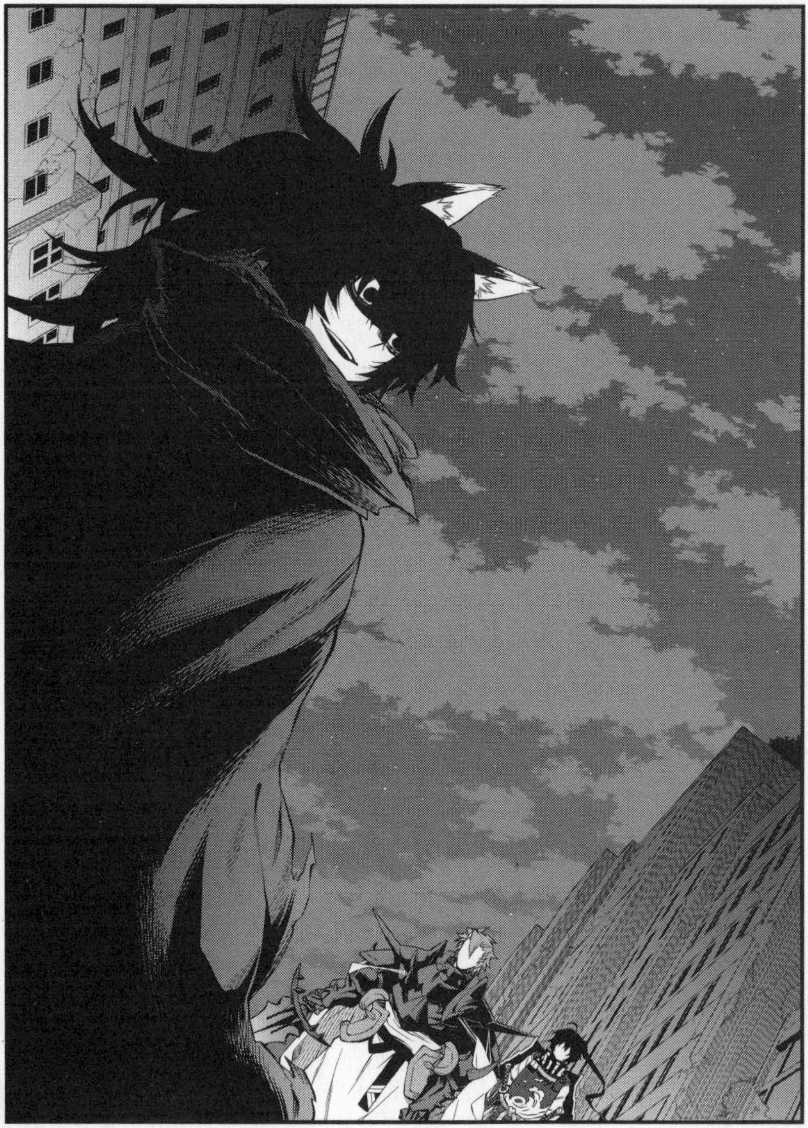

CHAPTER: 49 True Form

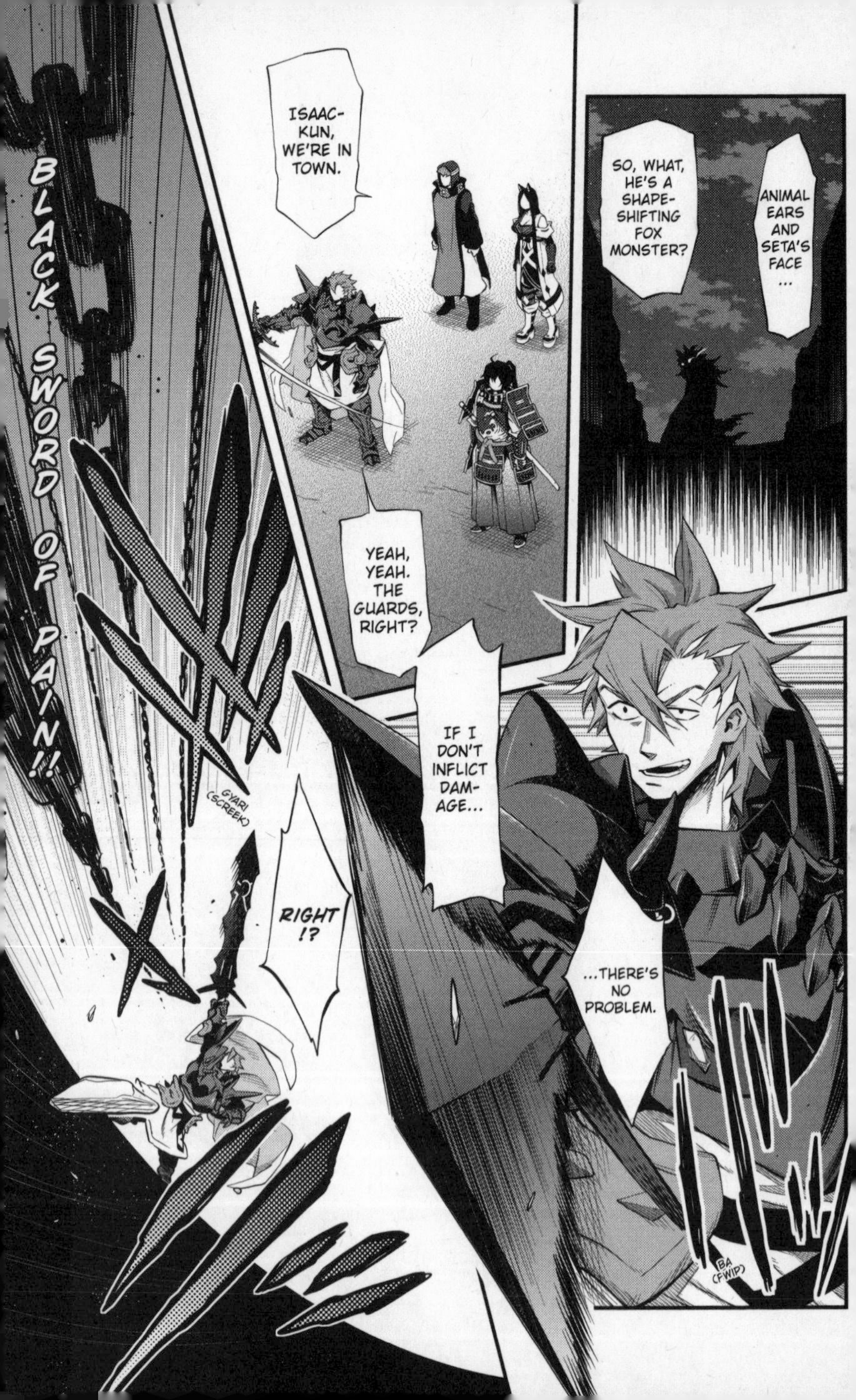

ANIMAL EARS AND SETA'S FACE...
SO, WHAT, HE'S A SHAPE-SHIFTING FOX MONSTER?
ISAAC-KUN, WE'RE IN TOWN.
YEAH, YEAH. THE GUARDS, RIGHT?
IF I DON'T INFLICT DAM-AGE...
...THERE'S NO PROBLEM.
BA (FWIP)
RIGHT!?
GYARI (SCREEK)
BLACK SWORD OF PAIN!!

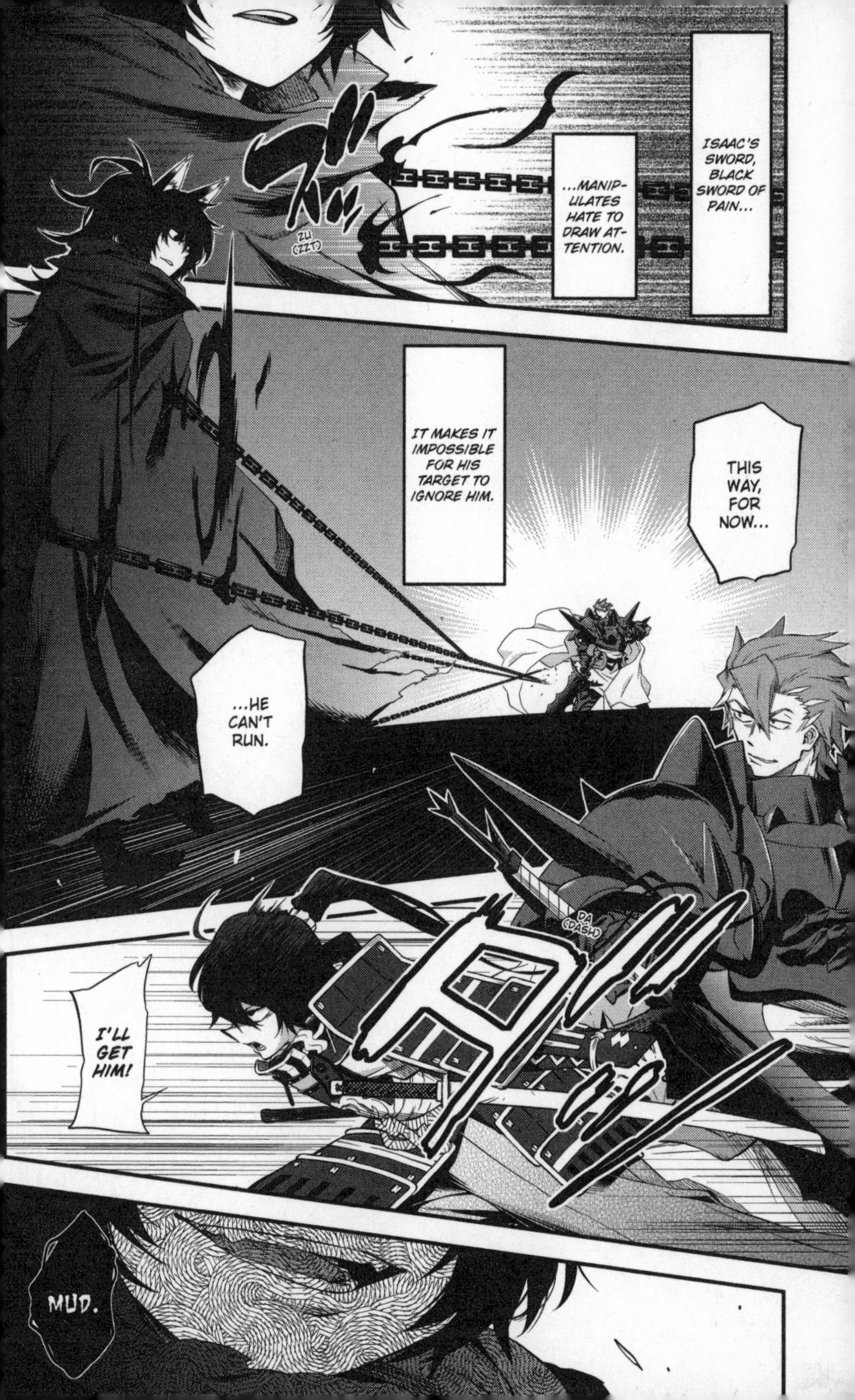
ISAAC'S SWORD, BLACK SWORD OF PAIN...
...MANIPULATES HATE TO DRAW ATTENTION.
ZU (ZZZT)
IT MAKES IT IMPOSSIBLE FOR HIS TARGET TO IGNORE HIM.
THIS WAY, FOR NOW...
...HE CAN'T RUN.
DA (DASH)
I'LL GET HIM!
MUD.

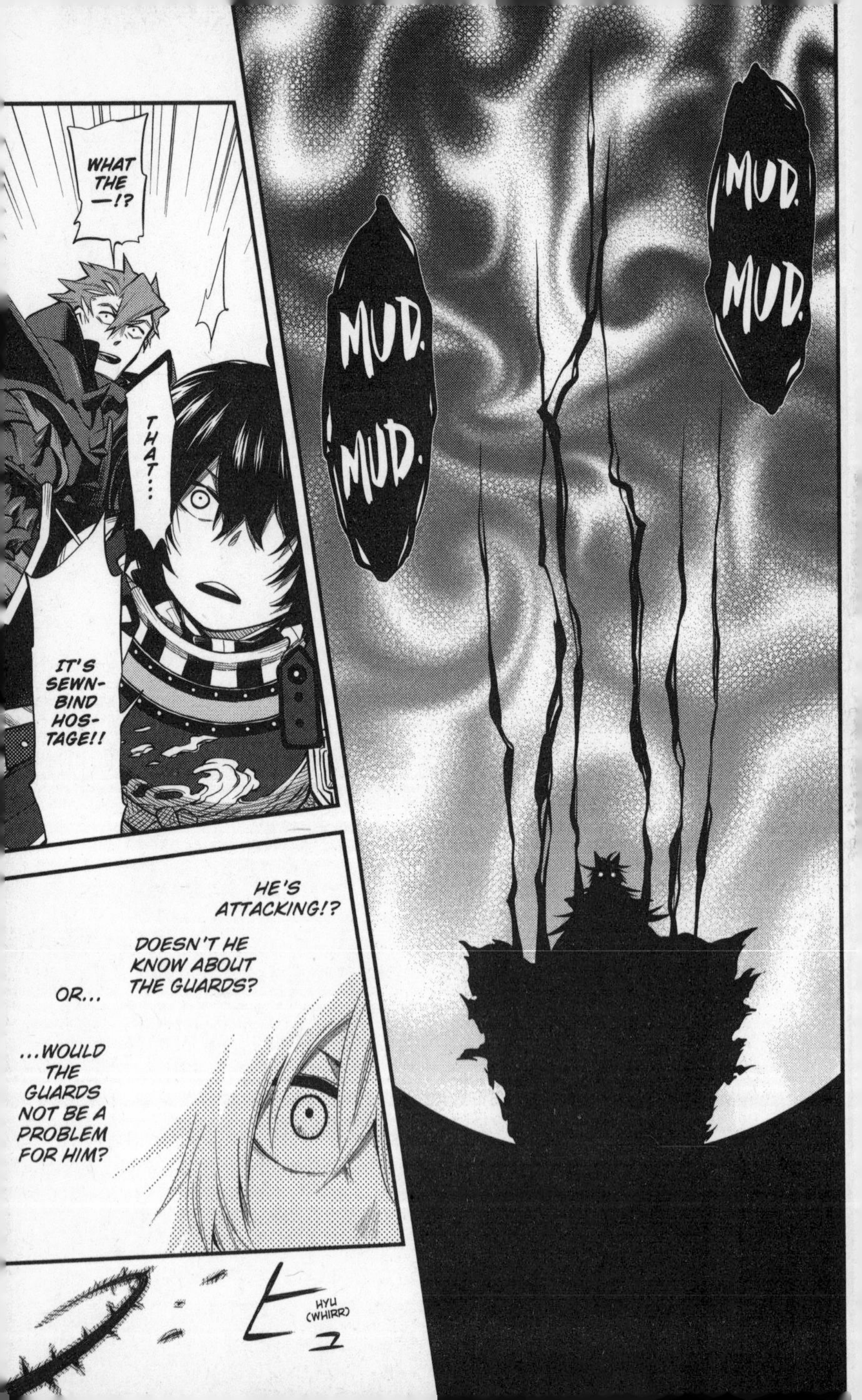
MUD. MUD.
MUD. MUD.
WHAT THE—!?
THAT...
IT'S SEWN-BIND HOSTAGE!!
HE'S ATTACKING!?
DOESN'T HE KNOW ABOUT THE GUARDS?
OR...
...WOULD THE GUARDS NOT BE A PROBLEM FOR HIM?
HYU (WHIRR)

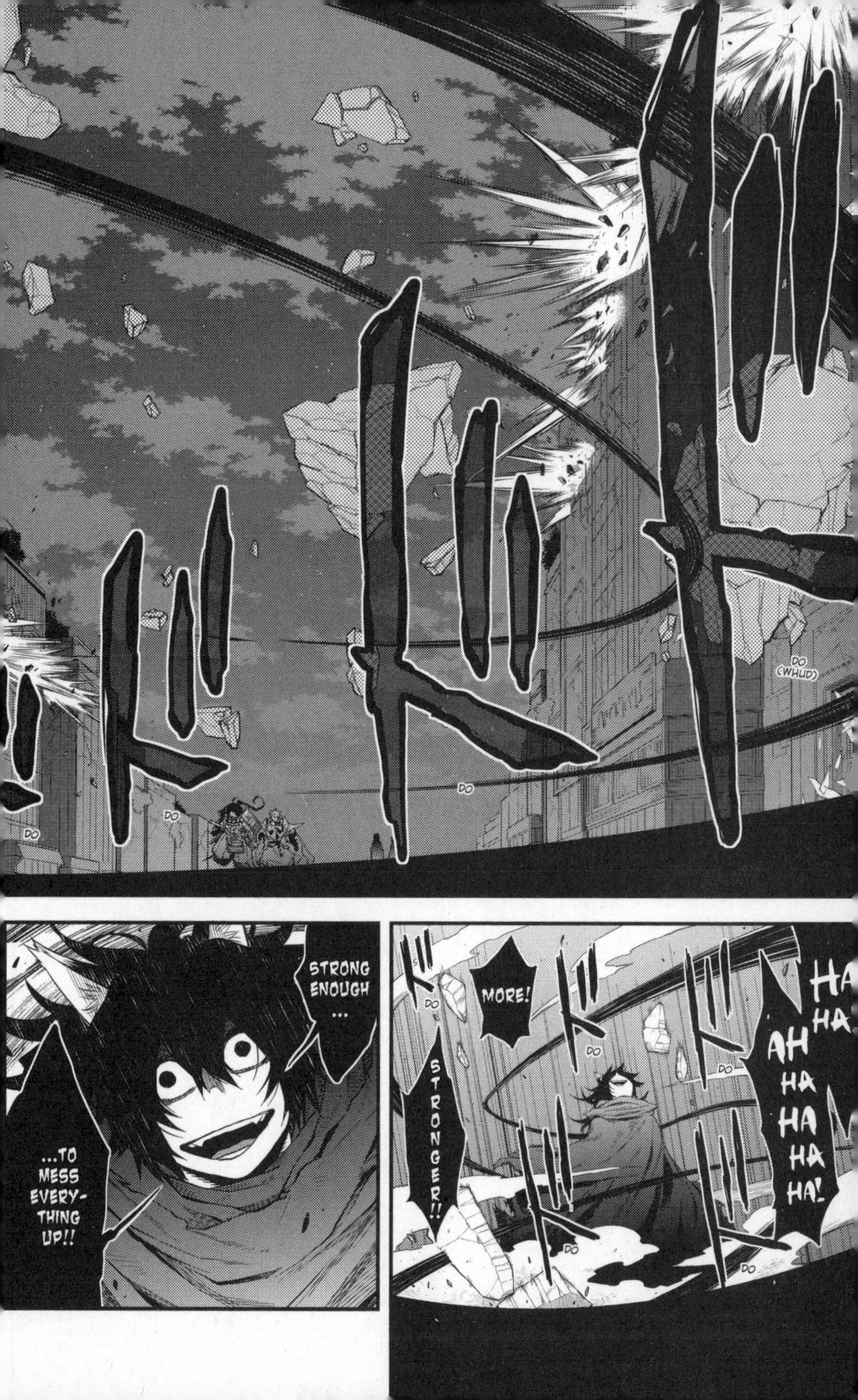
DO
(WHUD)
DO
DO
DO
HA HA
AH HA HA HA HA HA!
MORE!
STRONGER!!
DO
DO
DO
DO
DO
STRONG ENOUGH ...
...TO MESS EVERY-THING UP!!

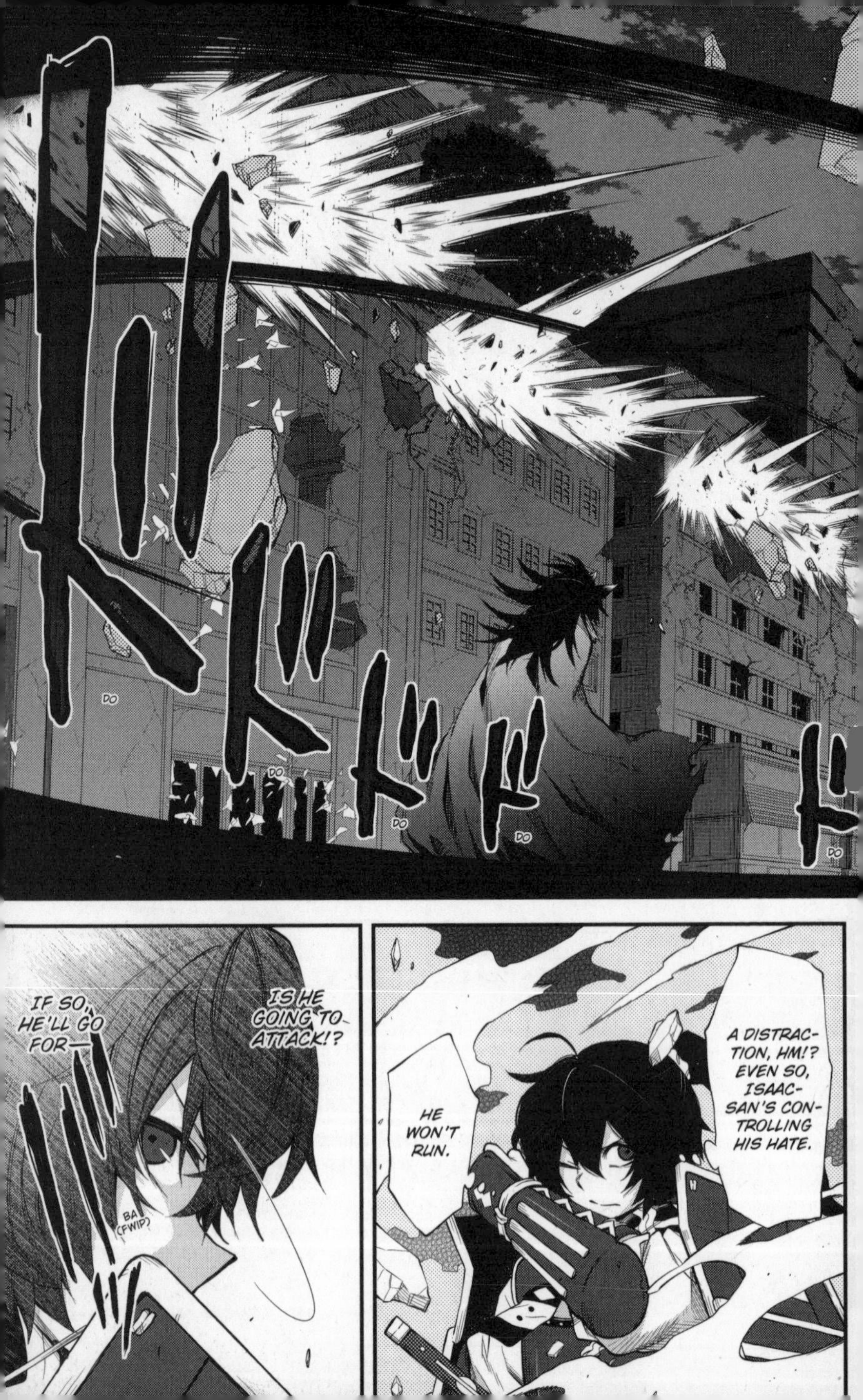
DO
DO
DO
DO
DO
A DISTRACTION, HM!? EVEN SO, ISAAC-SAN'S CONTROLLING HIS HATE.
HE WON'T RUN.
IS HE GOING TO ATTACK!?
IF SO, HE'LL GO FOR—
BA (FWIP)

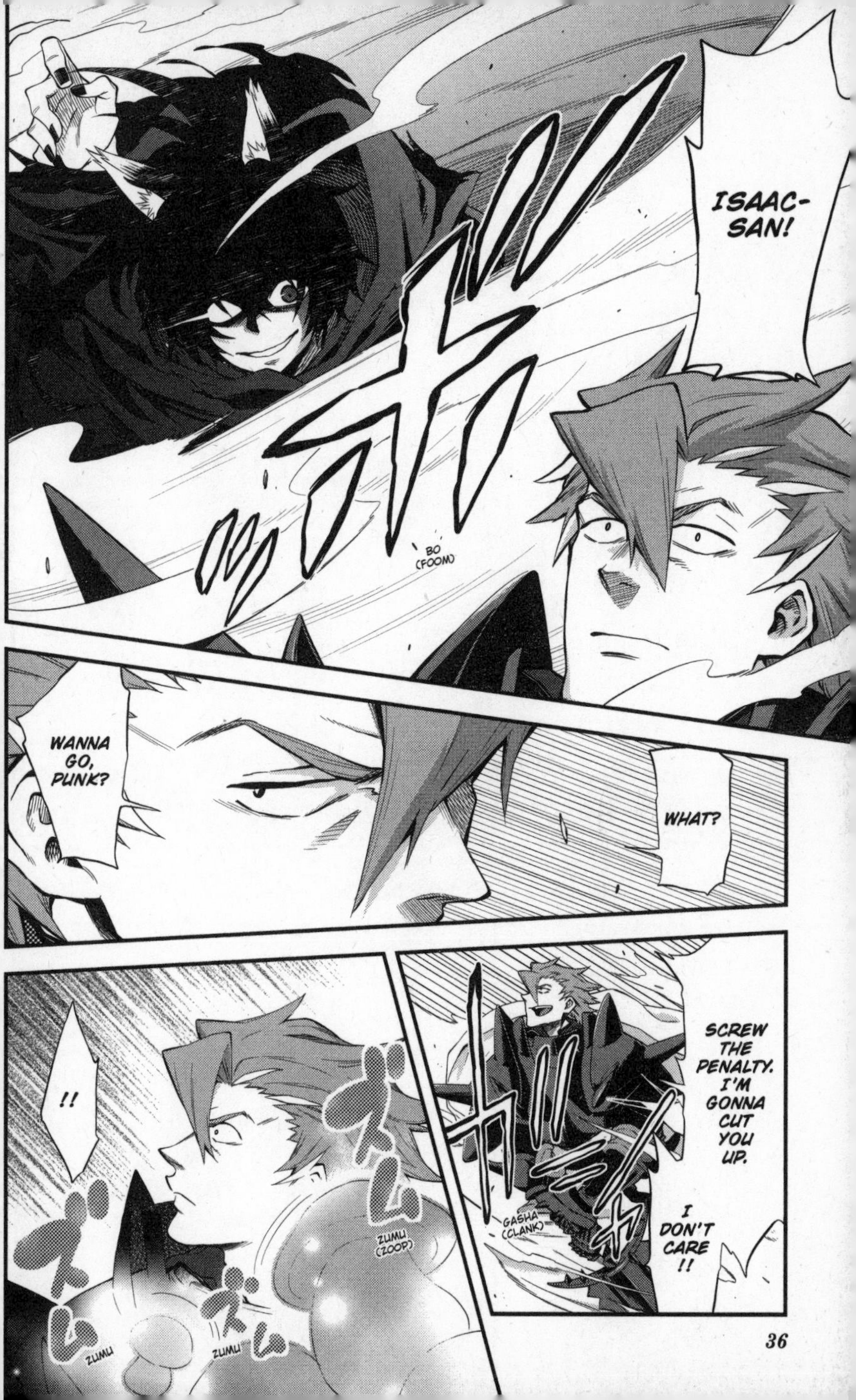
ISAAC-SAN!
BO (FOOM)
WHAT?
WANNA GO, PUNK?
SCREW THE PENALTY. I'M GONNA CUT YOU UP.
I DON'T CARE!!
GASHA (CLANK)
!!
ZUMU (ZOOP)
ZUMU
ZUMU

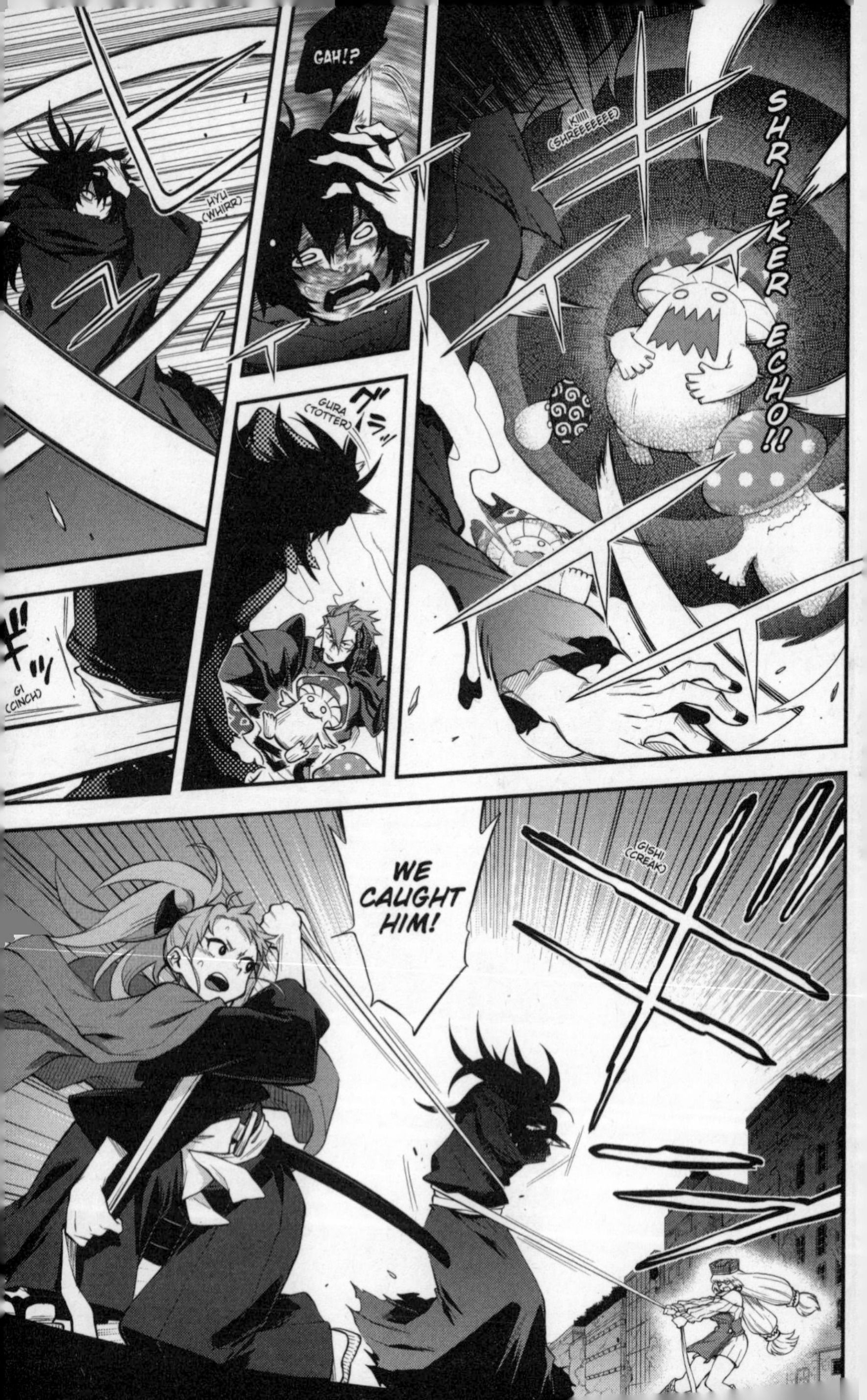
SHRIEKER ECHO!!
KIIII (SHREEEEEEE)
GAH!?
GURA (TOTTER)
HYU (WHIRR)
GI (CINCH)
GISHI (CREAK)
WE CAUGHT HIM!

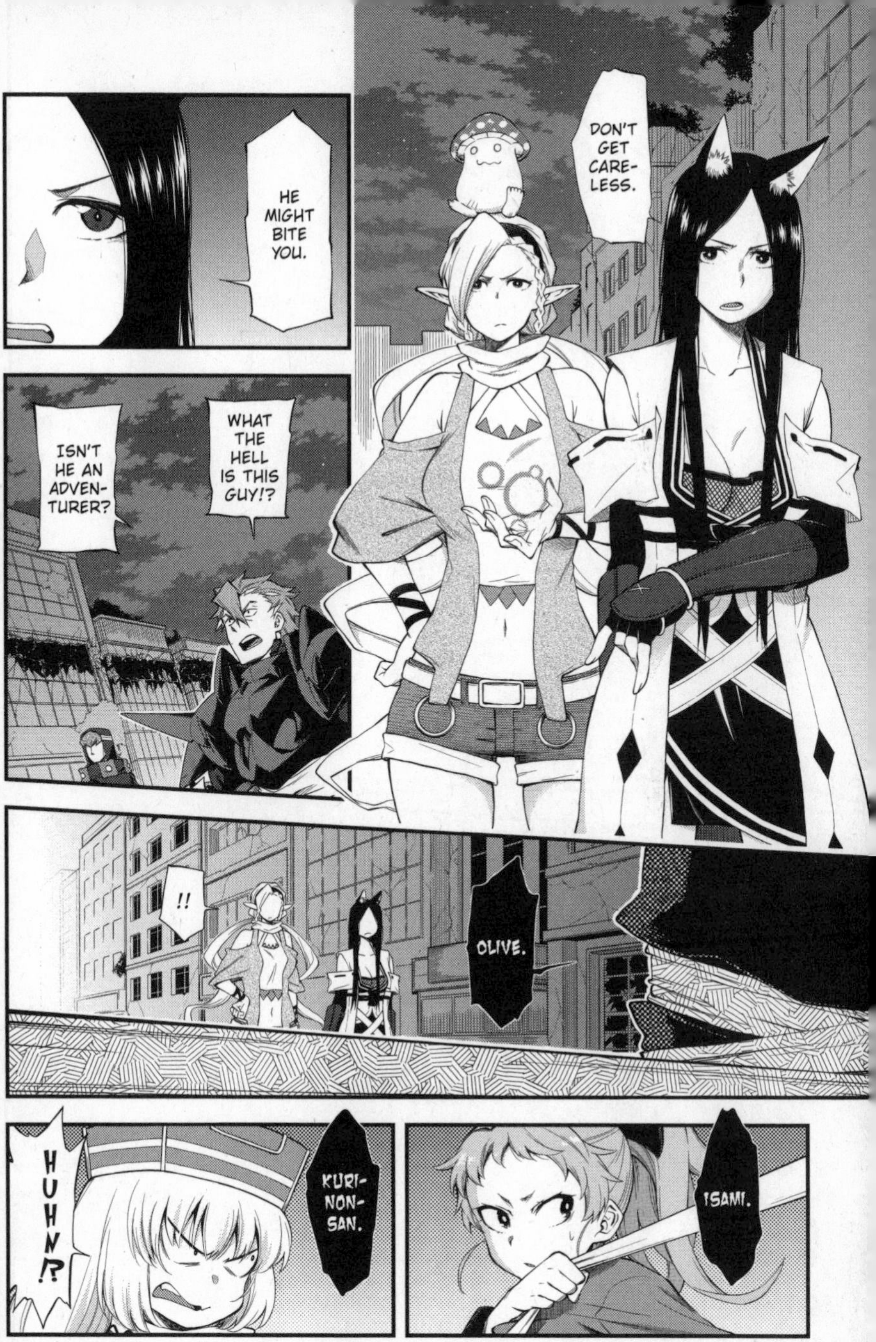
DON'T GET CARE-LESS.
HE MIGHT BITE YOU.
WHAT THE HELL IS THIS GUY!?
ISN'T HE AN ADVEN-TURER?
OLIVE.
!!
ISAMI.
KURI-NON-SAN.
HUHN!?

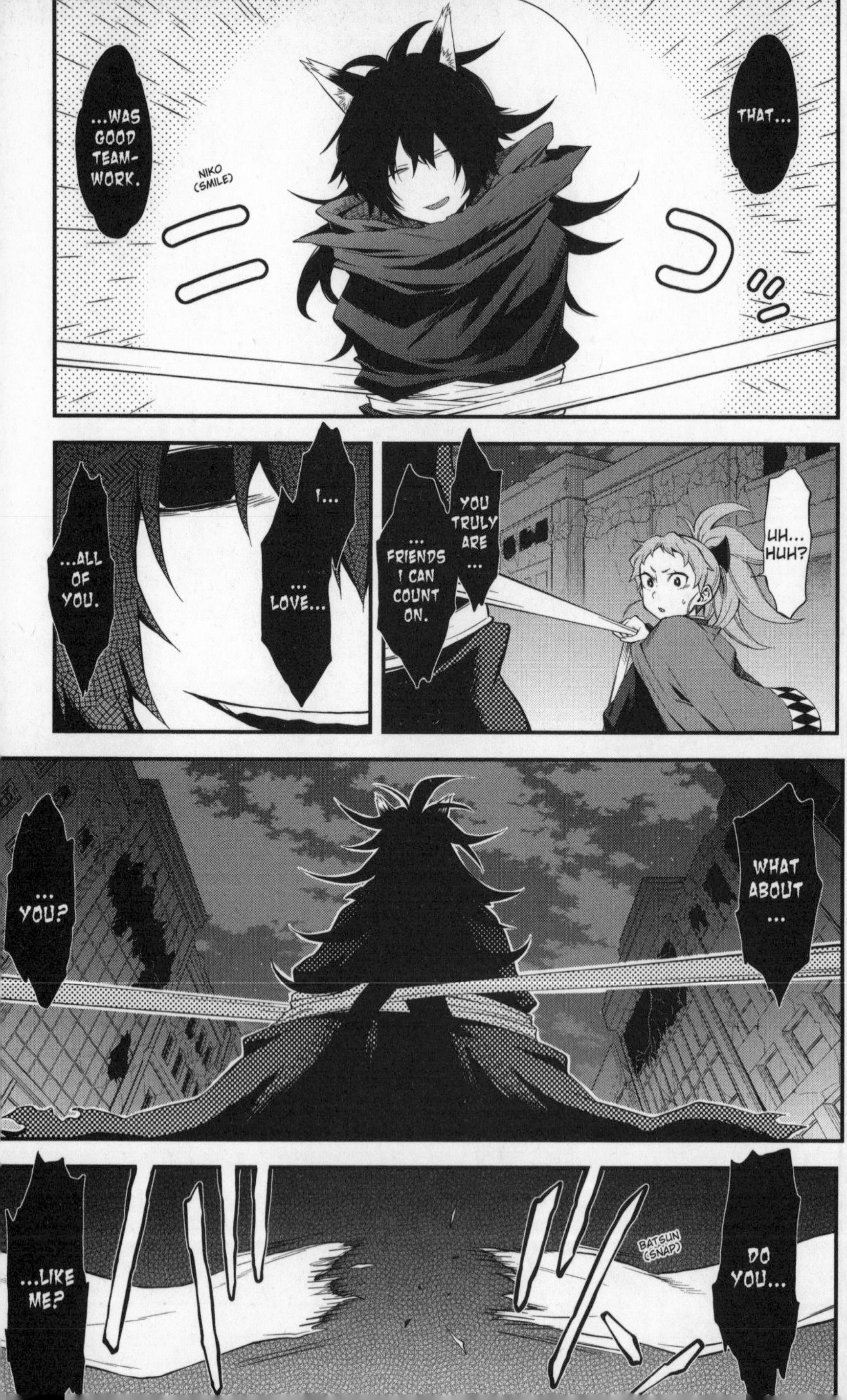
THAT...
...WAS GOOD TEAM-WORK.
NIKO (SMILE)
UH... HUH?
YOU TRULY ARE...
...FRIENDS I CAN COUNT ON.
I...
...LOVE...
...ALL OF YOU.
WHAT ABOUT...
...YOU?
DO YOU...
BATSUN (SNAP)
...LIKE ME?

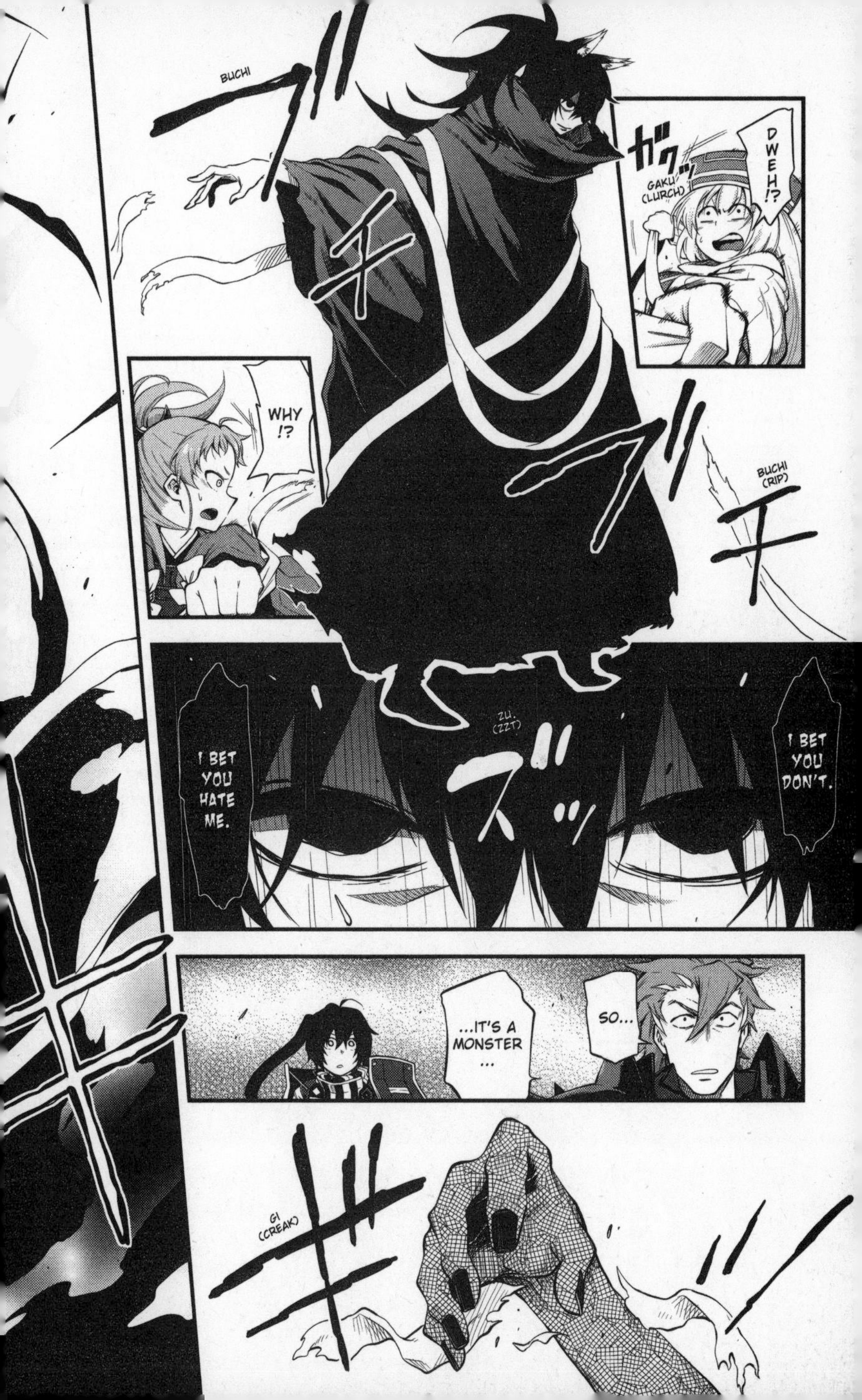
DWEH!?
ガク
GAKU (LURCH)
BUCHI (RIP)
BUCHI
WHY!?
I BET YOU DON'T.
ZU. (ZZT)
I BET YOU HATE ME.
SO...
...IT'S A MONSTER ...
GI (CREAK)

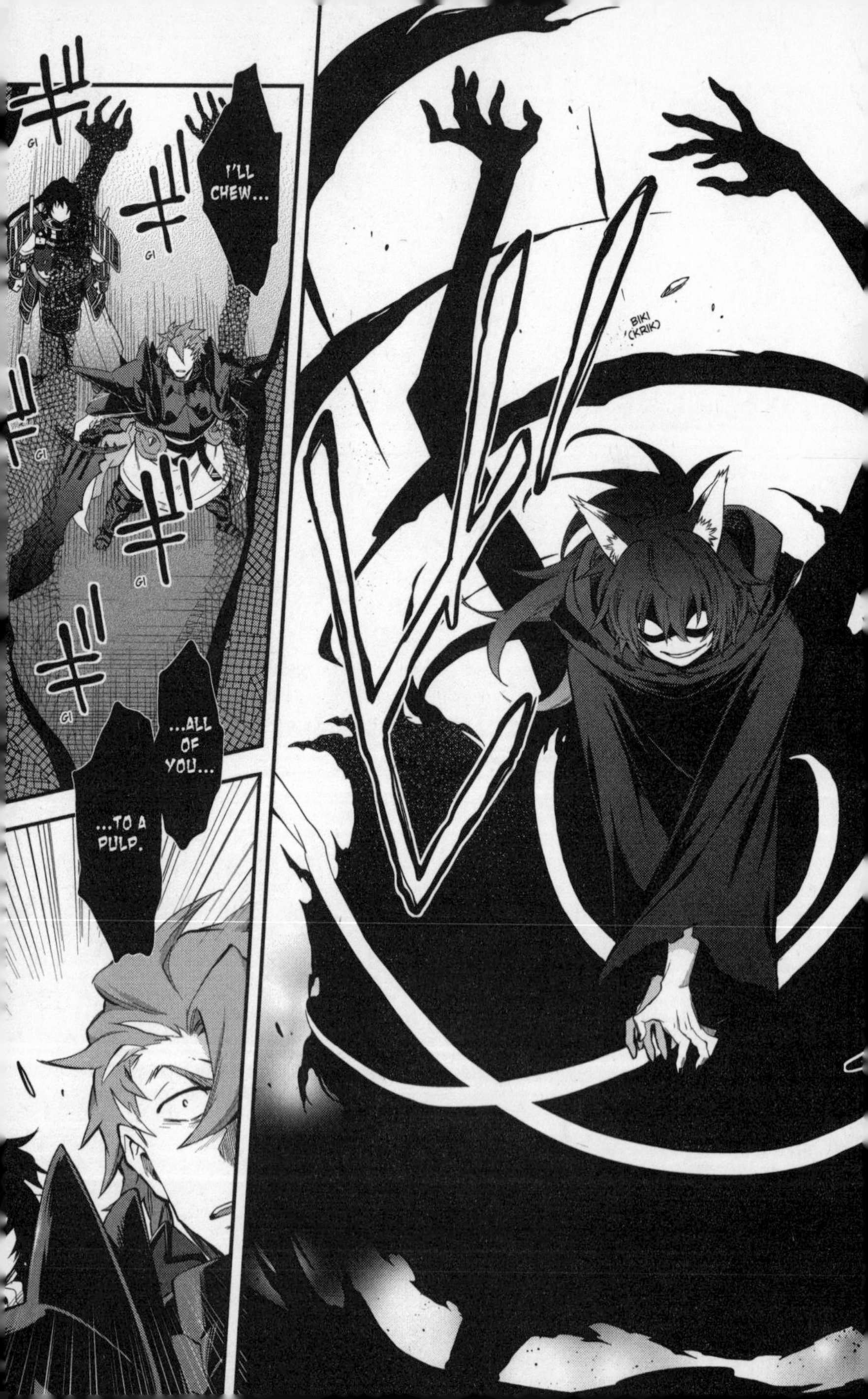
BIKI
(KRIK)
I'LL CHEW...
GI
GI
GI
GI
GI
...ALL OF YOU...
...TO A PULP.

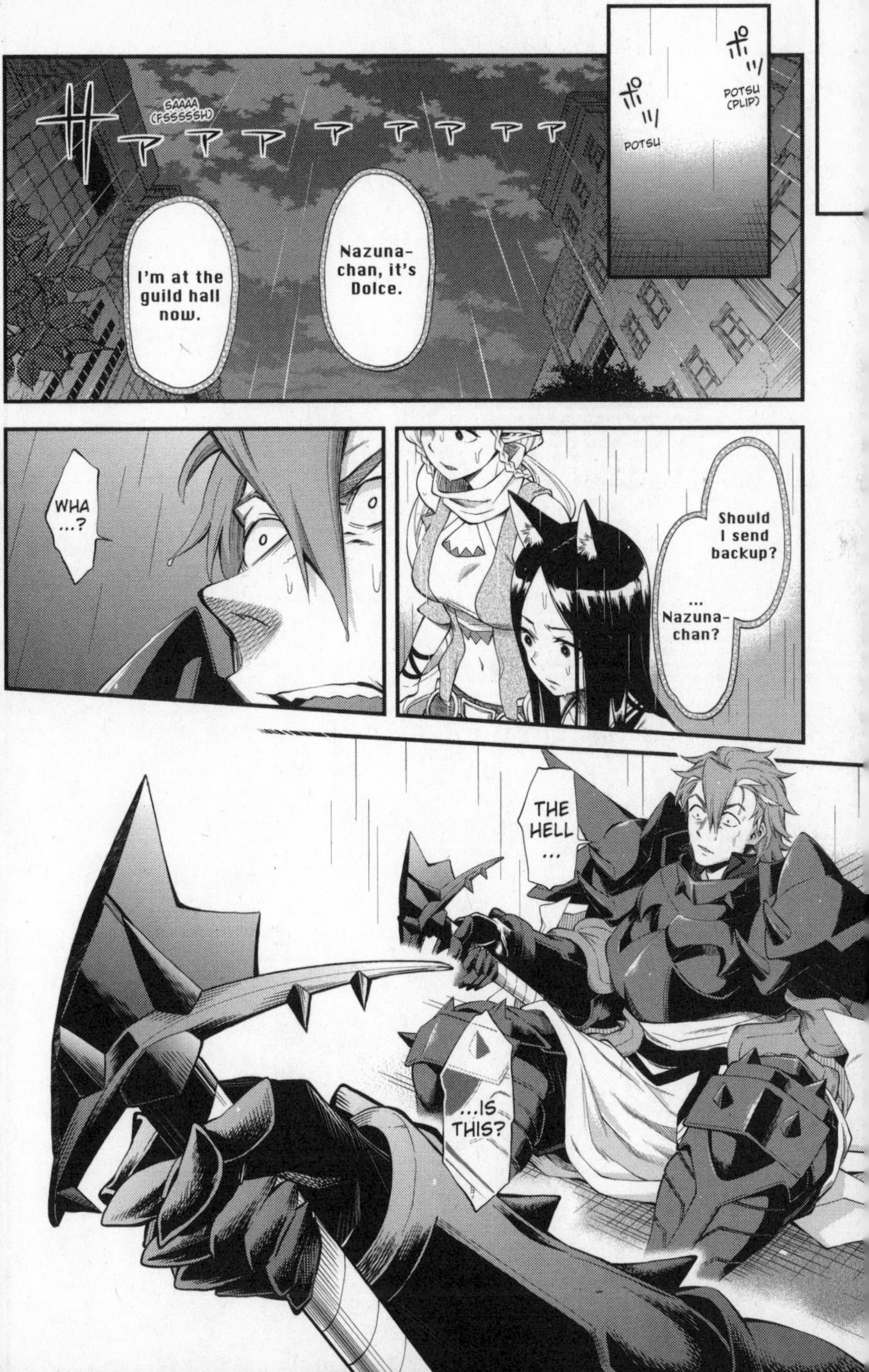
POTSU (PLIP)
POTSU
SAAAA (FSSSSSH)
Nazuna-chan, it's Dolce.
I'm at the guild hall now.
Should I send backup?
... Nazuna-chan?
WHA ...?
THE HELL ...
...IS THIS?

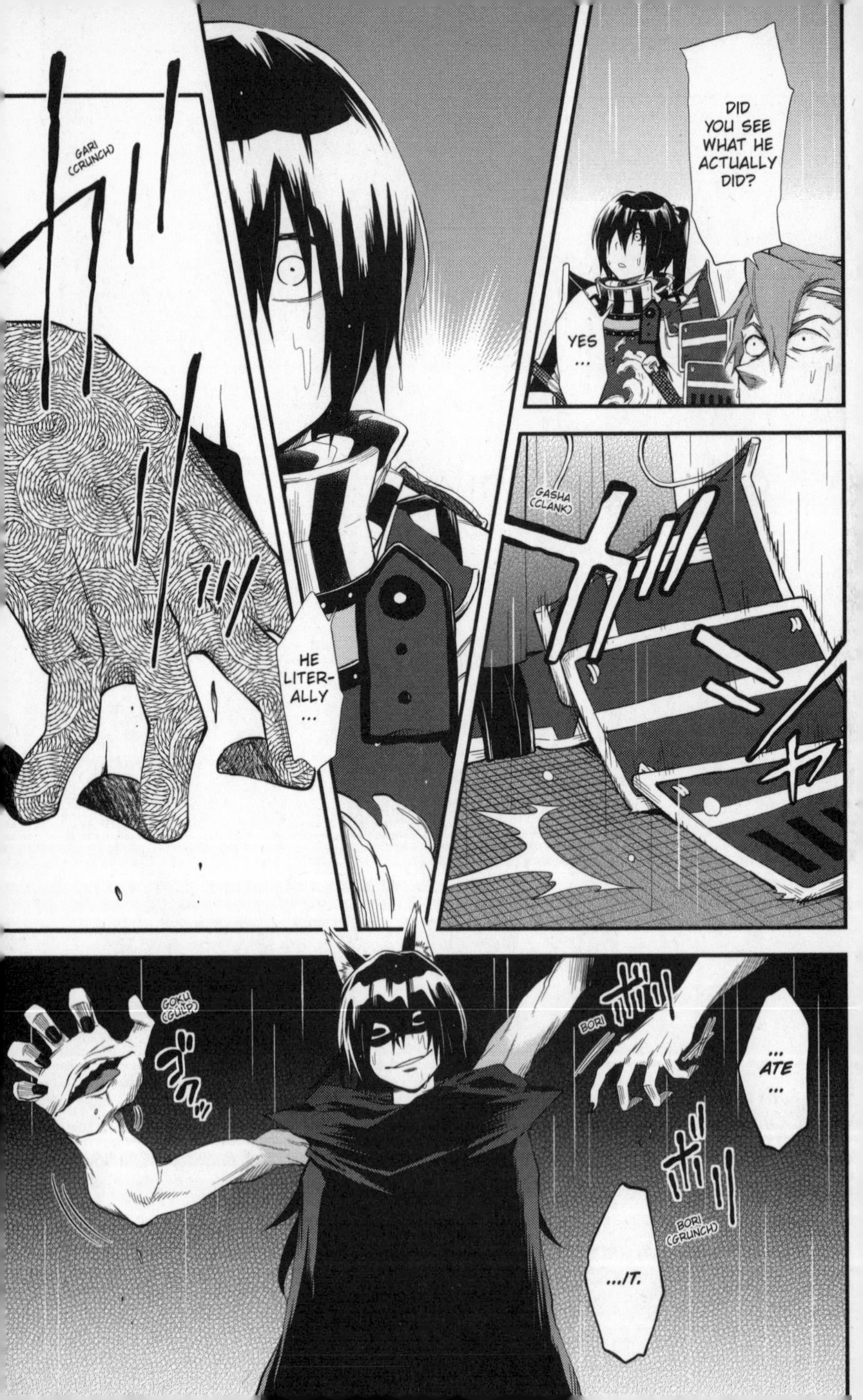
DID YOU SEE WHAT HE ACTUALLY DID?
YES ...
GASHA (CLANK)
HE LITER-ALLY ...
GARI (CRUNCH)
... ATE ...
BORI
GOKU (GULP)
BORI (CRUNCH)
...IT.

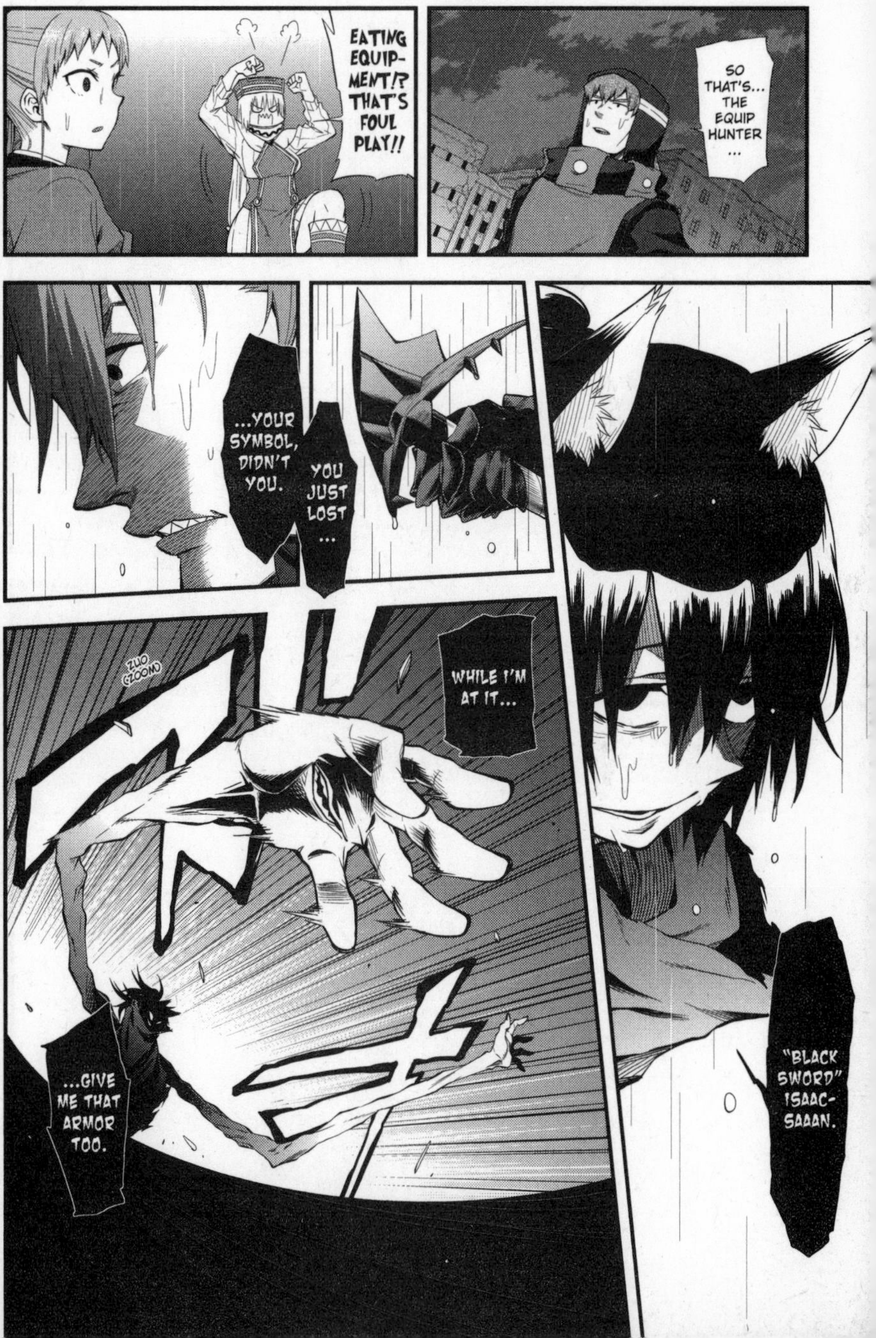
SO THAT'S... THE EQUIP HUNTER ...
EATING EQUIP-MENT!? THAT'S FOUL PLAY!!
"BLACK SWORD" ISAAC-SAAAN.
YOU JUST LOST ...
...YOUR SYMBOL, DIDN'T YOU.
WHILE I'M AT IT...
ZUO (ZOOM)
...GIVE ME THAT ARMOR TOO.

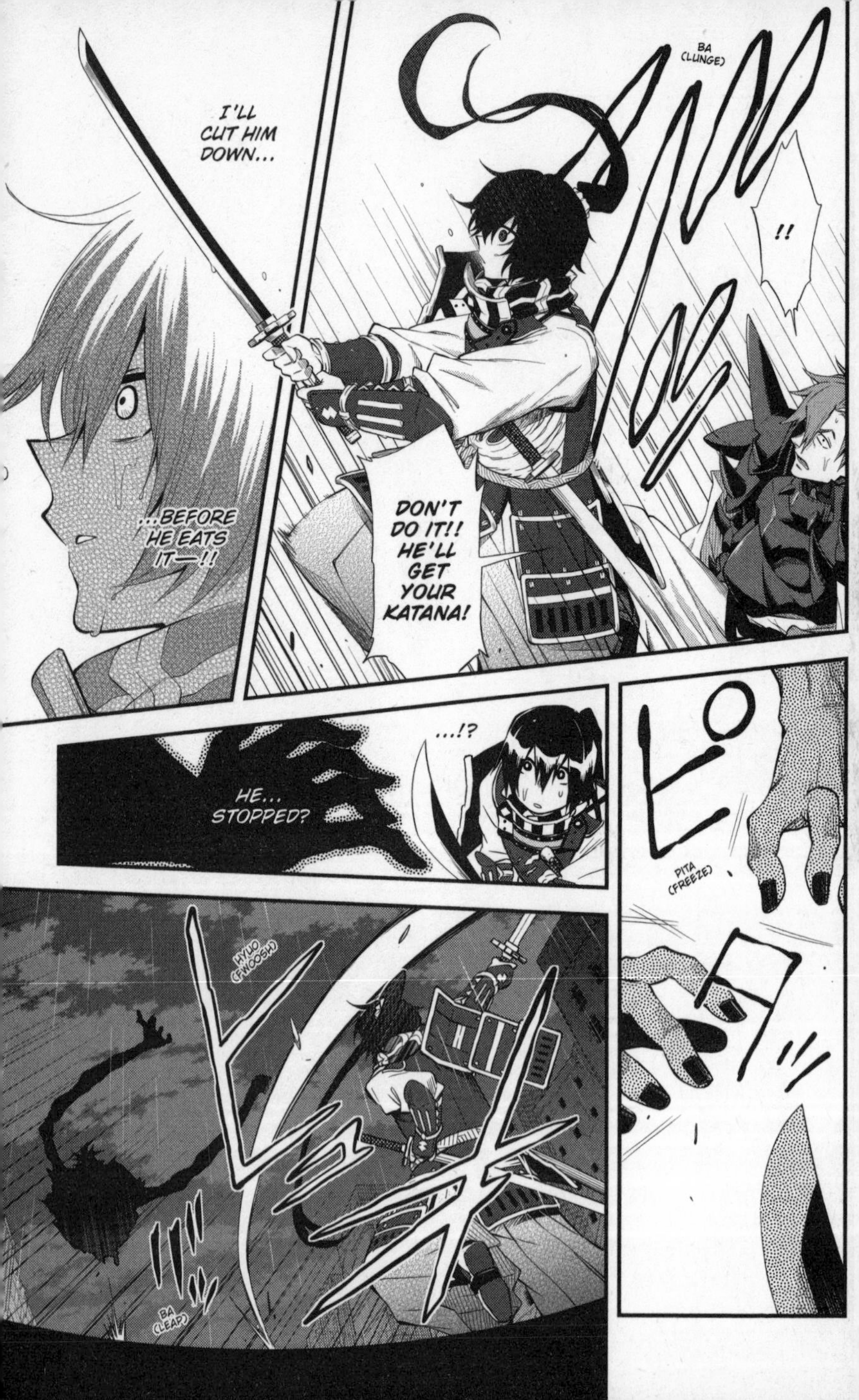
BA
(LUNGE)
!!
DON'T DO IT!! HE'LL GET YOUR KATANA!
I'LL CUT HIM DOWN...
...BEFORE HE EATS IT—!!
PITA
(FREEZE)
...!?
HE... STOPPED?
HYUO
(FWOOSH)
BA
(LEAP)

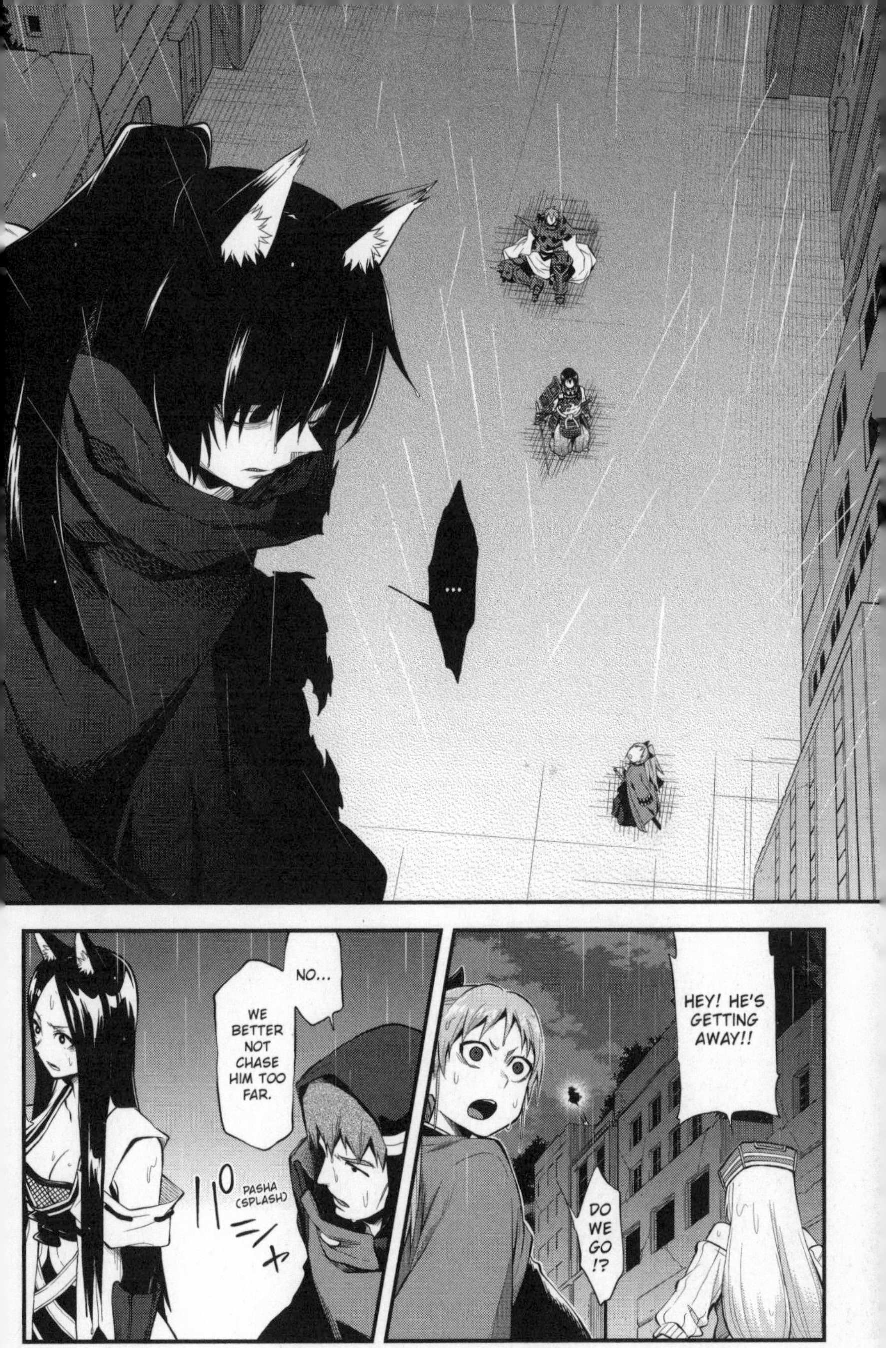
...
HEY! HE'S GETTING AWAY!!
DO WE GO !?
NO...
WE BETTER NOT CHASE HIM TOO FAR.
PASHA (SPLASH)

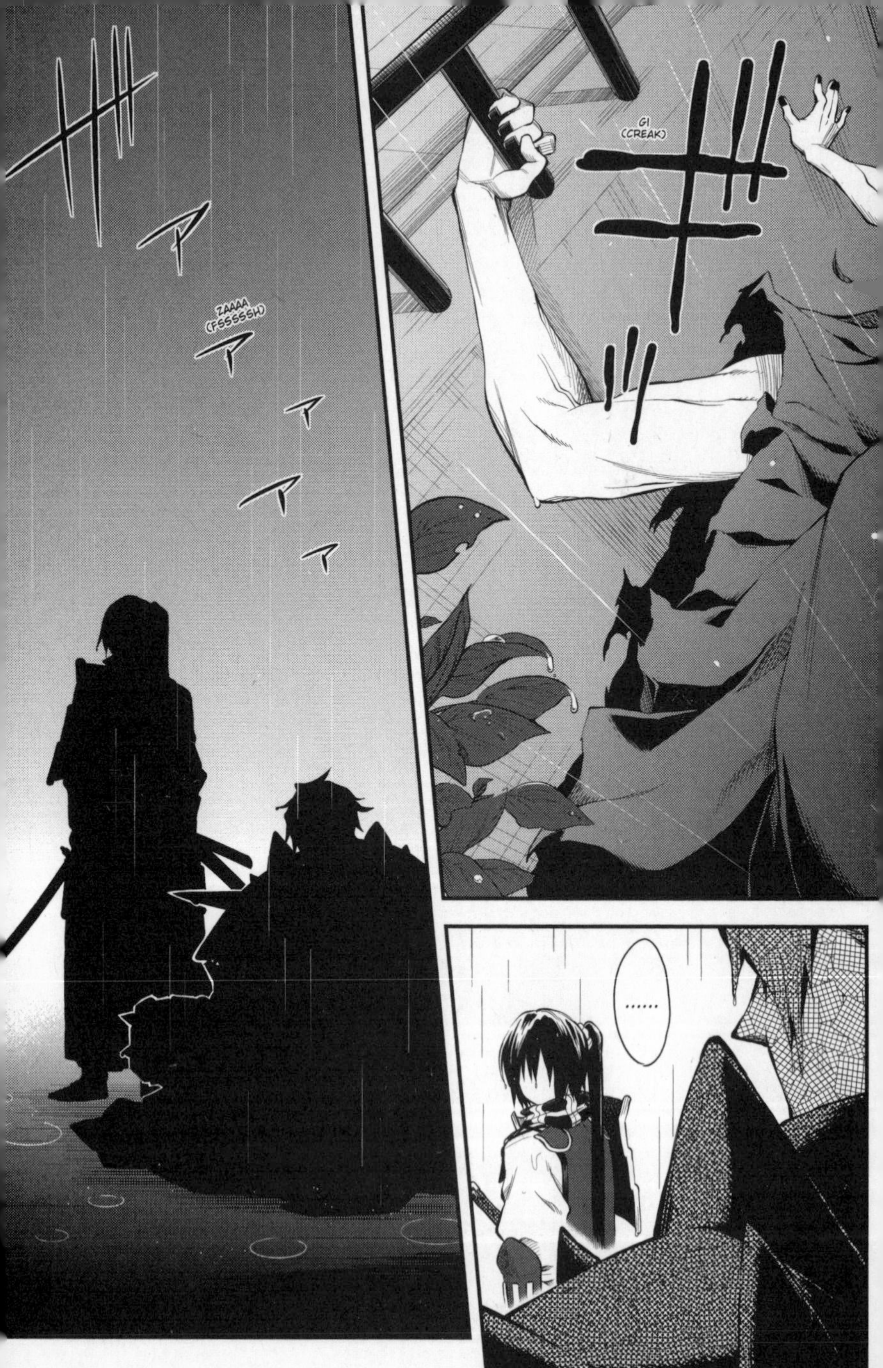
GI
(CREAK)
......
ZAAAA
(FSSSSSH)

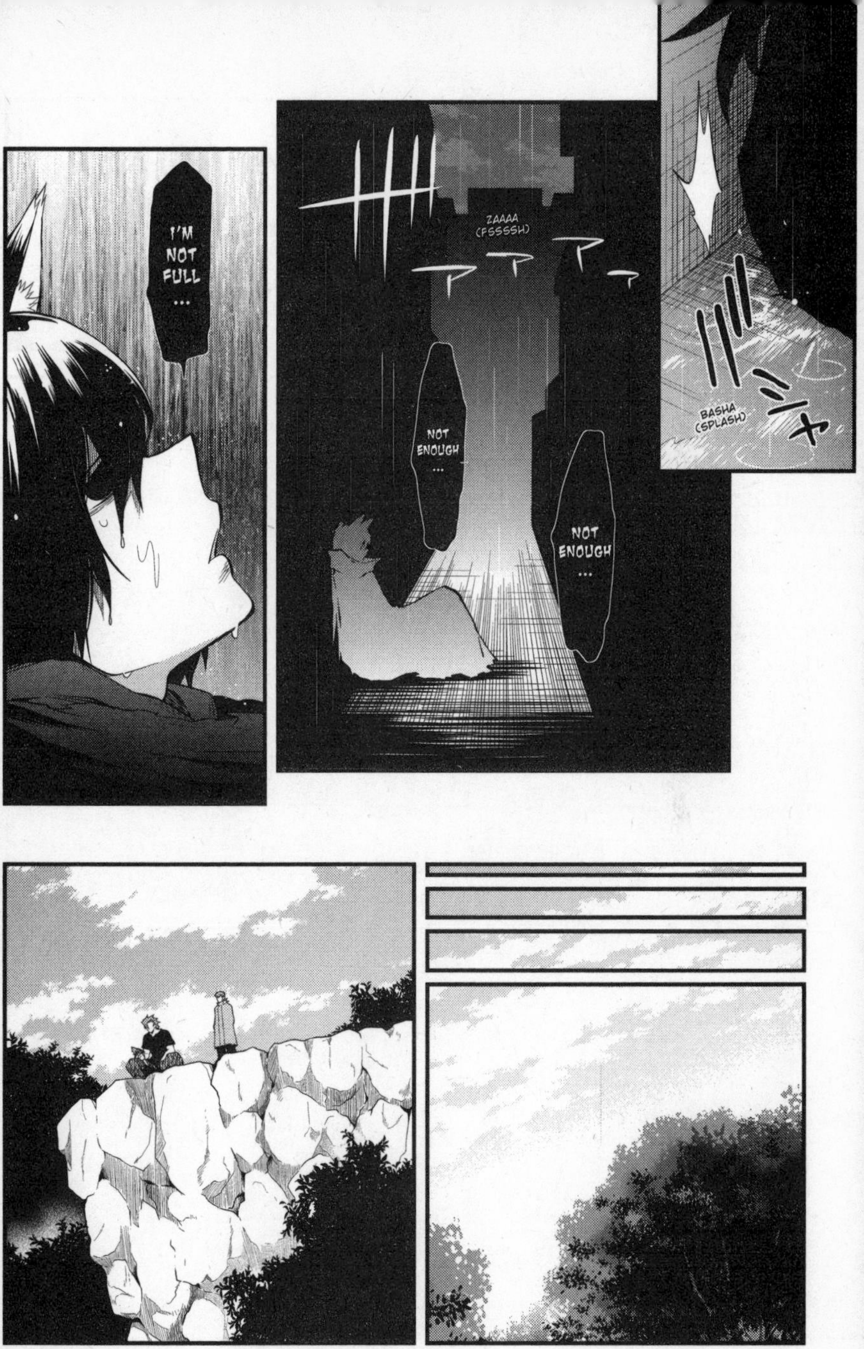
BASHA (SPLASH)
ZAAAA (FSSSSH)
NOT ENOUGH ...
NOT ENOUGH ...
I'M NOT FULL ...

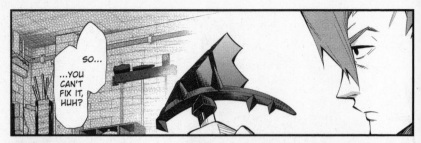

SO...
...YOU CAN'T FIX IT, HUH?
YOUR ARMOR'S ONE THING, BUT THE SWORD'S JUST...
IT'S NOT "BROKEN" SO MUCH AS "GONE."
SORRY I CAN'T HELP.
NO...
IT'S FINE. DON'T WORRY ABOUT IT.
JUST TAKE CARE OF THE ARMOR FOR ME, THEN.
ISAAC-KUN...
ARE YOU CRYING?
AS IF, YOU IDIOT!!

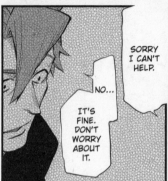

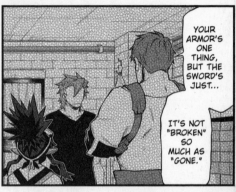

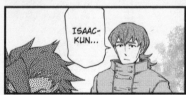

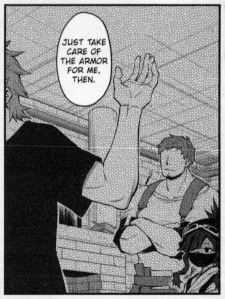

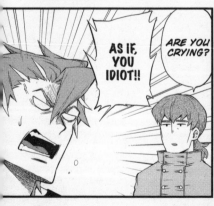

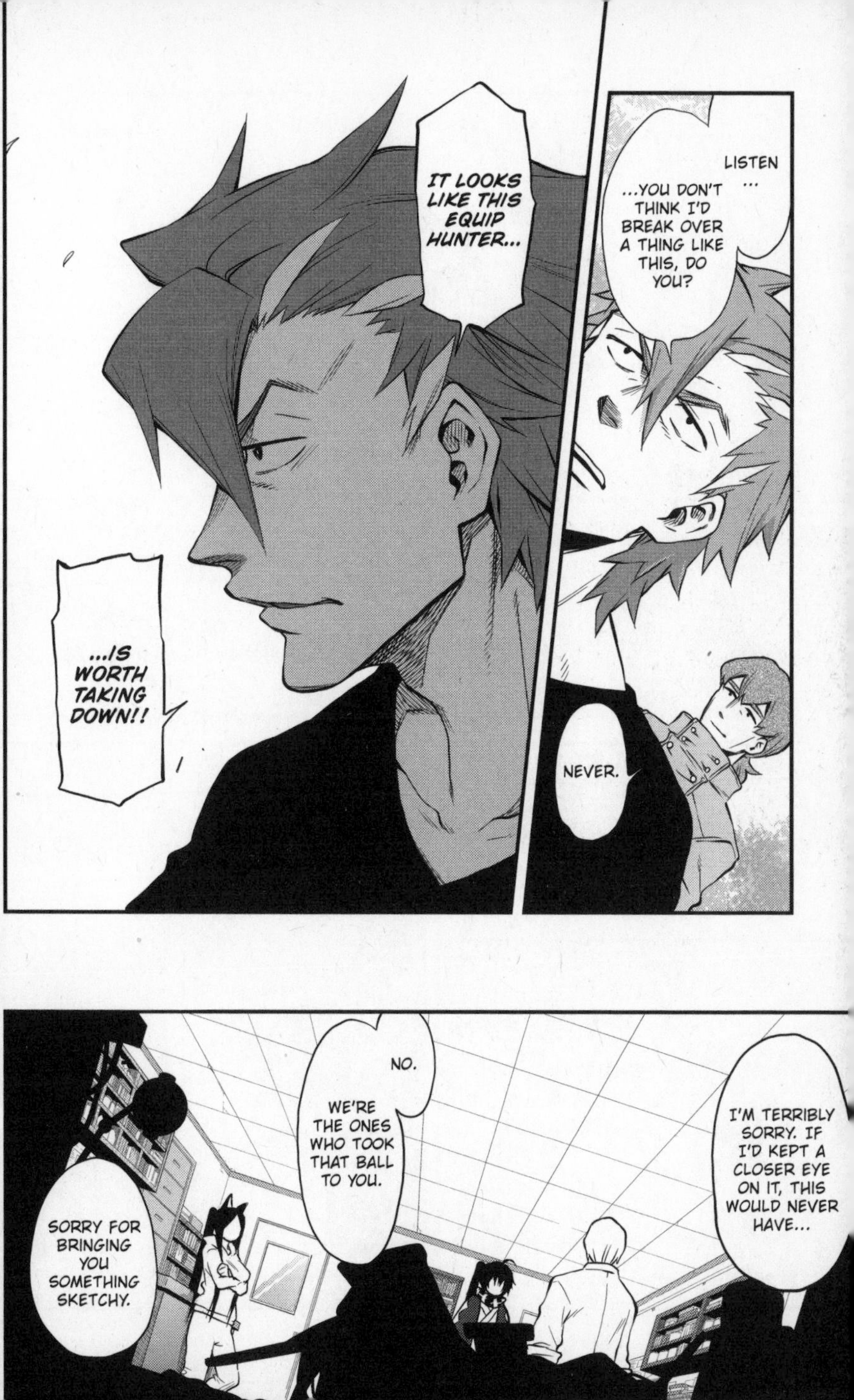

LISTEN ...
...YOU DON'T THINK I'D BREAK OVER A THING LIKE THIS, DO YOU?
NEVER.
IT LOOKS LIKE THIS EQUIP HUNTER...
...IS WORTH TAKING DOWN!!
I'M TERRIBLY SORRY. IF I'D KEPT A CLOSER EYE ON IT, THIS WOULD NEVER HAVE...
NO.
WE'RE THE ONES WHO TOOK THAT BALL TO YOU.
SORRY FOR BRINGING YOU SOMETHING SKETCHY.

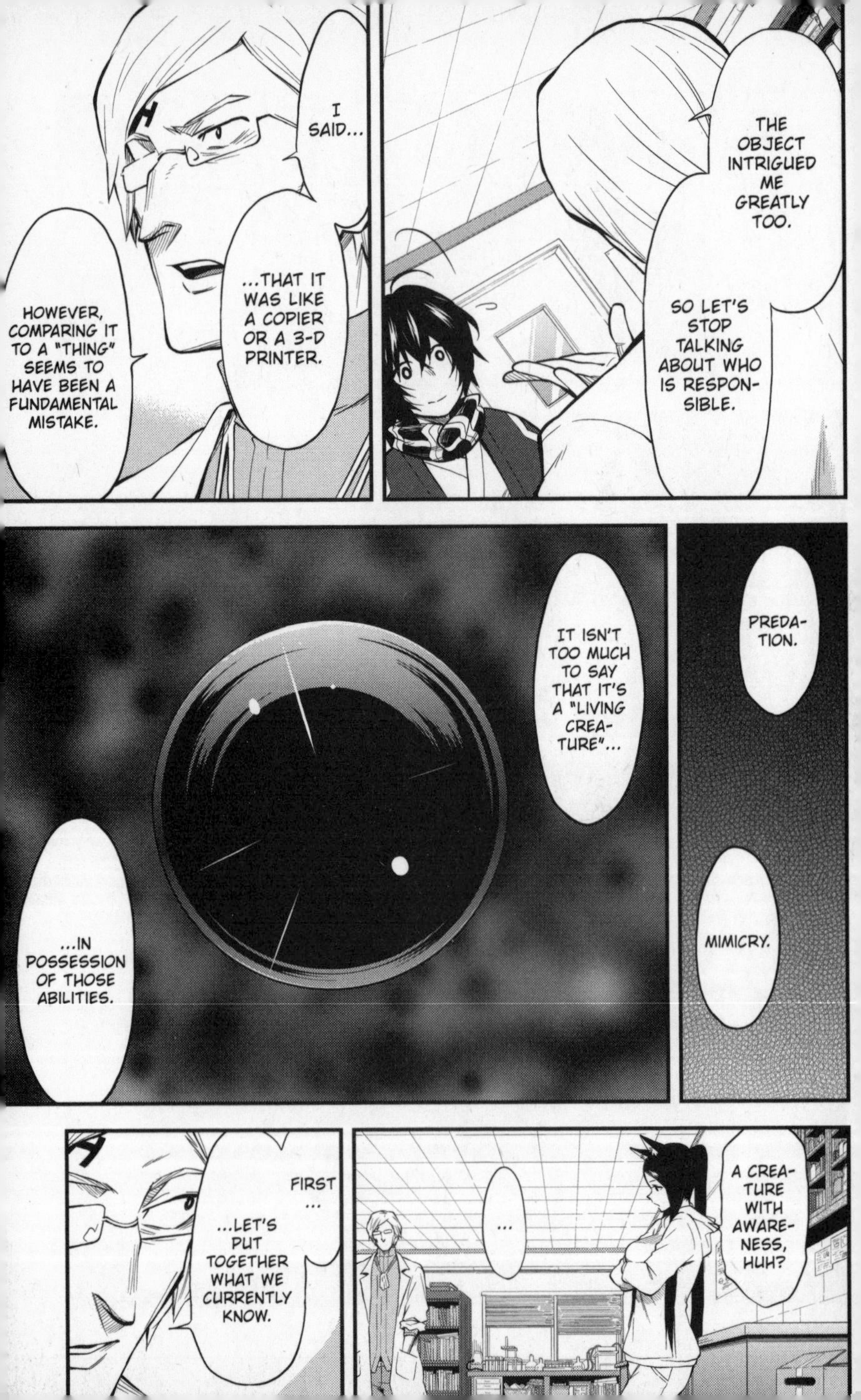
THE OBJECT INTRIGUED ME GREATLY TOO.
SO LET'S STOP TALKING ABOUT WHO IS RESPONSIBLE.
I SAID...
...THAT IT WAS LIKE A COPIER OR A 3-D PRINTER.
HOWEVER, COMPARING IT TO A "THING" SEEMS TO HAVE BEEN A FUNDAMENTAL MISTAKE.
PREDATION.
MIMICRY.
IT ISN'T TOO MUCH TO SAY THAT IT'S A "LIVING CREATURE"...
...IN POSSESSION OF THOSE ABILITIES.
A CREATURE WITH AWARENESS, HUH?
...
FIRST...
...LET'S PUT TOGETHER WHAT WE CURRENTLY KNOW.

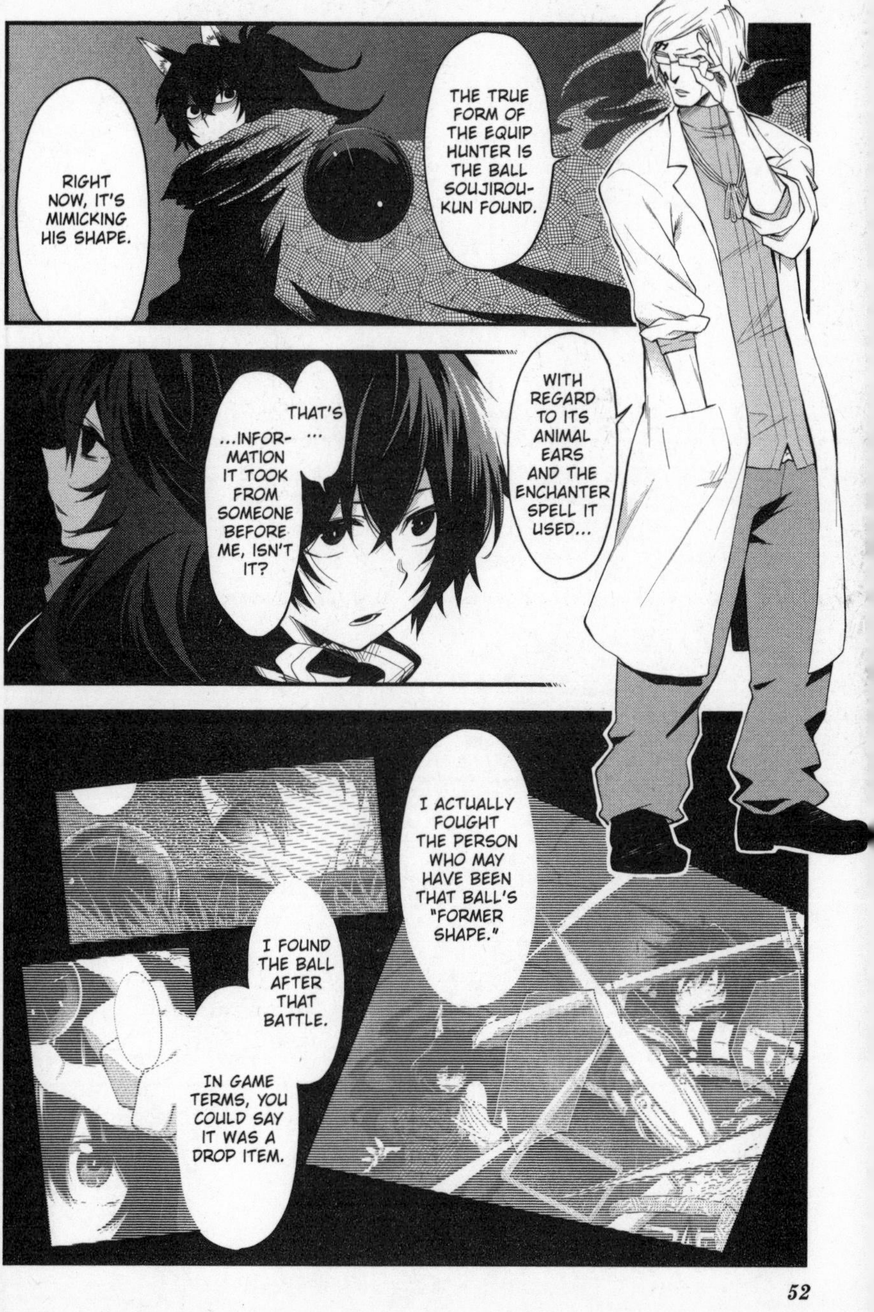
THE TRUE FORM OF THE EQUIP HUNTER IS THE BALL SOUJIROU-KUN FOUND.
RIGHT NOW, IT'S MIMICKING HIS SHAPE.
WITH REGARD TO ITS ANIMAL EARS AND THE ENCHANTER SPELL IT USED...
THAT'S ...
...INFORMATION IT TOOK FROM SOMEONE BEFORE ME, ISN'T IT?
I ACTUALLY FOUGHT THE PERSON WHO MAY HAVE BEEN THAT BALL'S "FORMER SHAPE."
I FOUND THE BALL AFTER THAT BATTLE.
IN GAME TERMS, YOU COULD SAY IT WAS A DROP ITEM.

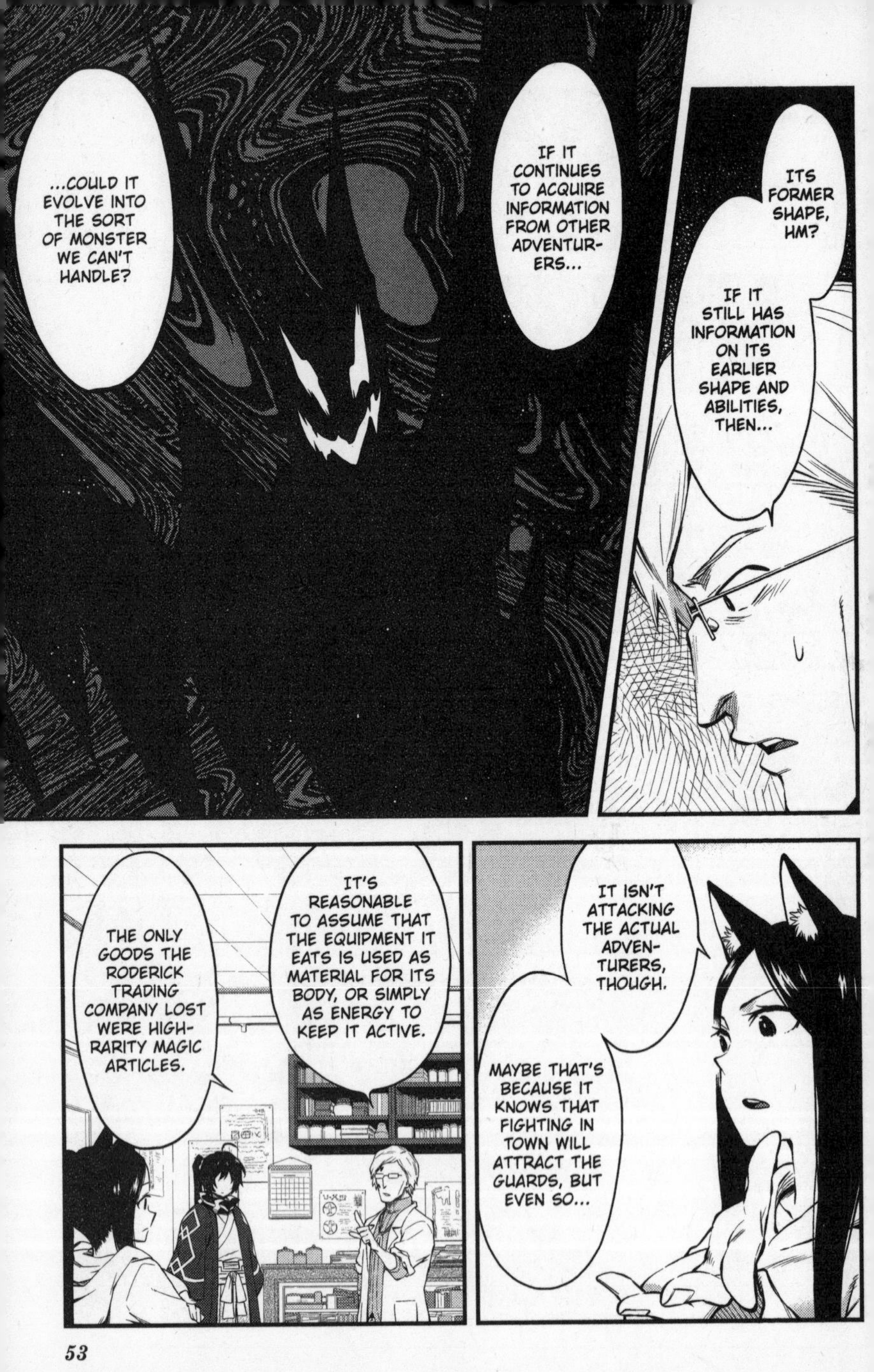
ITS FORMER SHAPE, HM?
IF IT STILL HAS INFORMATION ON ITS EARLIER SHAPE AND ABILITIES, THEN...
IF IT CONTINUES TO ACQUIRE INFORMATION FROM OTHER ADVENTUR-ERS...
...COULD IT EVOLVE INTO THE SORT OF MONSTER WE CAN'T HANDLE?
IT ISN'T ATTACKING THE ACTUAL ADVEN-TURERS, THOUGH.
MAYBE THAT'S BECAUSE IT KNOWS THAT FIGHTING IN TOWN WILL ATTRACT THE GUARDS, BUT EVEN SO...
IT'S REASONABLE TO ASSUME THAT THE EQUIPMENT IT EATS IS USED AS MATERIAL FOR ITS BODY, OR SIMPLY AS ENERGY TO KEEP IT ACTIVE.
THE ONLY GOODS THE RODERICK TRADING COMPANY LOST WERE HIGH-RARITY MAGIC ARTICLES.

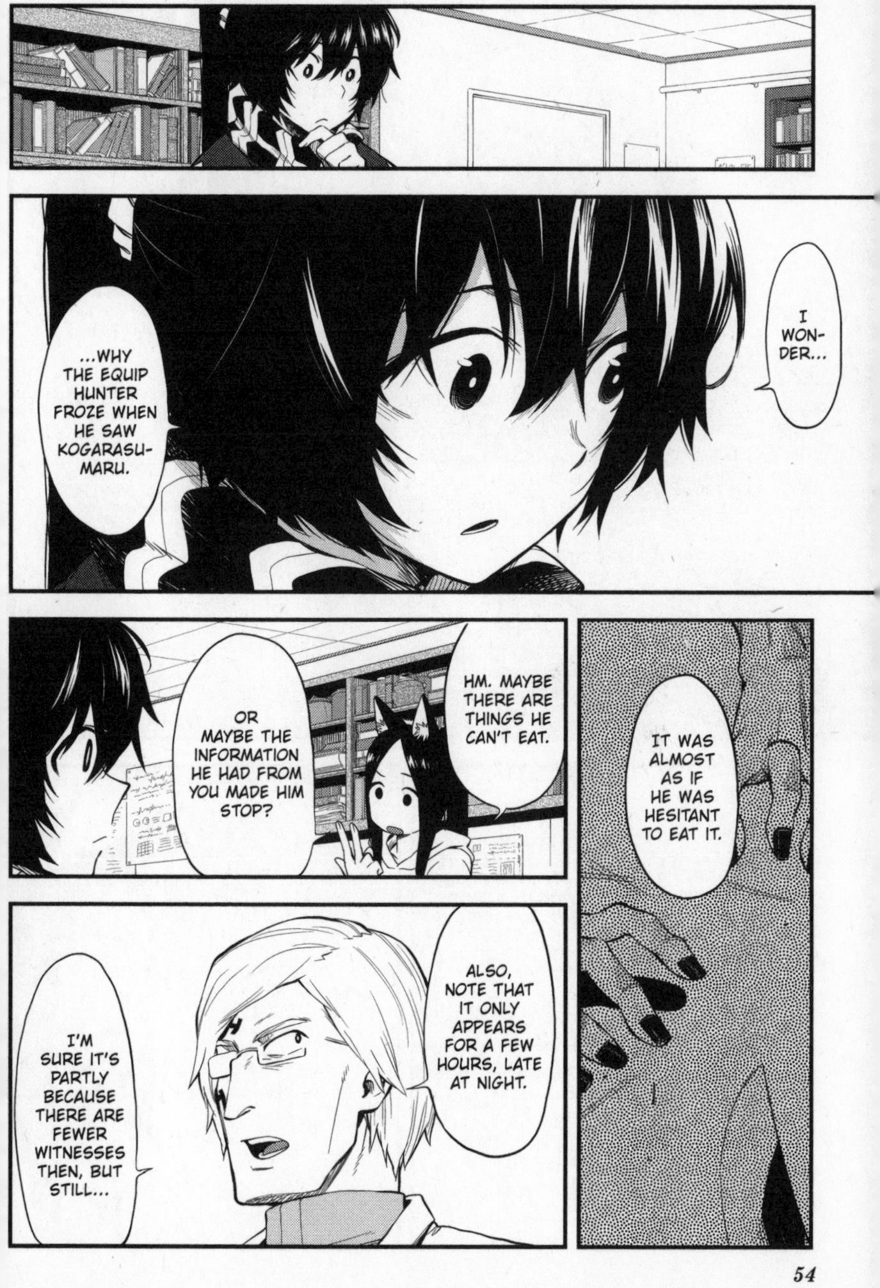
I WONDER...
...WHY THE EQUIP HUNTER FROZE WHEN HE SAW KOGARASU-MARU.
IT WAS ALMOST AS IF HE WAS HESITANT TO EAT IT.
HM. MAYBE THERE ARE THINGS HE CAN'T EAT.
OR MAYBE THE INFORMATION HE HAD FROM YOU MADE HIM STOP?
ALSO, NOTE THAT IT ONLY APPEARS FOR A FEW HOURS, LATE AT NIGHT.
I'M SURE IT'S PARTLY BECAUSE THERE ARE FEWER WITNESSES THEN, BUT STILL...

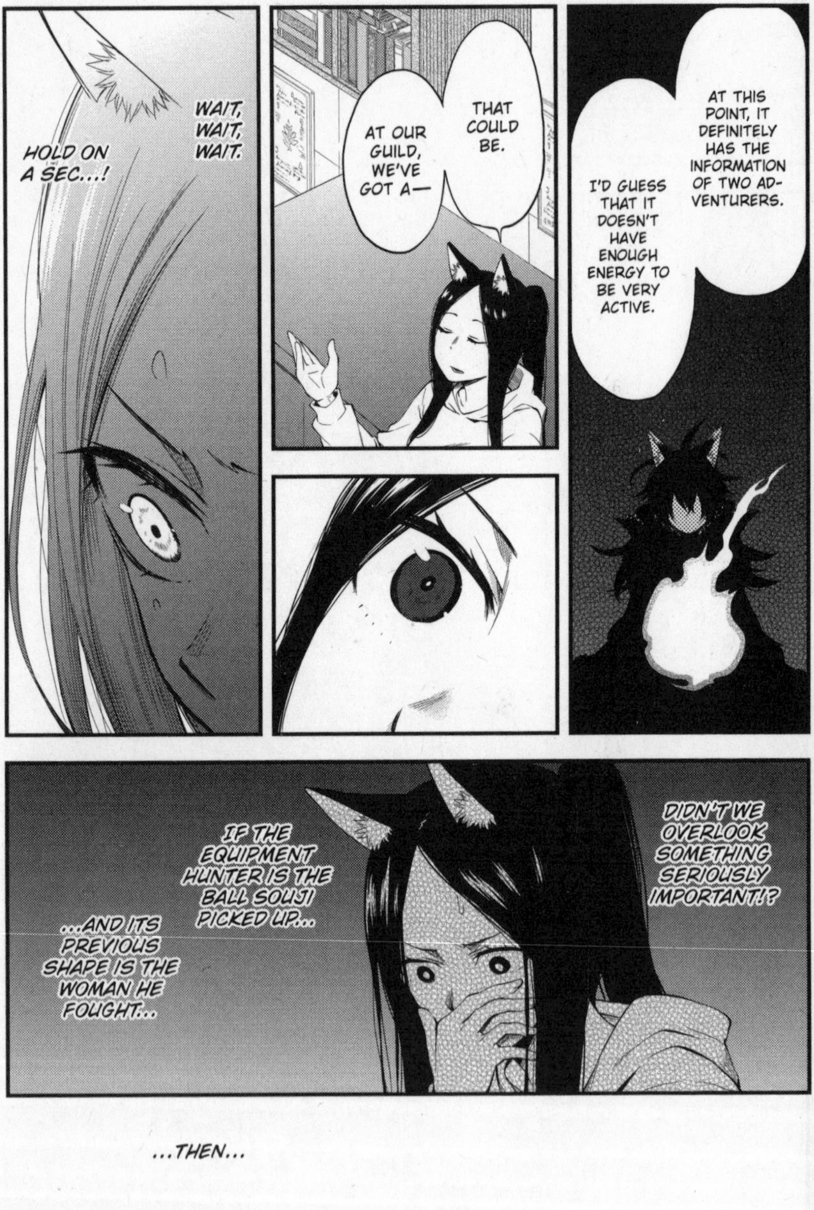
AT THIS POINT, IT DEFINITELY HAS THE INFORMATION OF TWO ADVENTURERS.
I'D GUESS THAT IT DOESN'T HAVE ENOUGH ENERGY TO BE VERY ACTIVE.
THAT COULD BE.
AT OUR GUILD, WE'VE GOT A—
WAIT, WAIT, WAIT.
HOLD ON A SEC...!
DIDN'T WE OVERLOOK SOMETHING SERIOUSLY IMPORTANT!?
IF THE EQUIPMENT HUNTER IS THE BALL SOUJI PICKED UP...
...AND ITS PREVIOUS SHAPE IS THE WOMAN HE FOUGHT...

...THEN...

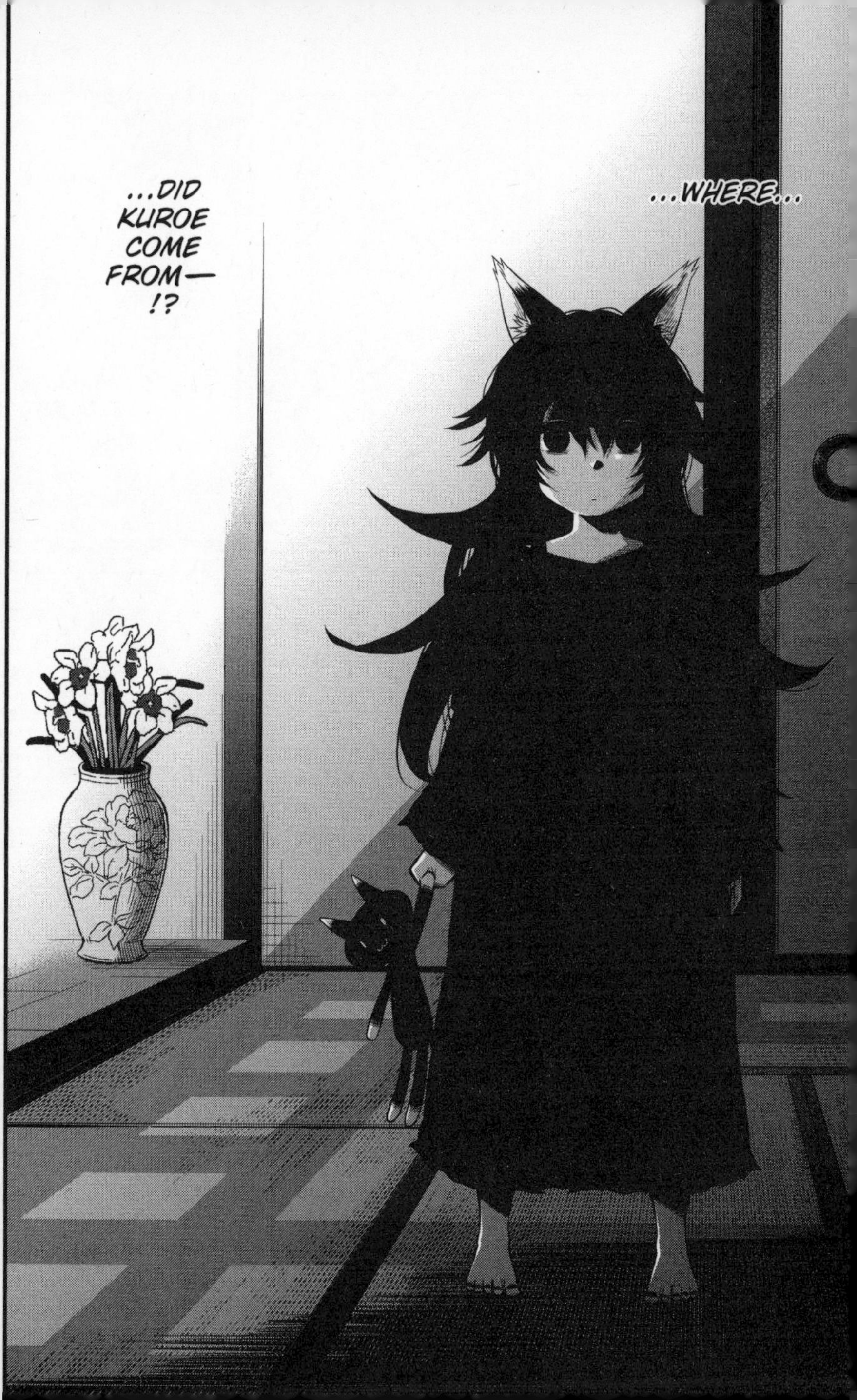
...WHERE...
...DID KUROE COME FROM—!?

LOG HORIZON
THE WEST WIND BRIGADE

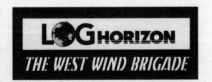

LOG HORIZON

THE WEST WIND BRIGADE

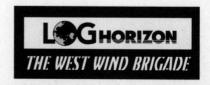

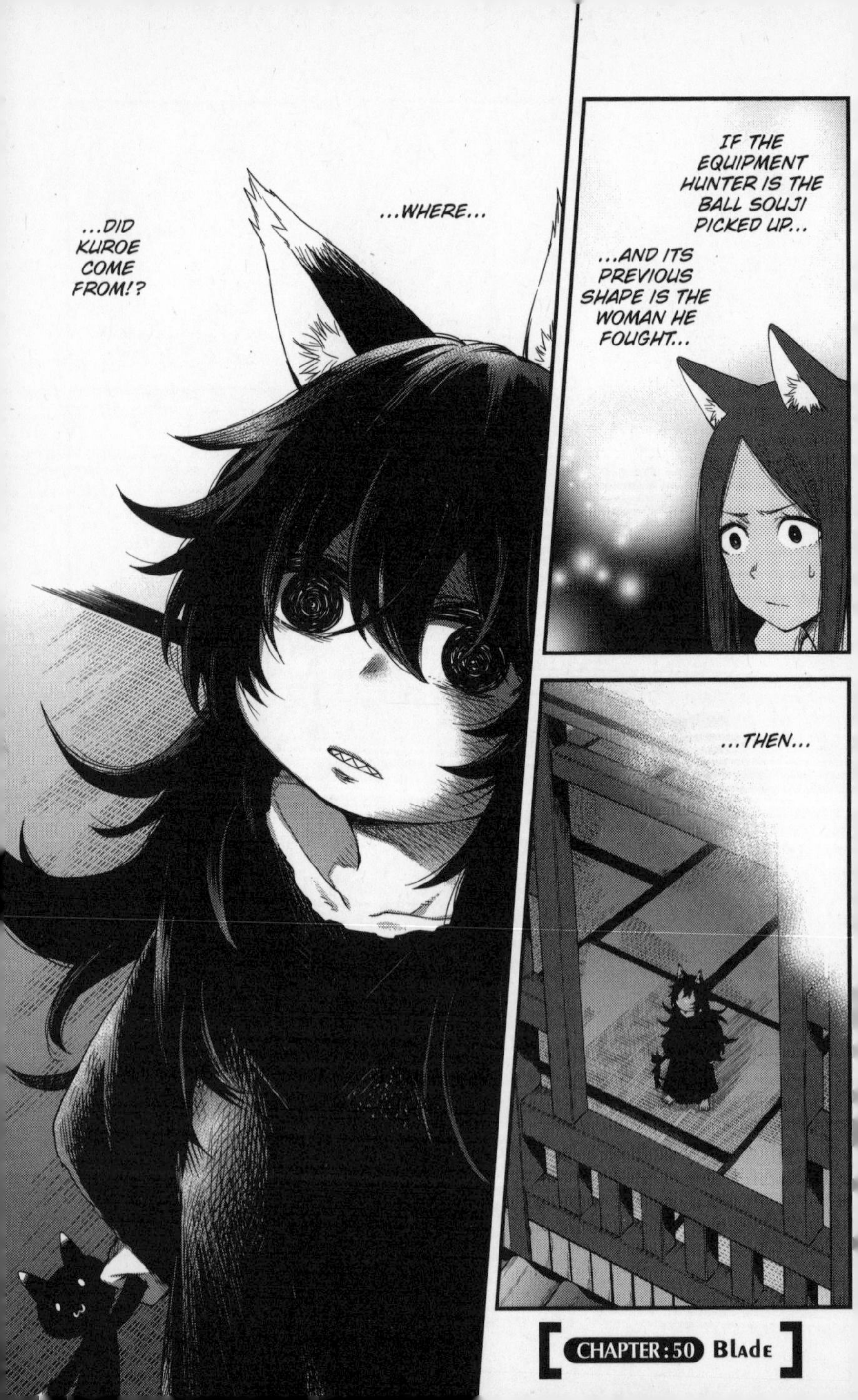
IF THE EQUIPMENT HUNTER IS THE BALL SOUJI PICKED UP...
...AND ITS PREVIOUS SHAPE IS THE WOMAN HE FOUGHT...
...THEN...
...WHERE...
...DID KUROE COME FROM!?
CHAPTER: 50 Blade

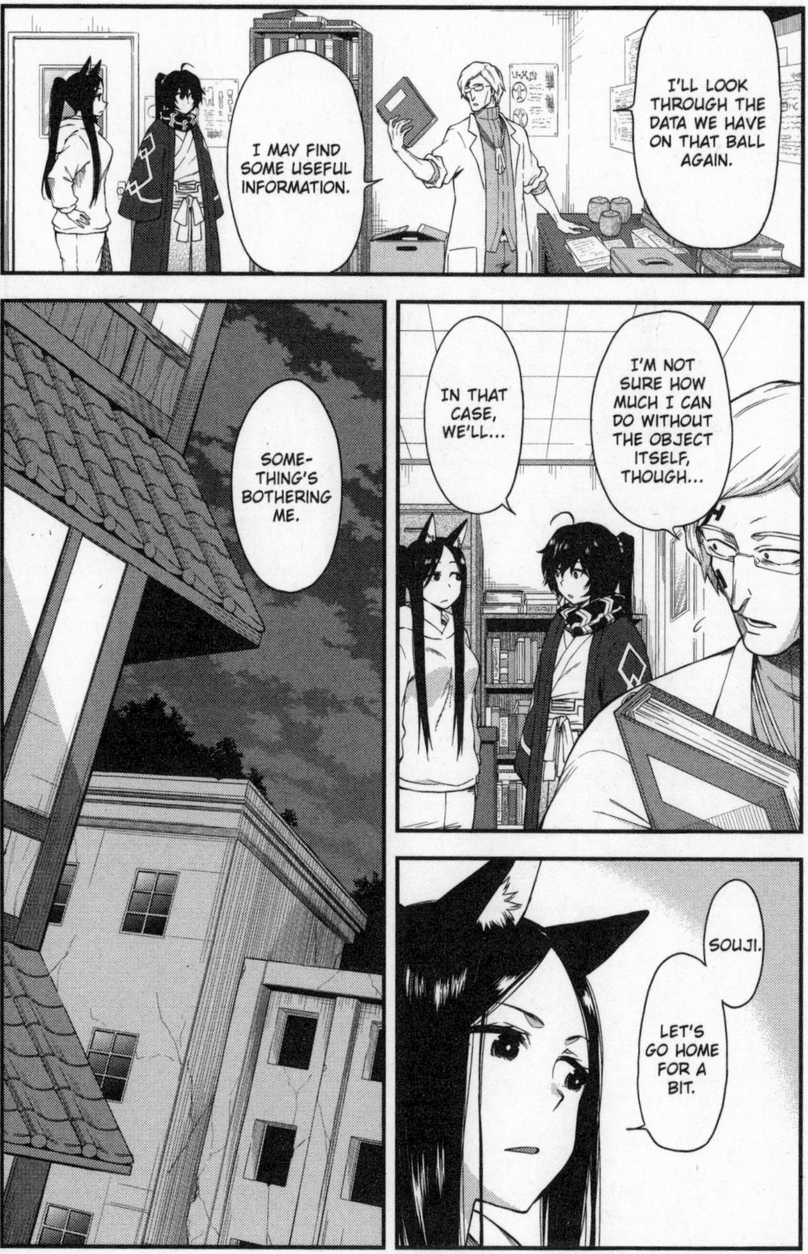
I'LL LOOK THROUGH THE DATA WE HAVE ON THAT BALL AGAIN.
I MAY FIND SOME USEFUL INFORMATION.
I'M NOT SURE HOW MUCH I CAN DO WITHOUT THE OBJECT ITSELF, THOUGH...
IN THAT CASE, WE'LL...
SOUJI.
LET'S GO HOME FOR A BIT.
SOME-THING'S BOTHERING ME.

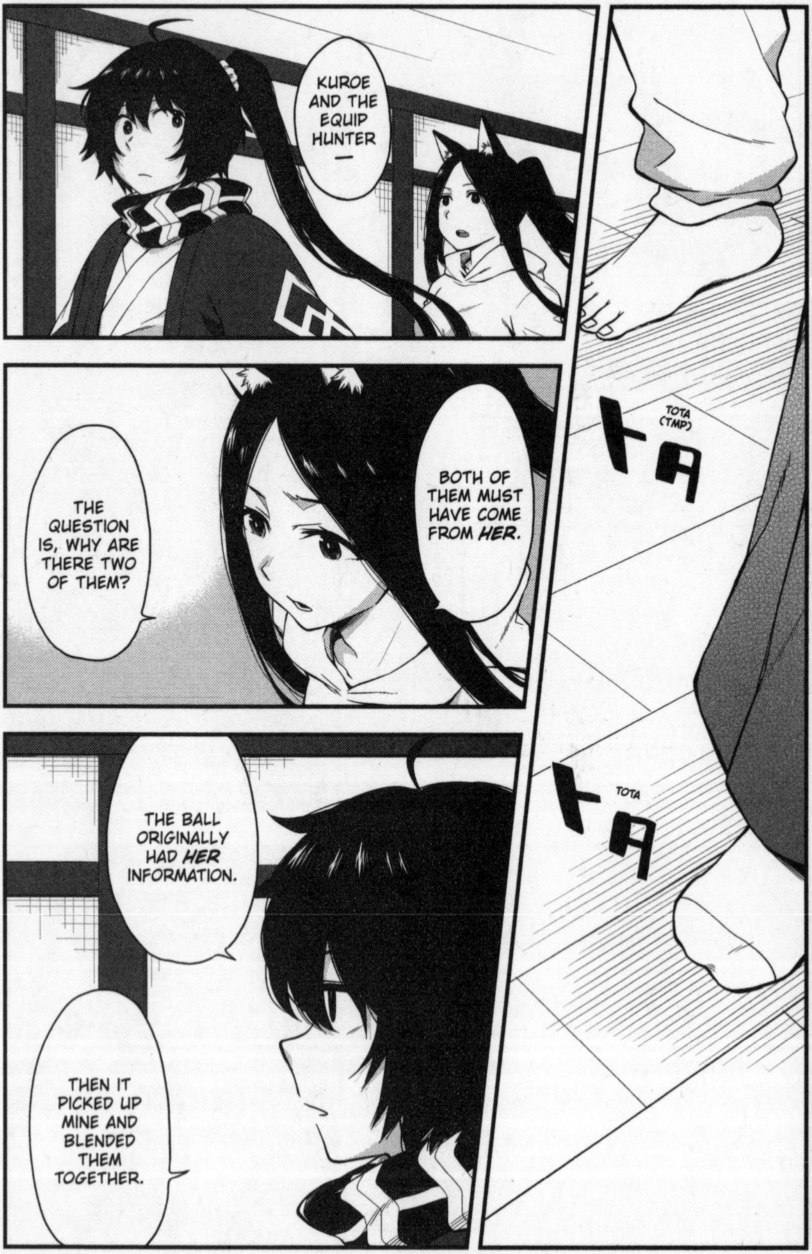

トタ
TOTA (TMP)
トタ
TOTA
KUROE AND THE EQUIP HUNTER —
BOTH OF THEM MUST HAVE COME FROM *HER*.
THE QUESTION IS, WHY ARE THERE TWO OF THEM?
THE BALL ORIGINALLY HAD *HER* INFORMATION.
THEN IT PICKED UP MINE AND BLENDED THEM TOGETHER.

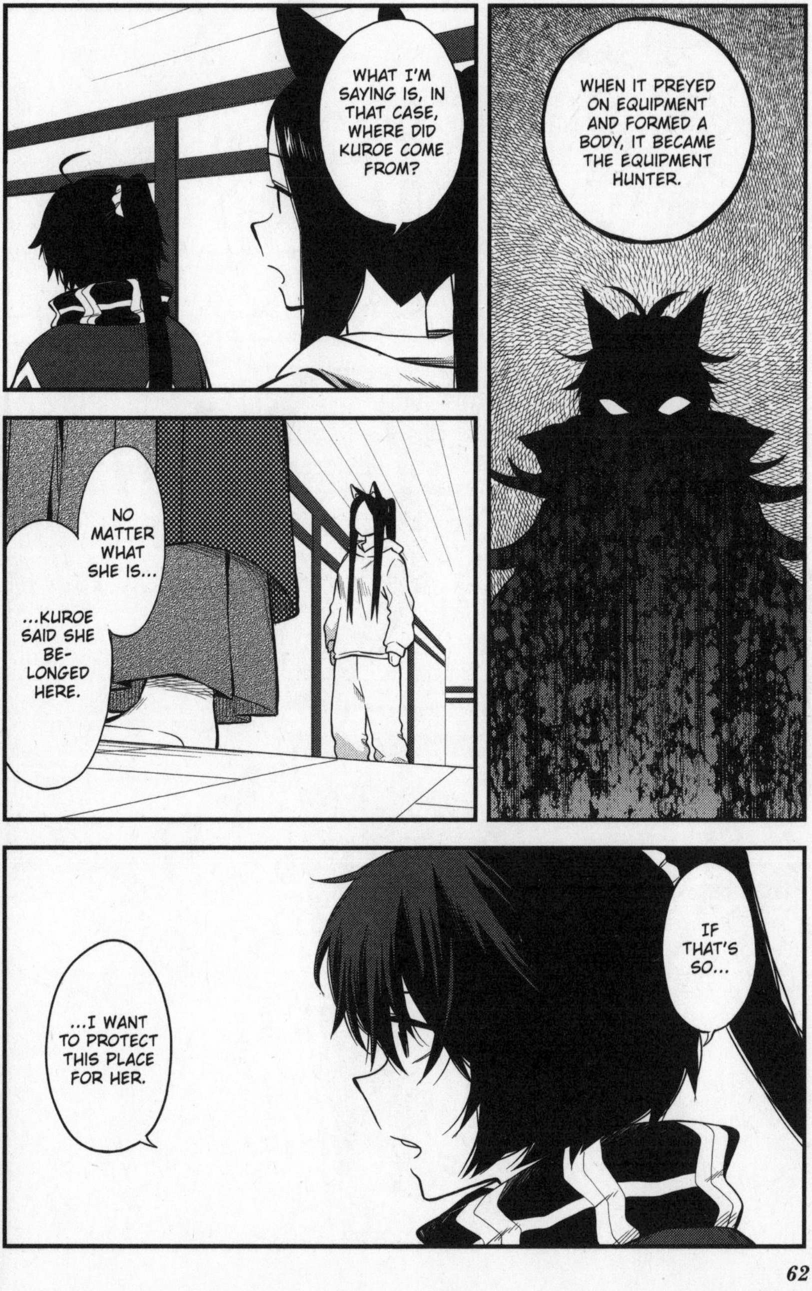
WHEN IT PREYED ON EQUIPMENT AND FORMED A BODY, IT BECAME THE EQUIPMENT HUNTER.
WHAT I'M SAYING IS, IN THAT CASE, WHERE DID KUROE COME FROM?
NO MATTER WHAT SHE IS...
...KUROE SAID SHE BE-LONGED HERE.
IF THAT'S SO...
...I WANT TO PROTECT THIS PLACE FOR HER.

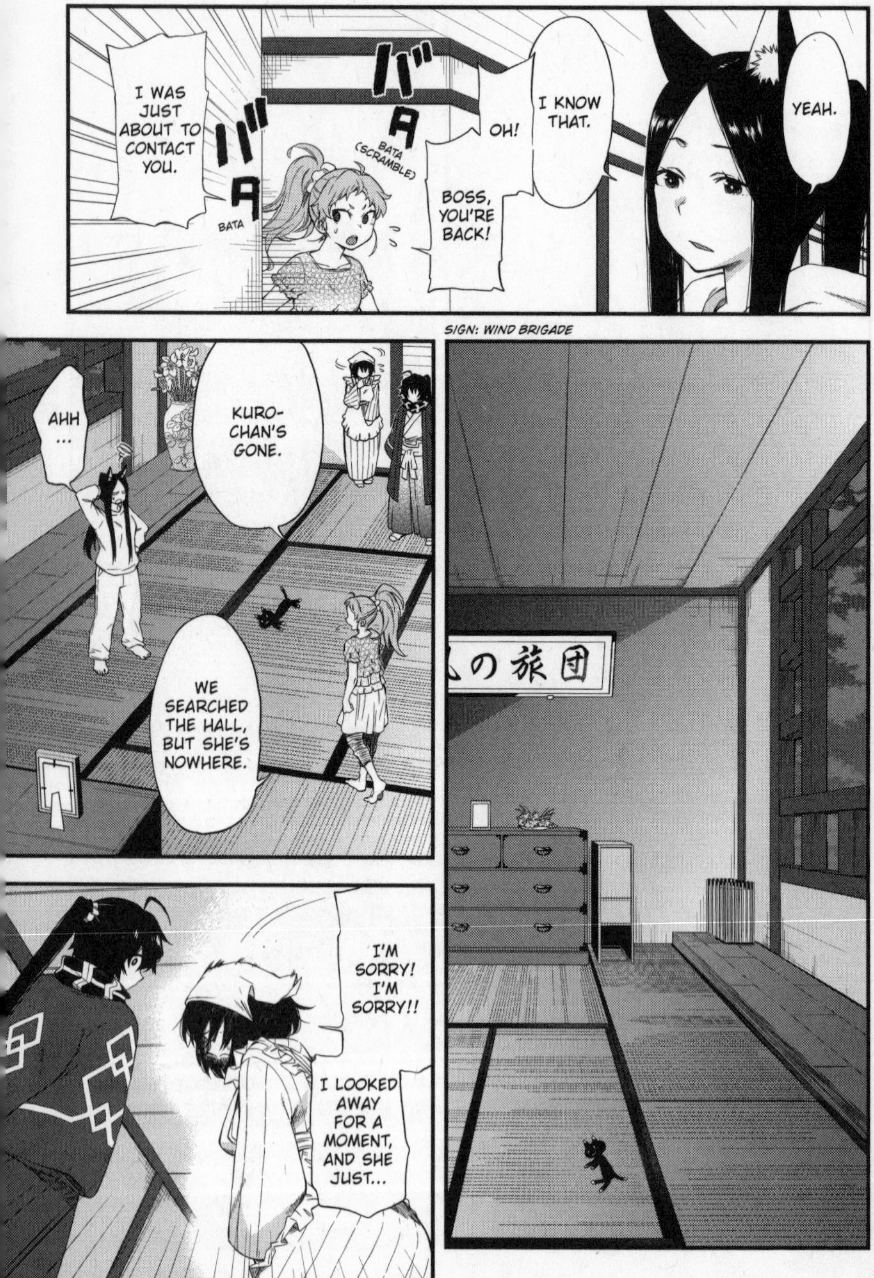
YEAH.
I KNOW THAT.
OH!
BOSS, YOU'RE BACK!
バタ
BATA (SCRAMBLE)
バタ
BATA
I WAS JUST ABOUT TO CONTACT YOU.
SIGN: WIND BRIGADE
の旅団
KURO-CHAN'S GONE.
AHH...
WE SEARCHED THE HALL, BUT SHE'S NOWHERE.
I'M SORRY! I'M SORRY!!
I LOOKED AWAY FOR A MOMENT, AND SHE JUST...

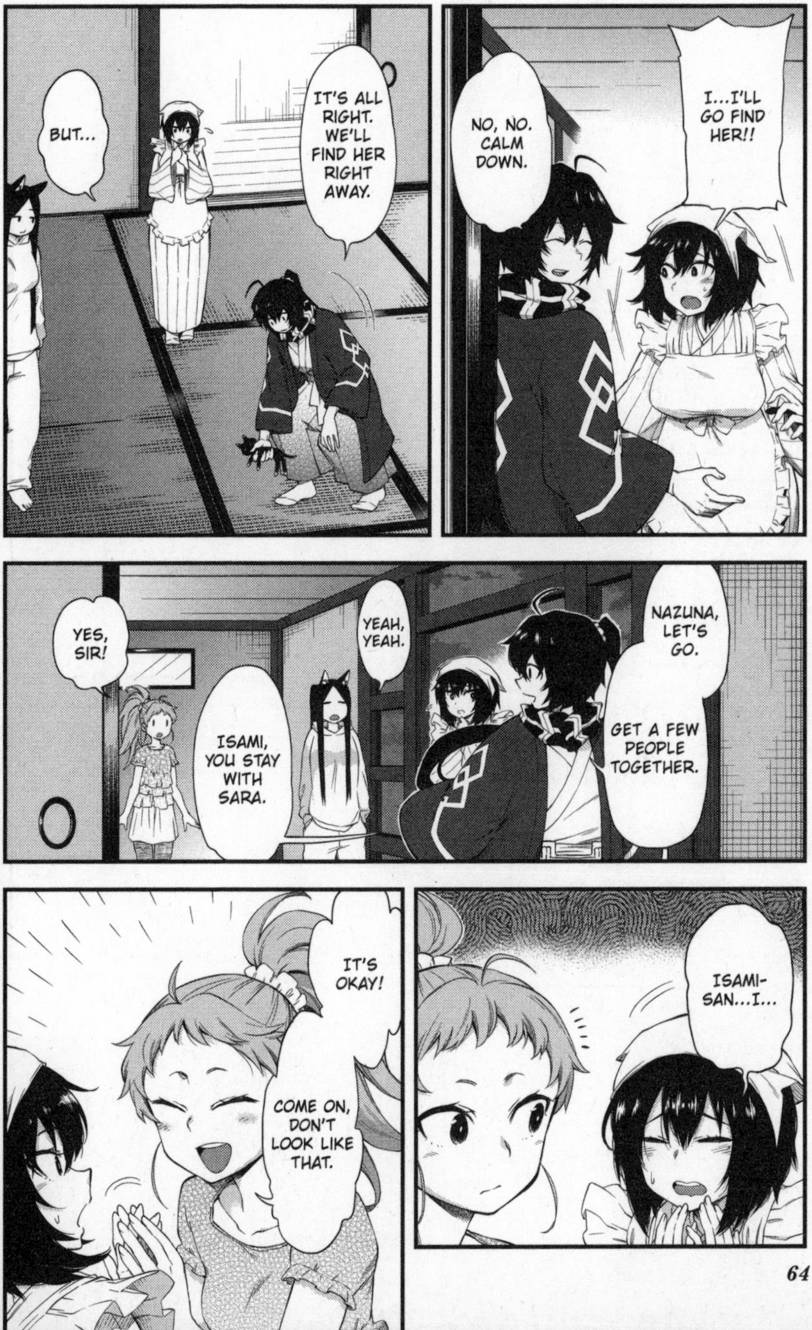
I...I'LL GO FIND HER!!
NO, NO. CALM DOWN.
IT'S ALL RIGHT. WE'LL FIND HER RIGHT AWAY.
BUT...
NAZUNA, LET'S GO.
GET A FEW PEOPLE TOGETHER.
YEAH, YEAH.
ISAMI, YOU STAY WITH SARA.
YES, SIR!
ISAMI-SAN...I...
IT'S OKAY!
COME ON, DON'T LOOK LIKE THAT.

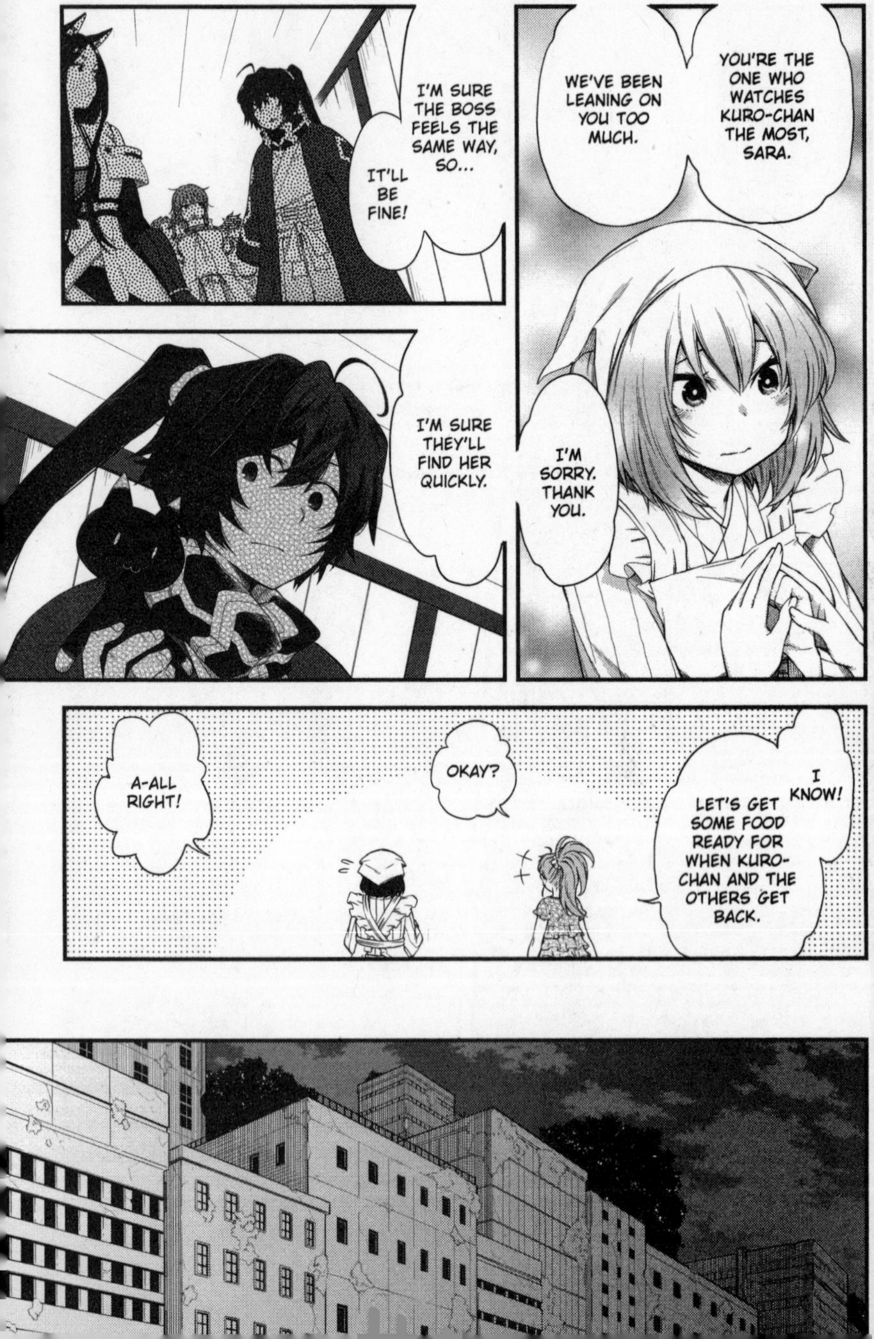
YOU'RE THE ONE WHO WATCHES KURO-CHAN THE MOST, SARA.
WE'VE BEEN LEANING ON YOU TOO MUCH.
I'M SORRY. THANK YOU.
I'M SURE THE BOSS FEELS THE SAME WAY, SO...
IT'LL BE FINE!
I'M SURE THEY'LL FIND HER QUICKLY.
I KNOW!
LET'S GET SOME FOOD READY FOR WHEN KURO-CHAN AND THE OTHERS GET BACK.
OKAY?
A-ALL RIGHT!

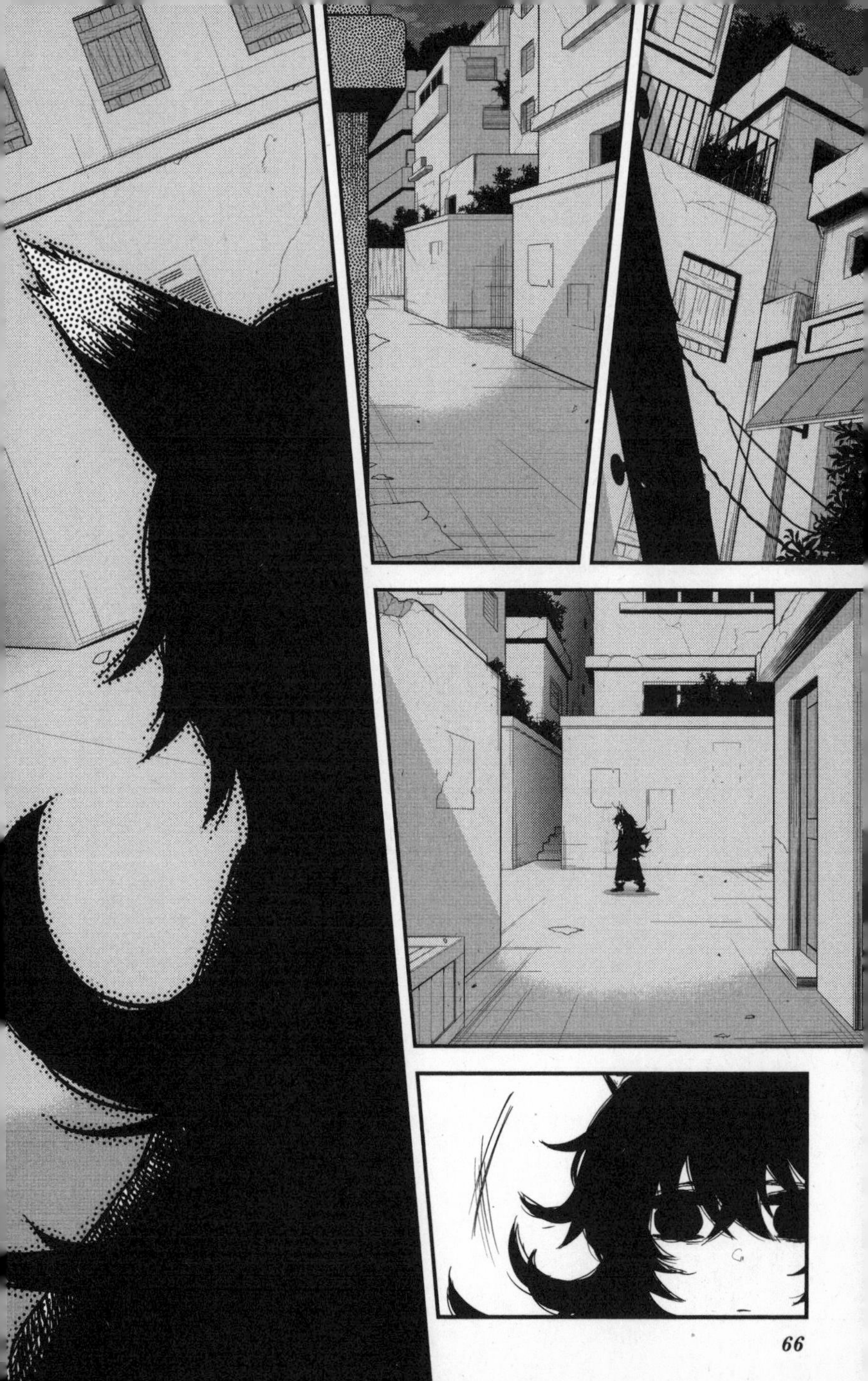

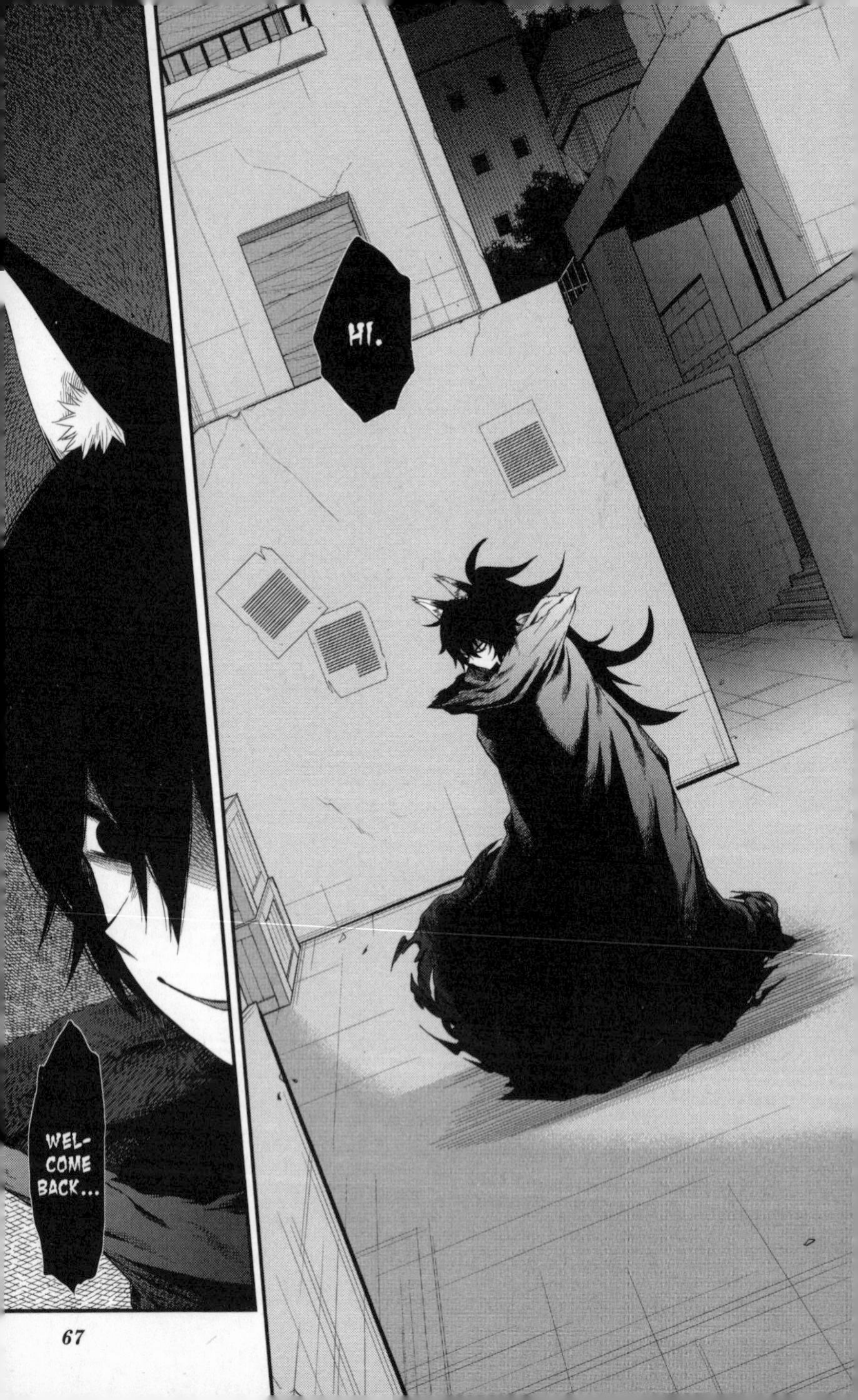
HI.
WEL-COME BACK...

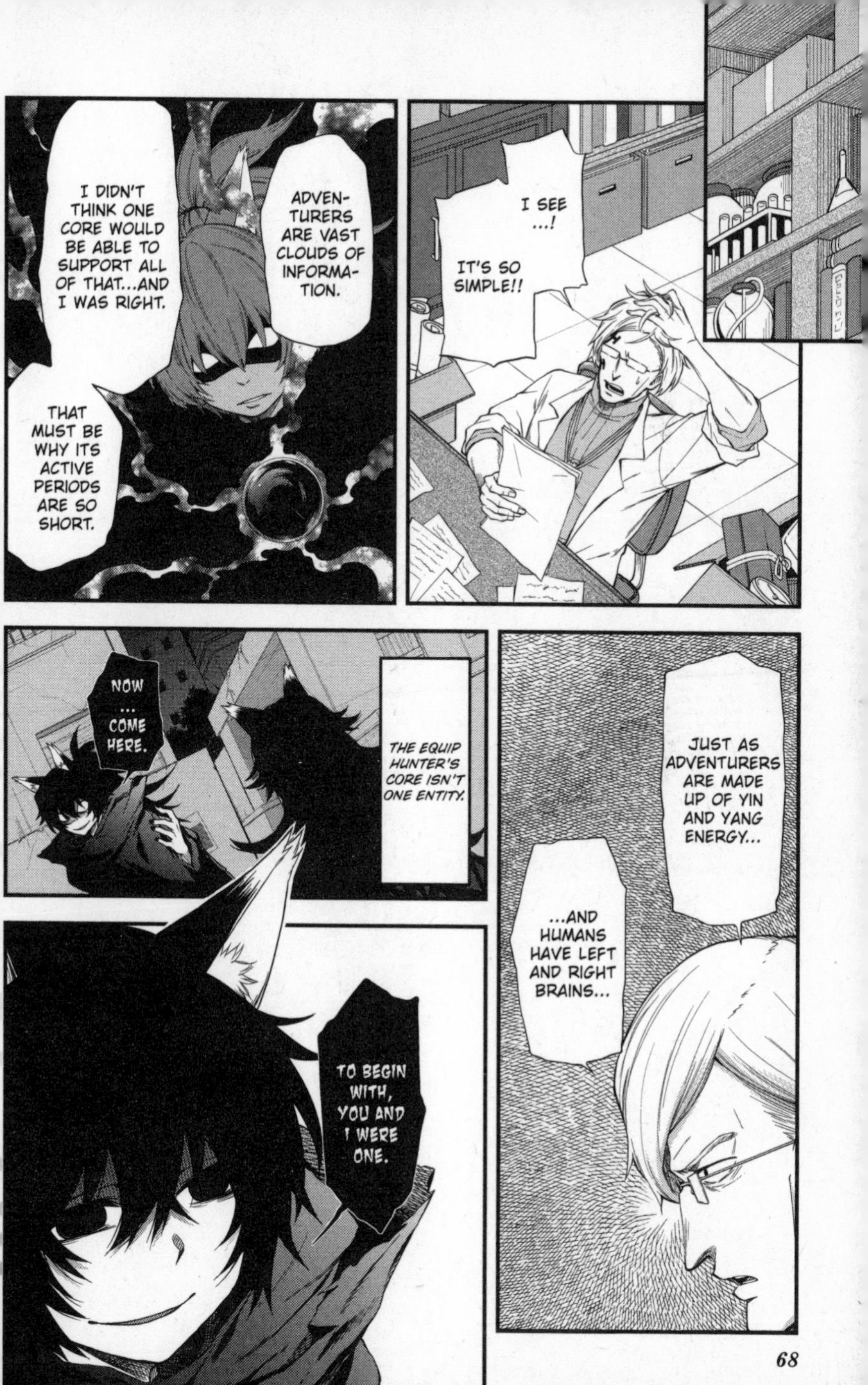
I SEE ...!
IT'S SO SIMPLE!!
ADVENTURERS ARE VAST CLOUDS OF INFORMATION.
I DIDN'T THINK ONE CORE WOULD BE ABLE TO SUPPORT ALL OF THAT...AND I WAS RIGHT.
THAT MUST BE WHY ITS ACTIVE PERIODS ARE SO SHORT.
JUST AS ADVENTURERS ARE MADE UP OF YIN AND YANG ENERGY...
...AND HUMANS HAVE LEFT AND RIGHT BRAINS...
THE EQUIP HUNTER'S CORE ISN'T ONE ENTITY.
NOW ... COME HERE.
TO BEGIN WITH, YOU AND I WERE ONE.

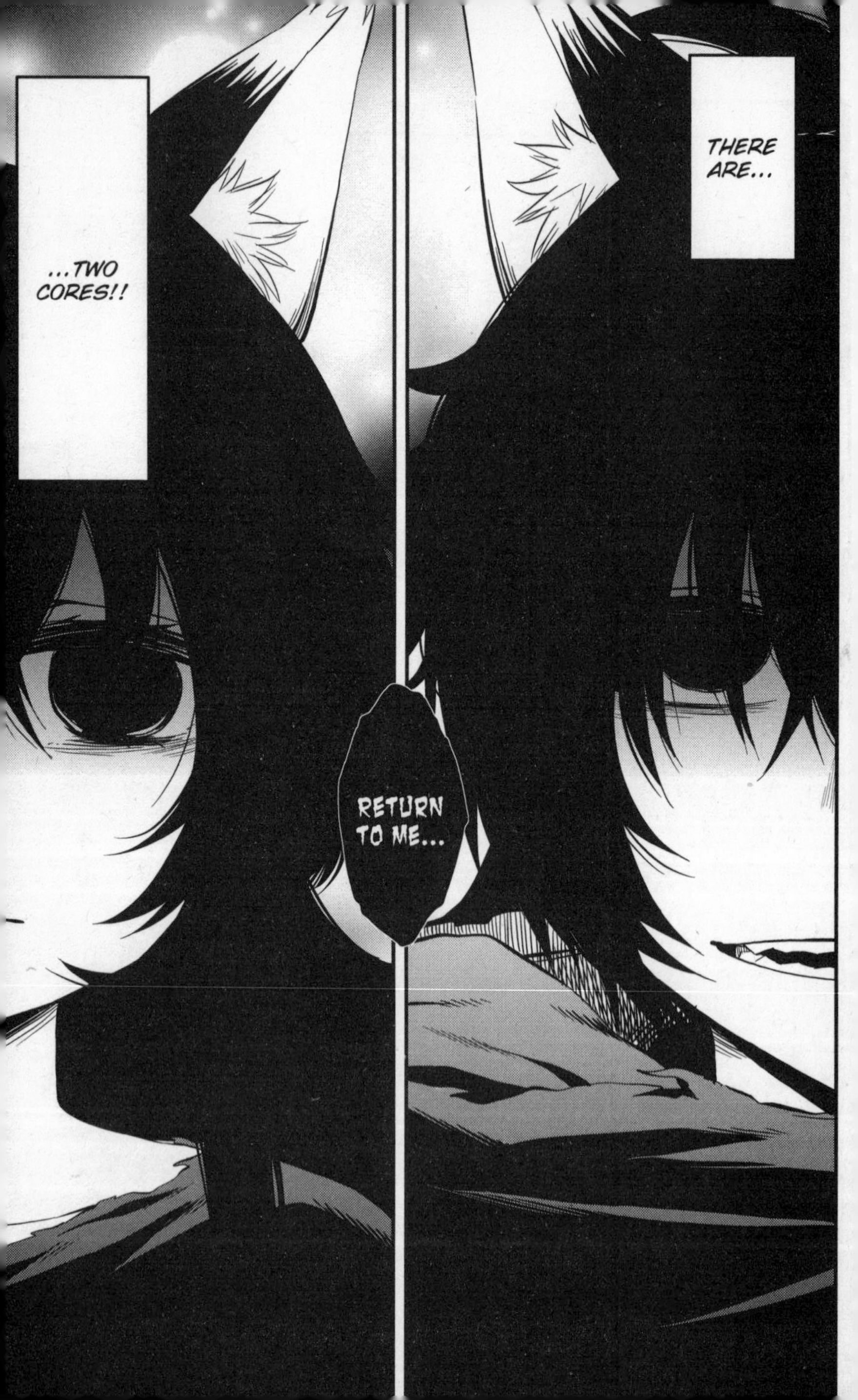
THERE ARE...
...TWO CORES!!
RETURN TO ME...

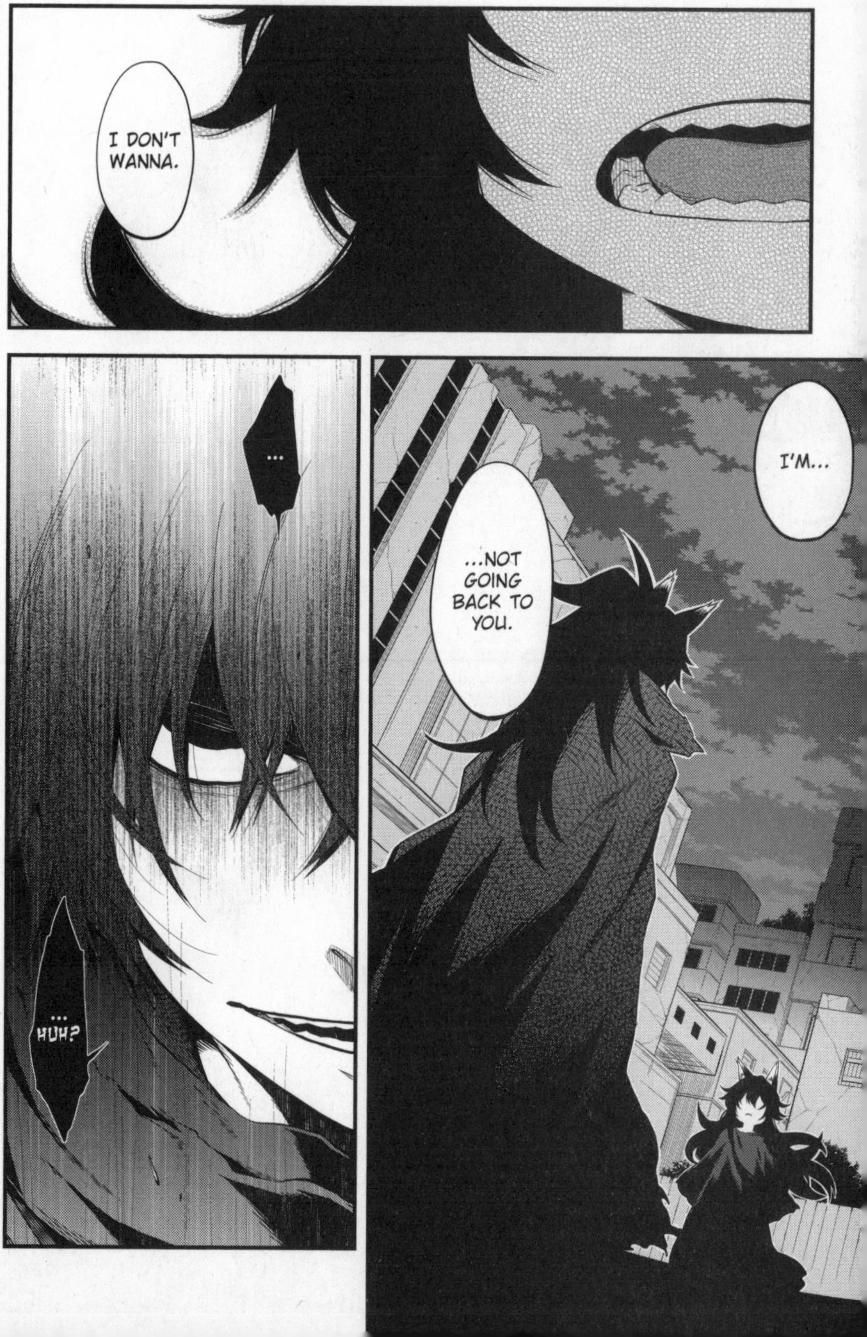
I DON'T WANNA.
I'M...
...NOT GOING BACK TO YOU.
...
...HUH?

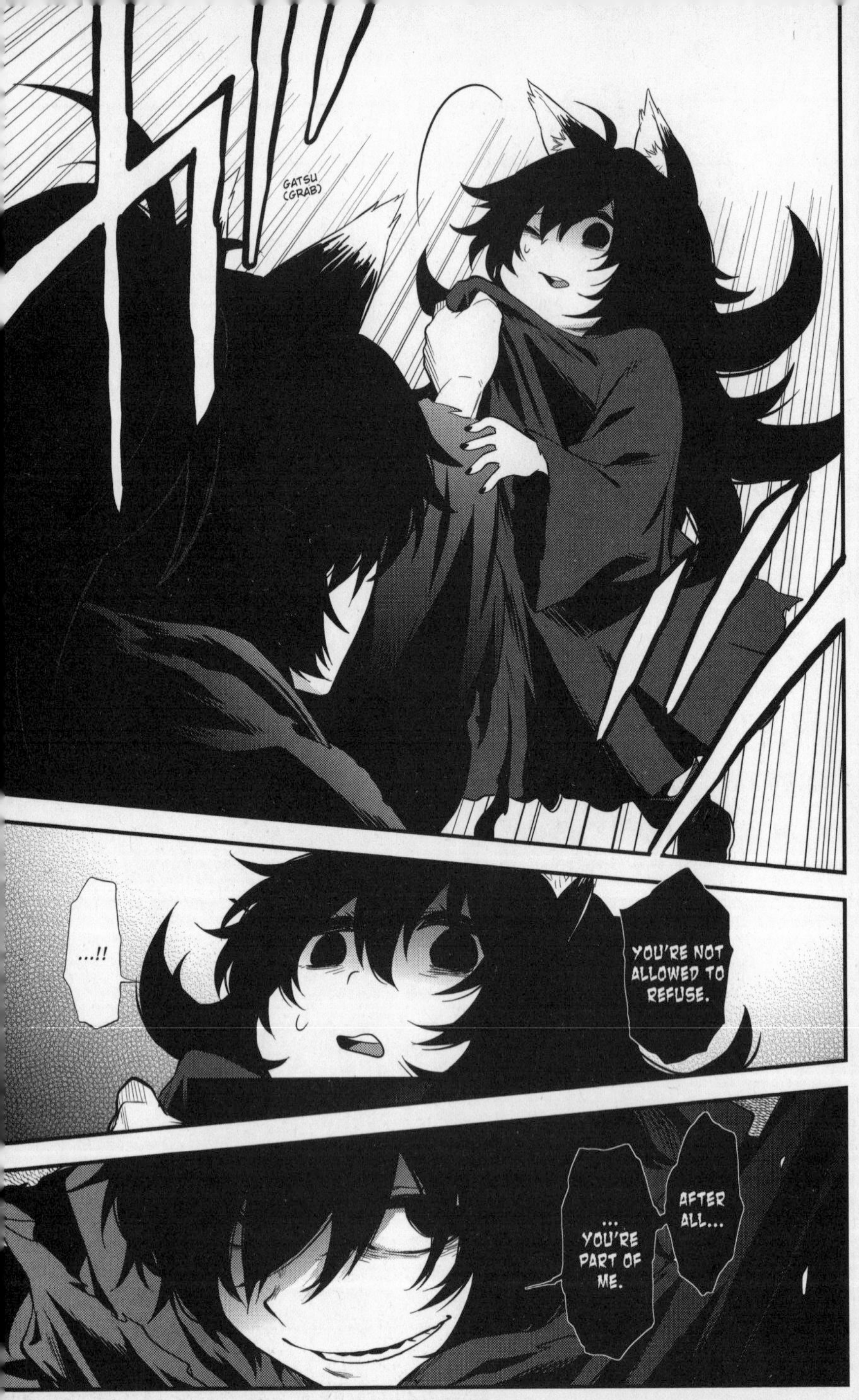
GATSU
(GRAB)
YOU'RE NOT ALLOWED TO REFUSE.
...!!
AFTER ALL...
... YOU'RE PART OF ME.

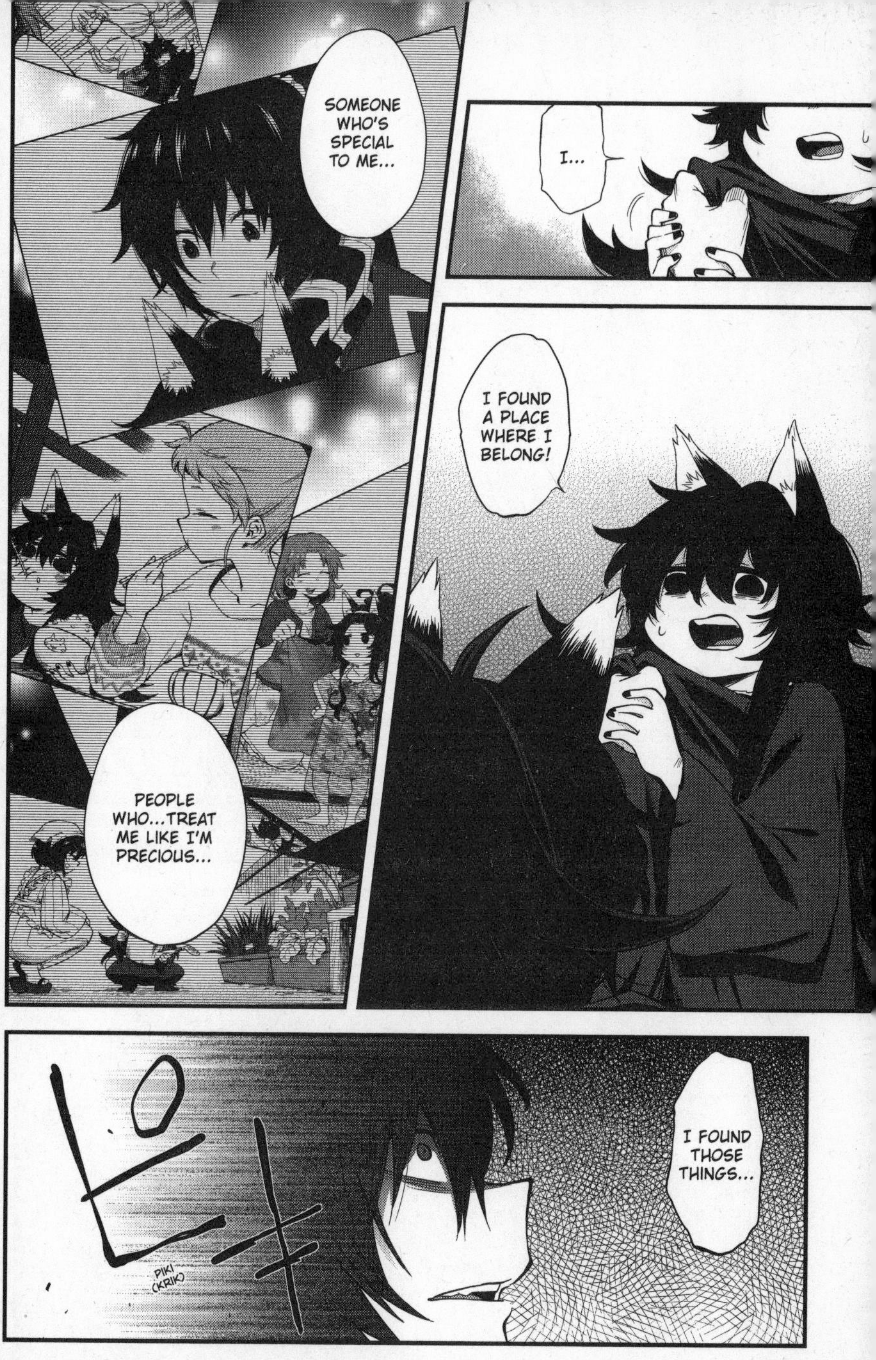
I...
I FOUND A PLACE WHERE I BELONG!
SOMEONE WHO'S SPECIAL TO ME...
PEOPLE WHO...TREAT ME LIKE I'M PRECIOUS...
I FOUND THOSE THINGS...
PIKI (KRIK)

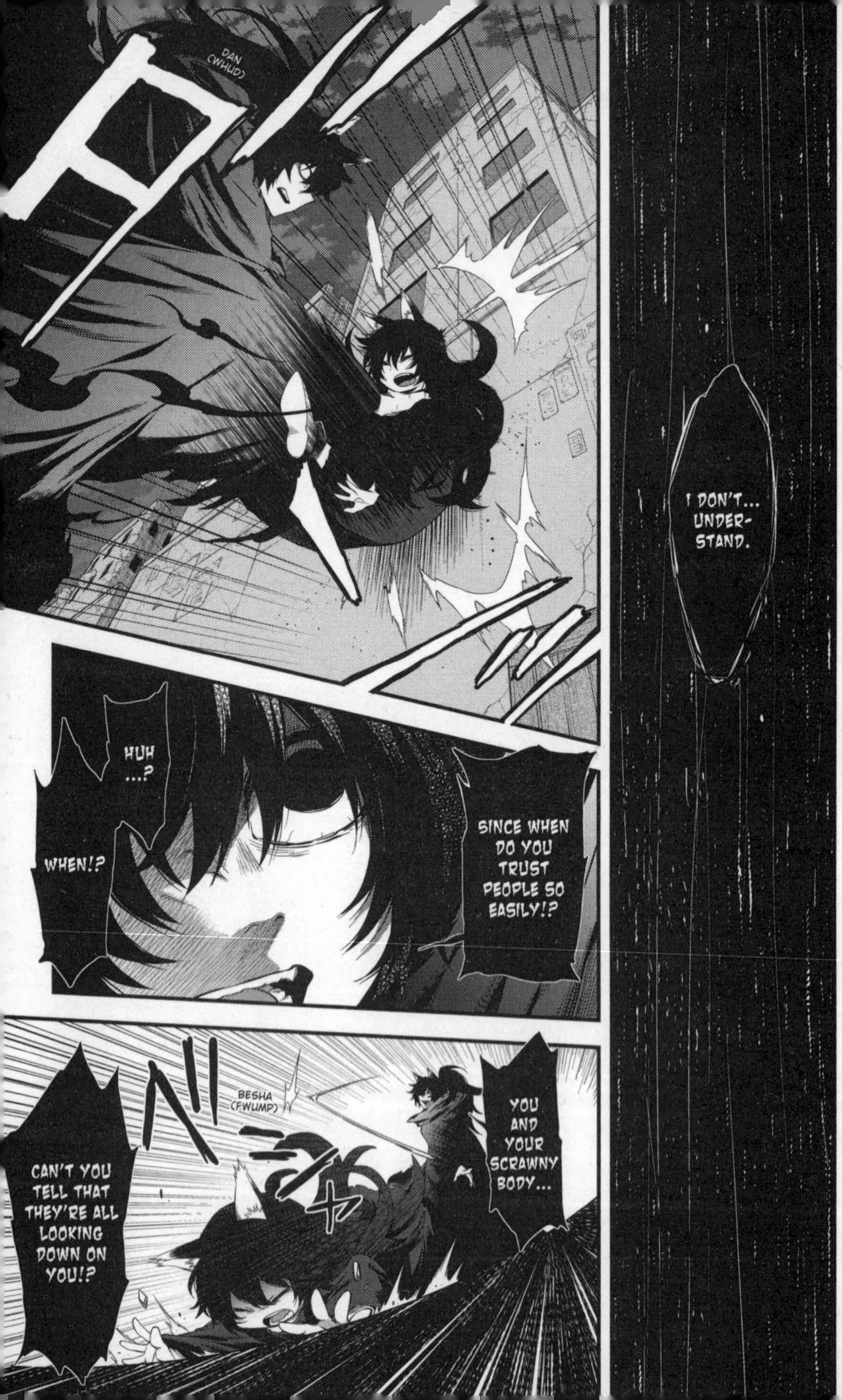
I DON'T... UNDER-STAND.
DAN (WHUD)
SINCE WHEN DO YOU TRUST PEOPLE SO EASILY!?
HUH ...?
WHEN!?
YOU AND YOUR SCRAWNY BODY...
BESHA (F.WUMP)
CAN'T YOU TELL THAT THEY'RE ALL LOOKING DOWN ON YOU!?

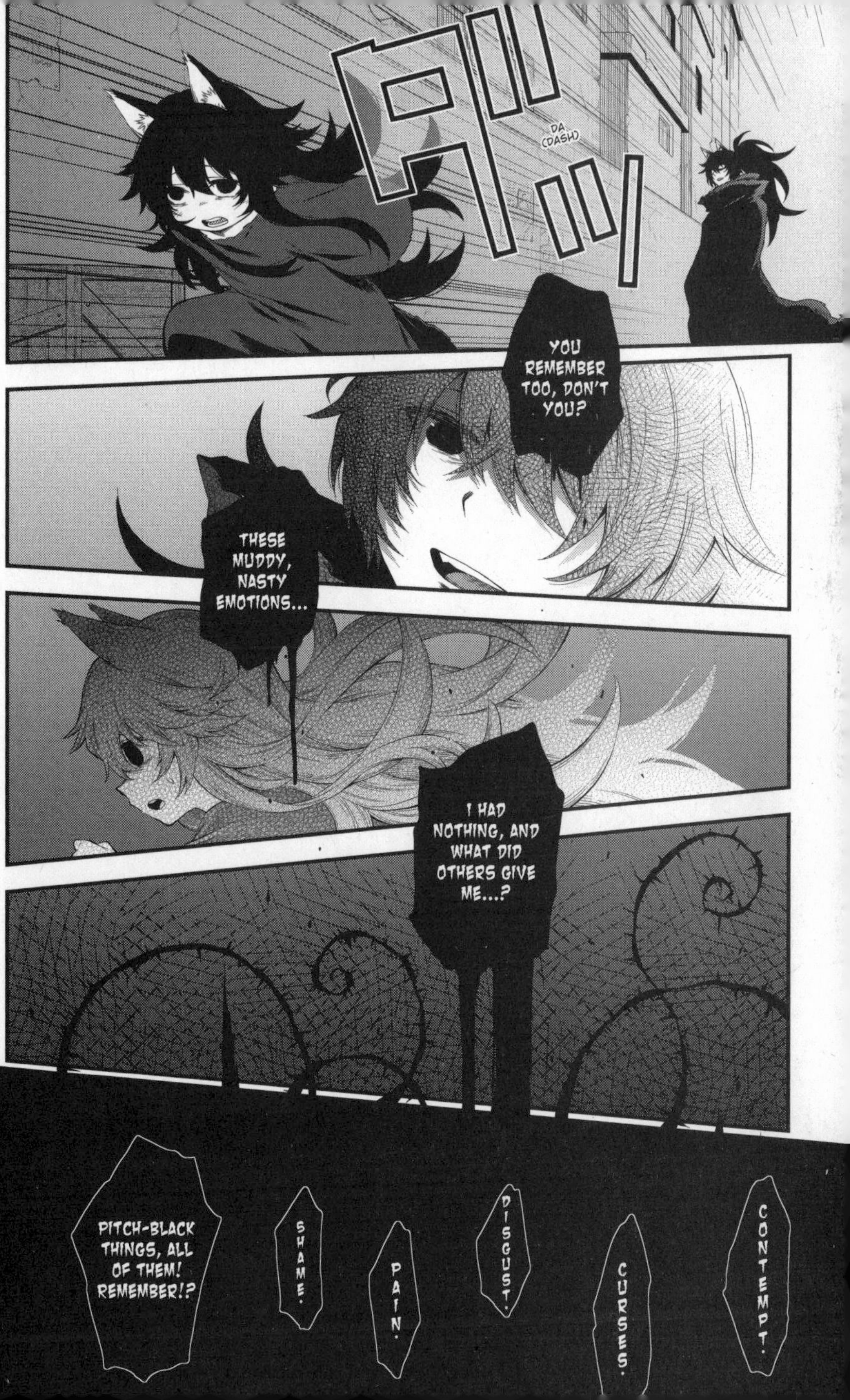
DA (DASH)
YOU REMEMBER TOO, DON'T YOU?
THESE MUDDY, NASTY EMOTIONS...
I HAD NOTHING, AND WHAT DID OTHERS GIVE ME...?
CONTEMPT.
CURSES.
DISGUST.
PAIN.
SHAME.
PITCH-BLACK THINGS, ALL OF THEM! REMEMBER!?

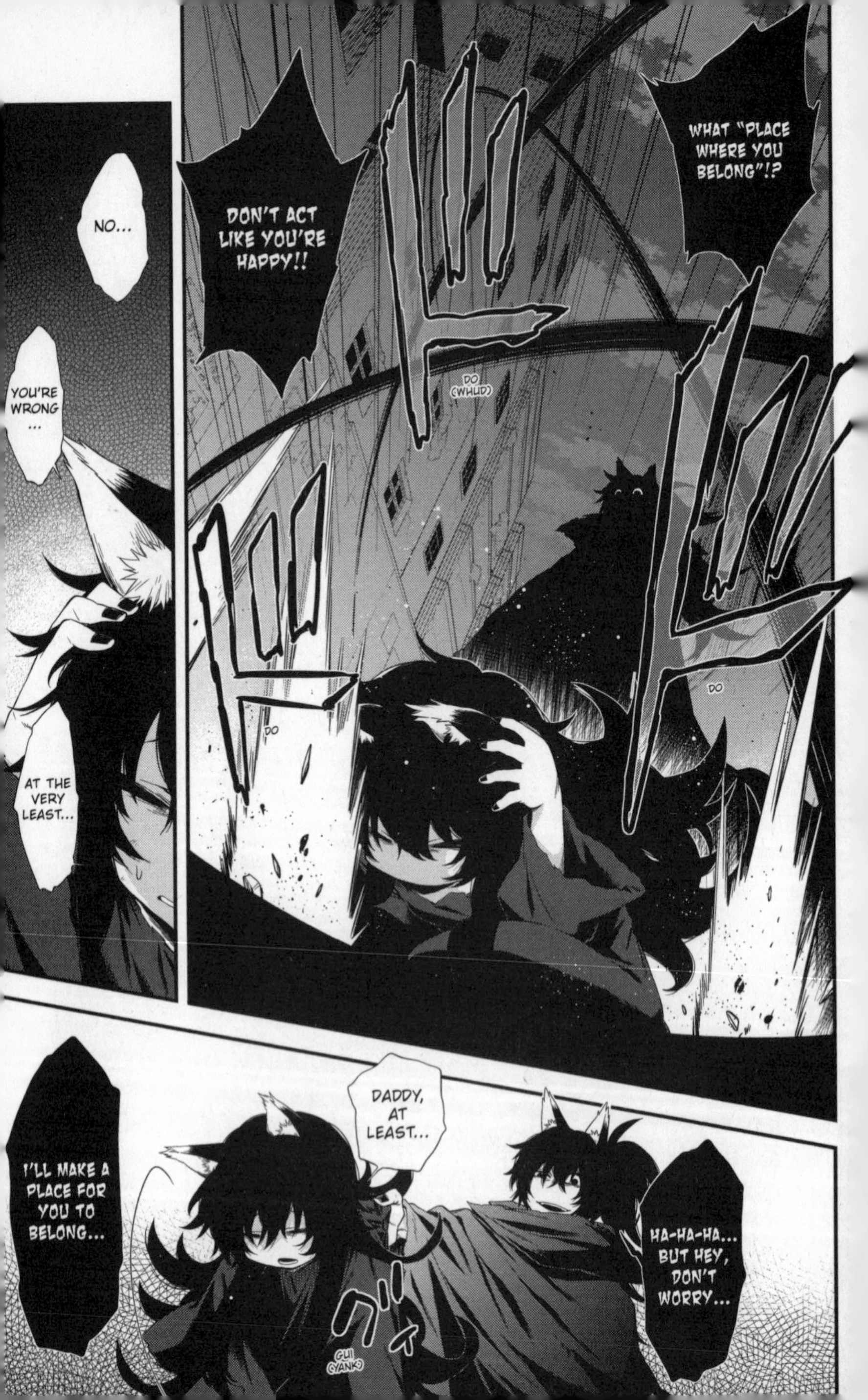
WHAT "PLACE WHERE YOU BELONG"!?
DON'T ACT LIKE YOU'RE HAPPY!!
DO (WHUD)
DO
DO
NO...
YOU'RE WRONG...
AT THE VERY LEAST...
HA-HA-HA... BUT HEY, DON'T WORRY...
DADDY, AT LEAST...
I'LL MAKE A PLACE FOR YOU TO BELONG...
GUI (YANK)

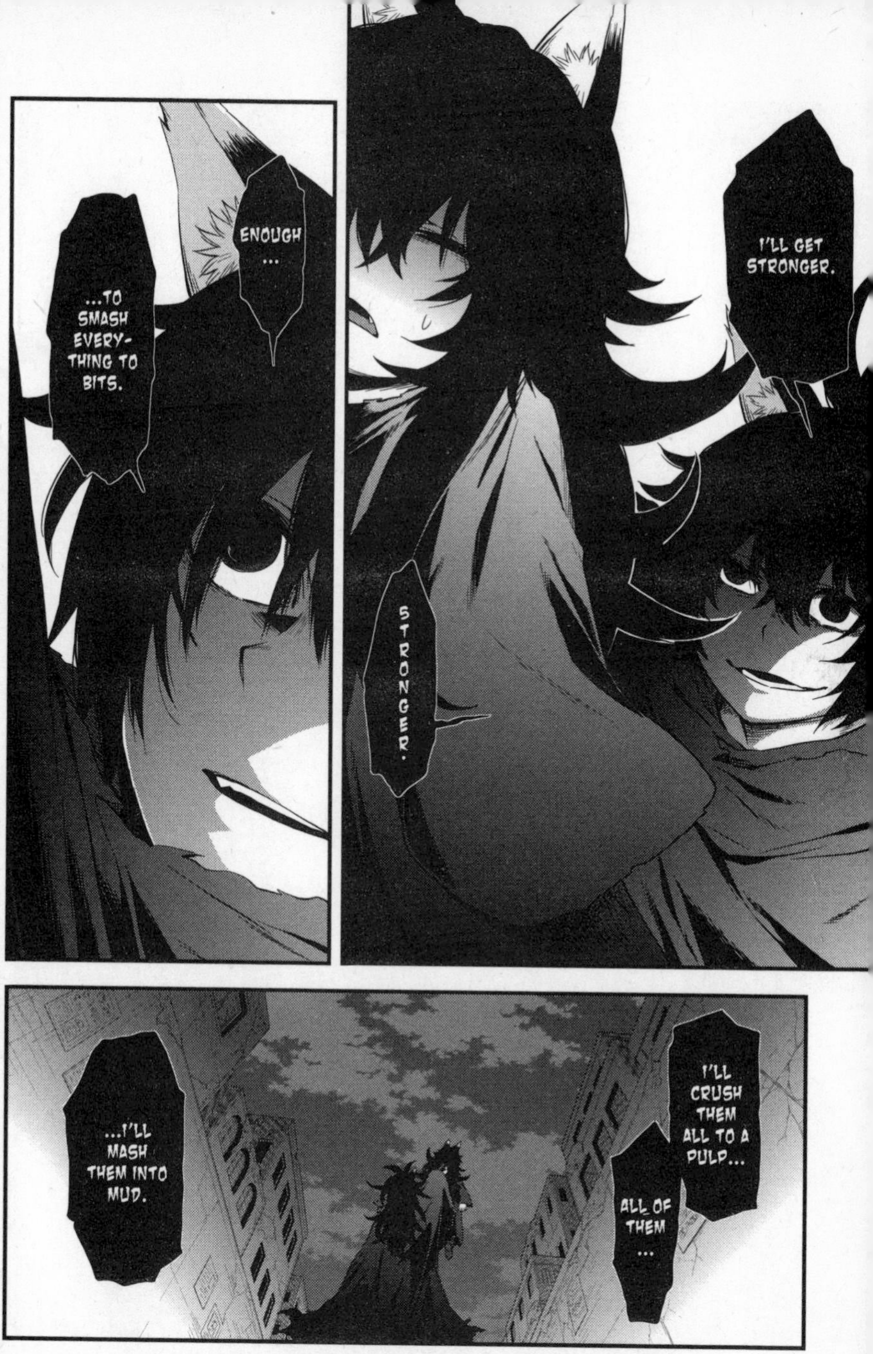
I'LL GET STRONGER.
STRONGER.
ENOUGH...
...TO SMASH EVERYTHING TO BITS.
I'LL CRUSH THEM ALL TO A PULP...
ALL OF THEM...
...I'LL MASH THEM INTO MUD.

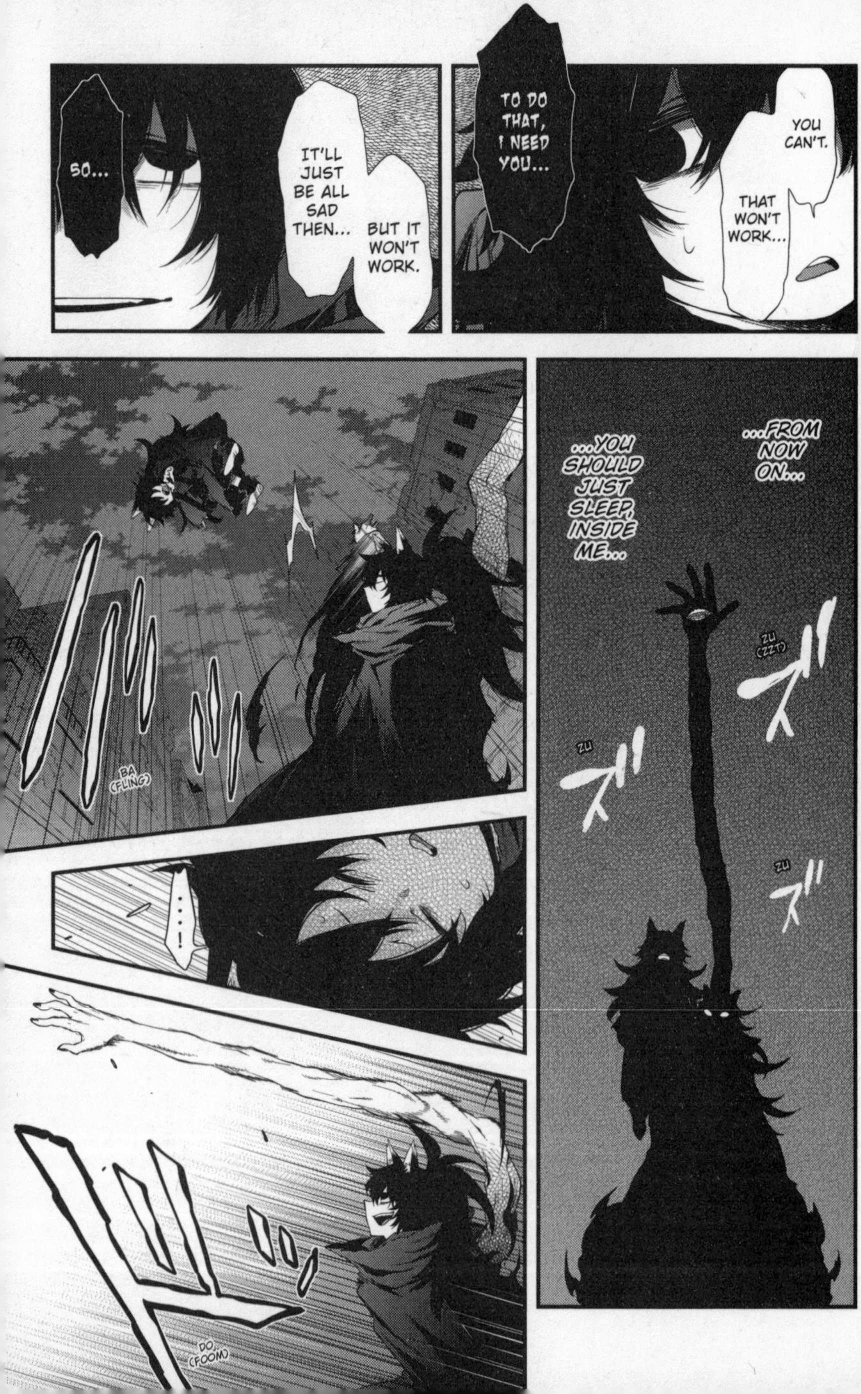
YOU CAN'T.
THAT WON'T WORK...
TO DO THAT, I NEED YOU...
IT'LL JUST BE ALL SAD THEN...
BUT IT WON'T WORK.
SO...
...FROM NOW ON...
...YOU SHOULD JUST SLEEP, INSIDE ME...
ZU (ZZZT)
ZU
ZU
BA (FLING)
...!
DO (FOOM)

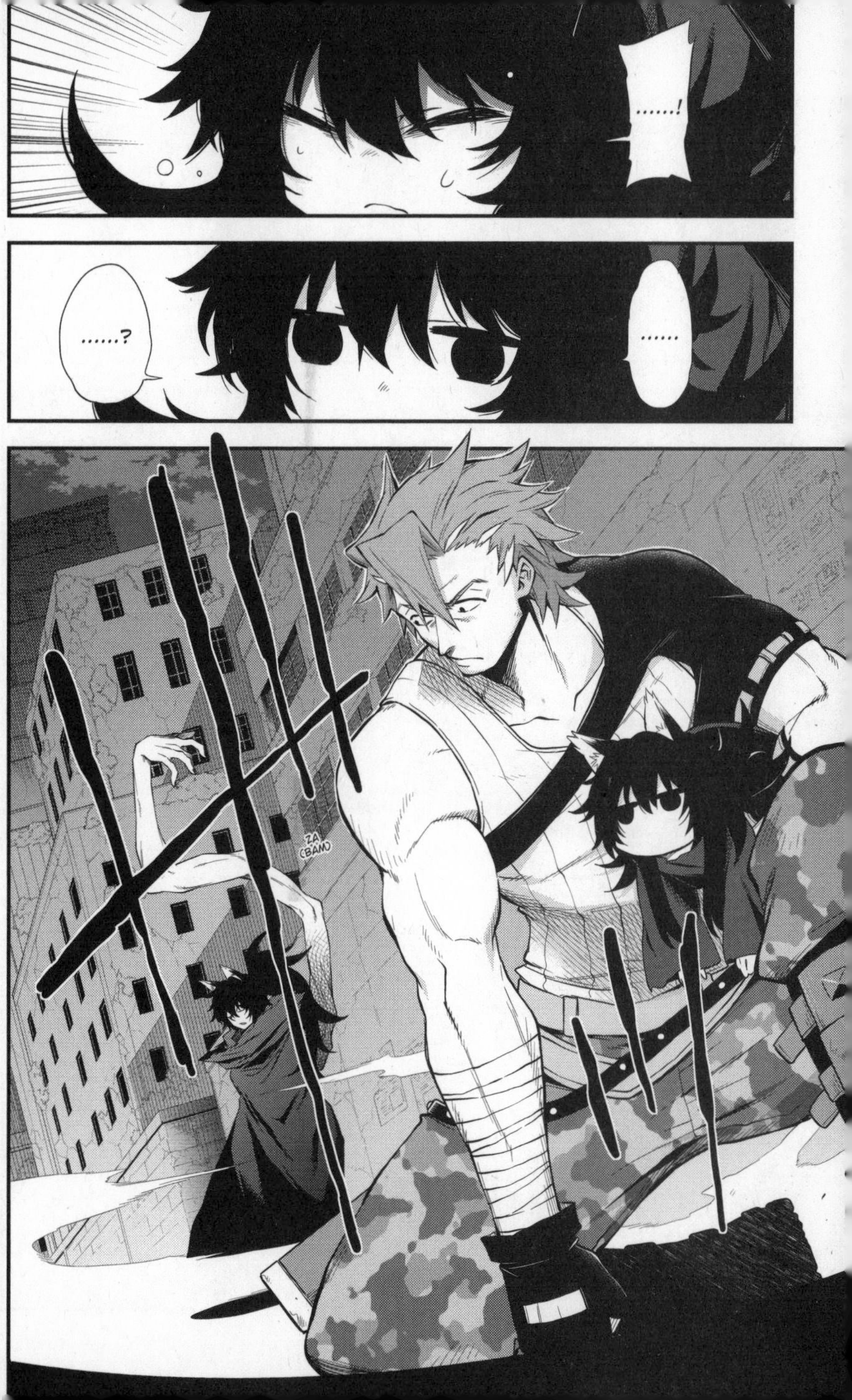
......!
......
......?
ZA
(BAM)

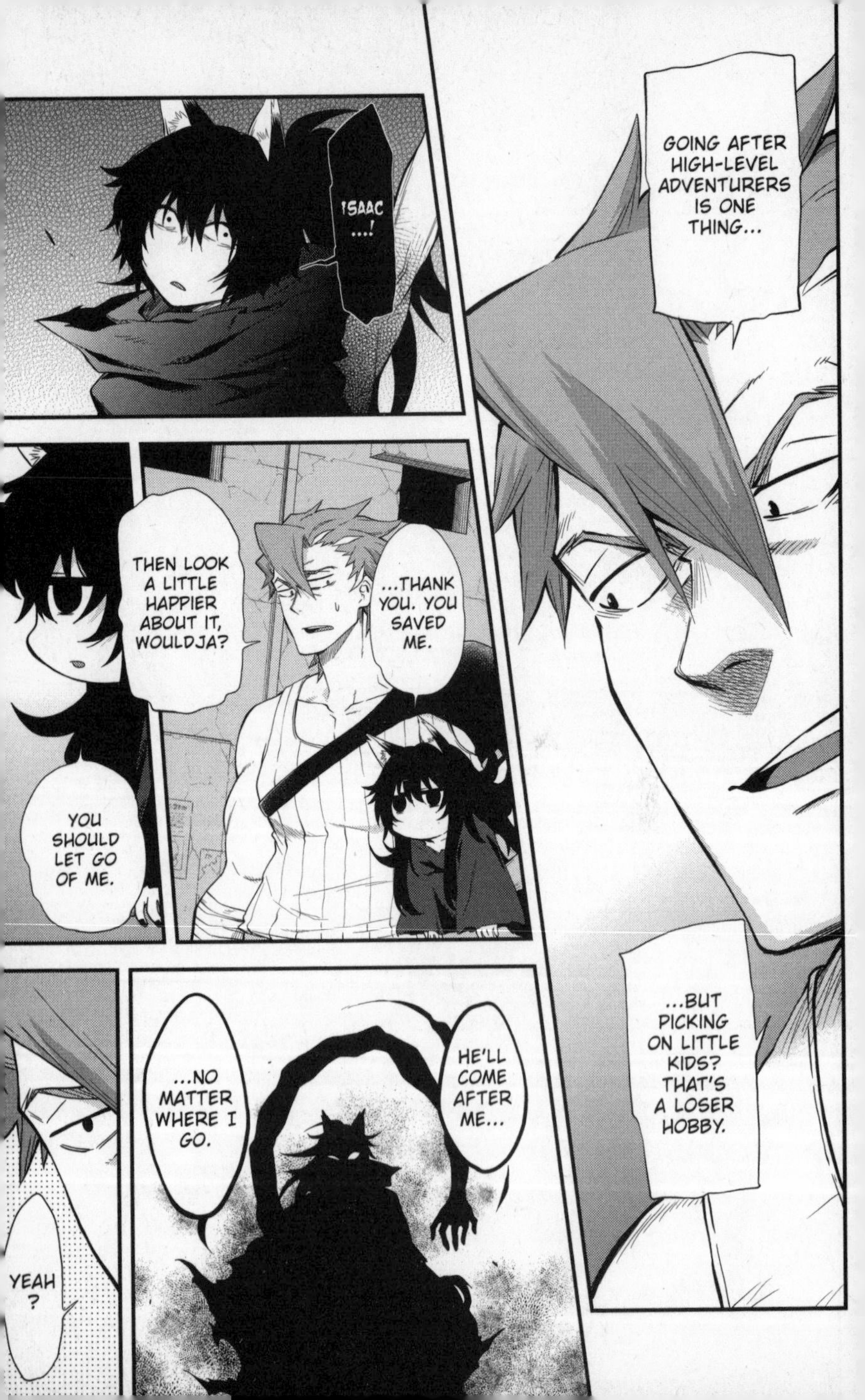
GOING AFTER HIGH-LEVEL ADVENTURERS IS ONE THING...
...BUT PICKING ON LITTLE KIDS? THAT'S A LOSER HOBBY.
ISAAC ...!
...THANK YOU. YOU SAVED ME.
THEN LOOK A LITTLE HAPPIER ABOUT IT, WOULDJA?
YOU SHOULD LET GO OF ME.
HE'LL COME AFTER ME...
...NO MATTER WHERE I GO.
YEAH?

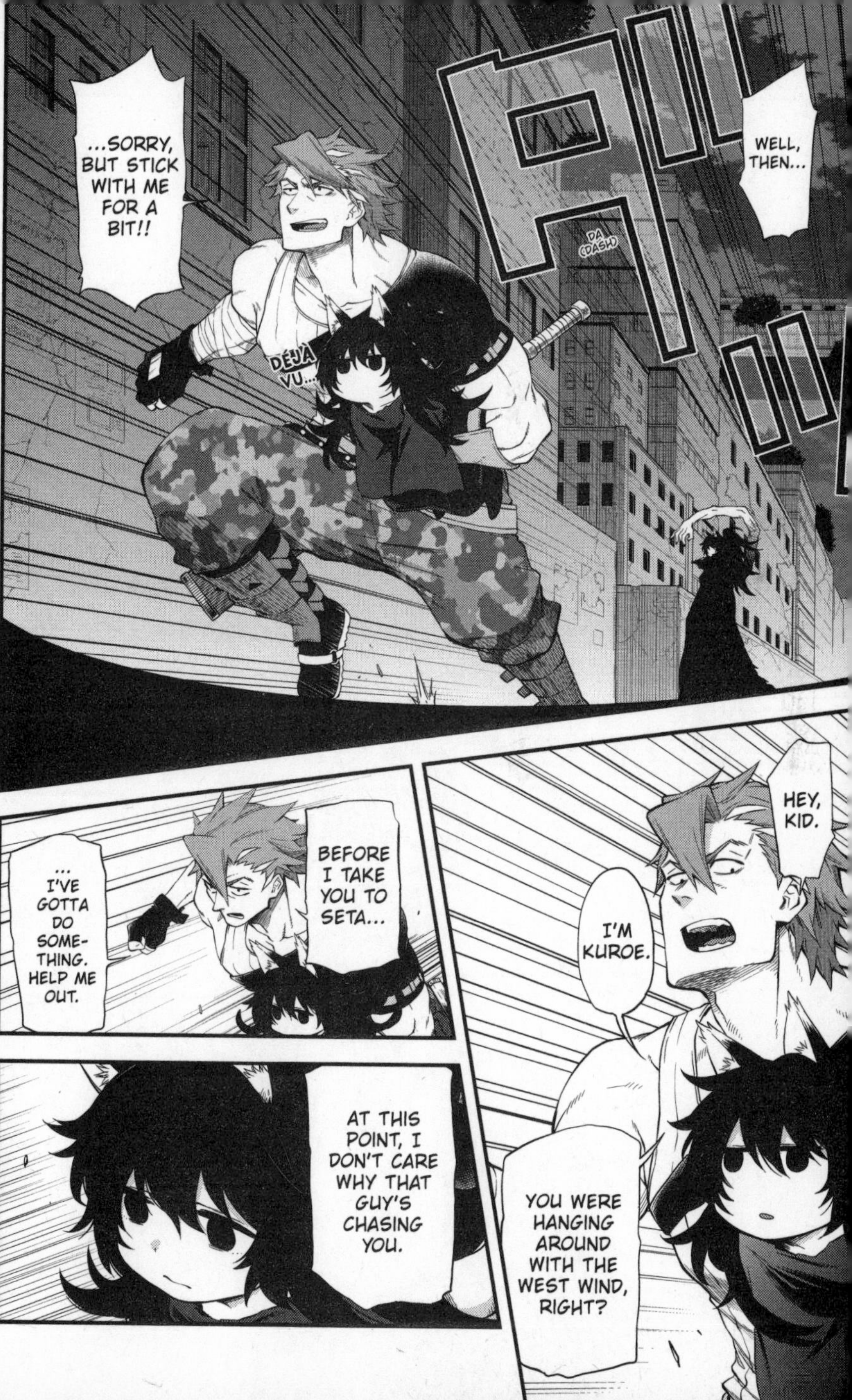
WELL, THEN...
DA (DASH)
...SORRY, BUT STICK WITH ME FOR A BIT!!
DÉJÀ VU...
HEY, KID.
I'M KUROE.
YOU WERE HANGING AROUND WITH THE WEST WIND, RIGHT?
BEFORE I TAKE YOU TO SETA...
...I'VE GOTTA DO SOMETHING. HELP ME OUT.
AT THIS POINT, I DON'T CARE WHY THAT GUY'S CHASING YOU.

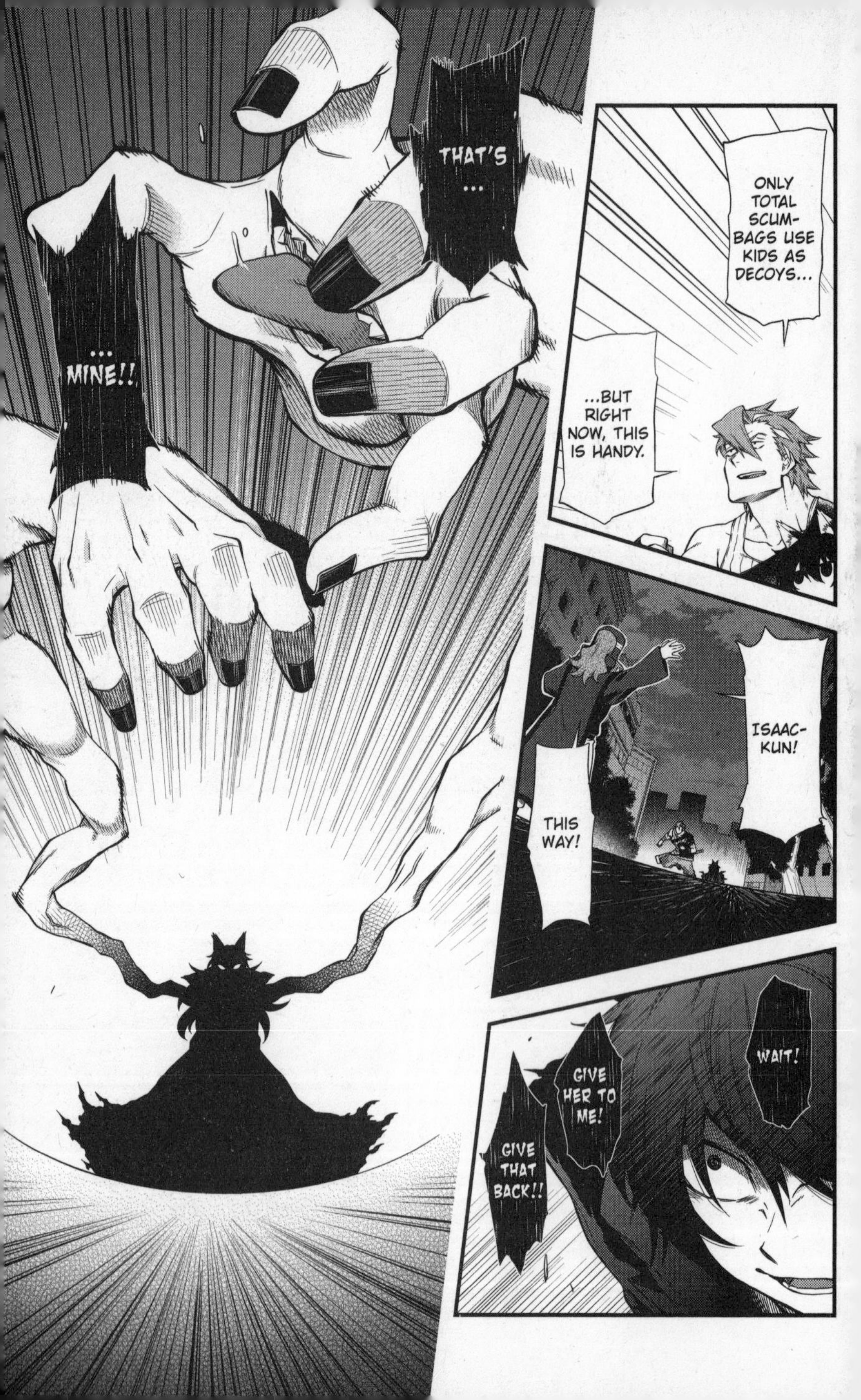
ONLY TOTAL SCUM-BAGS USE KIDS AS DECOYS...
...BUT RIGHT NOW, THIS IS HANDY.
ISAAC-KUN!
THIS WAY!
WAIT!
GIVE HER TO ME!
GIVE THAT BACK!!
THAT'S ...
... MINE!!

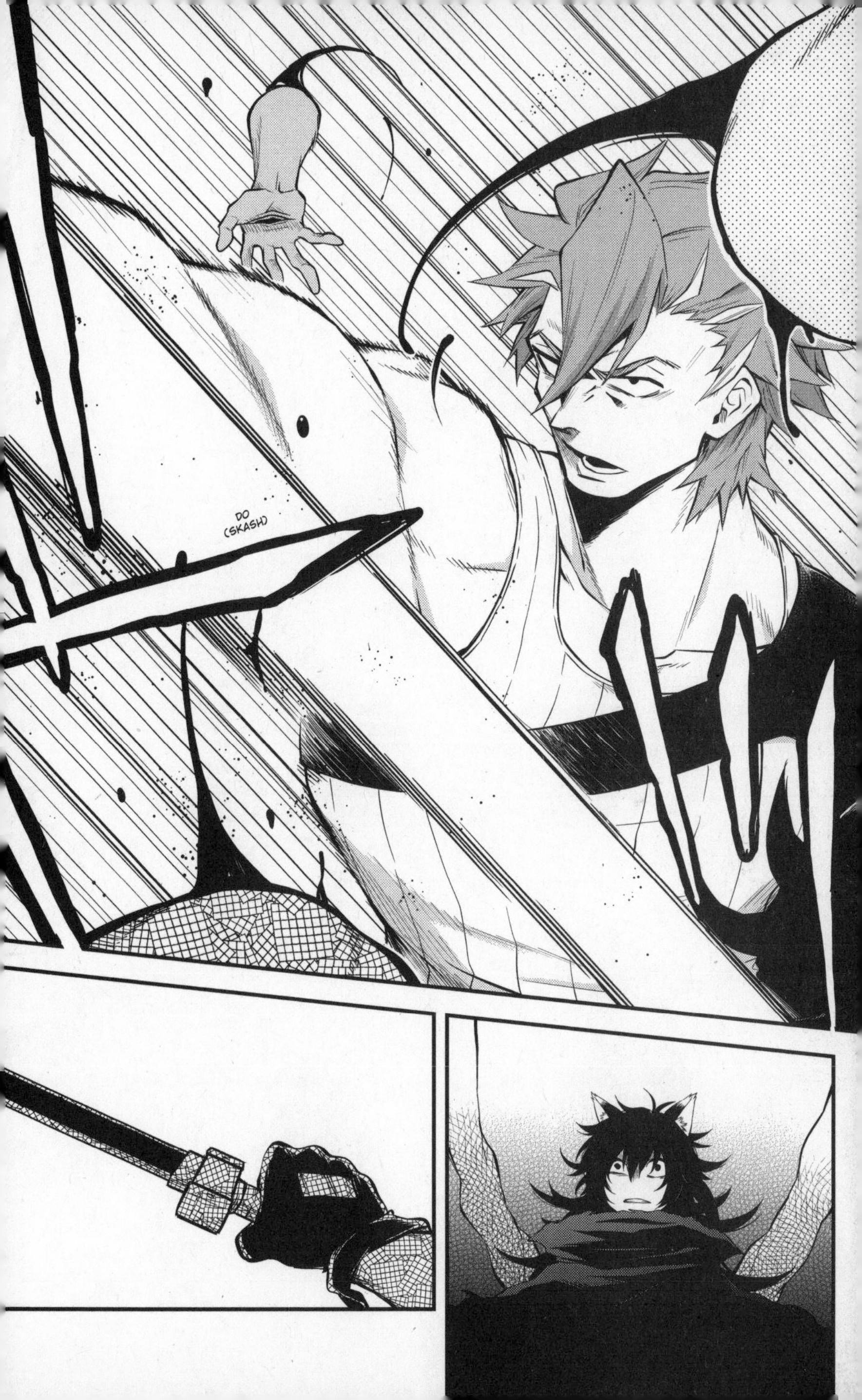
DO
(SKASH)

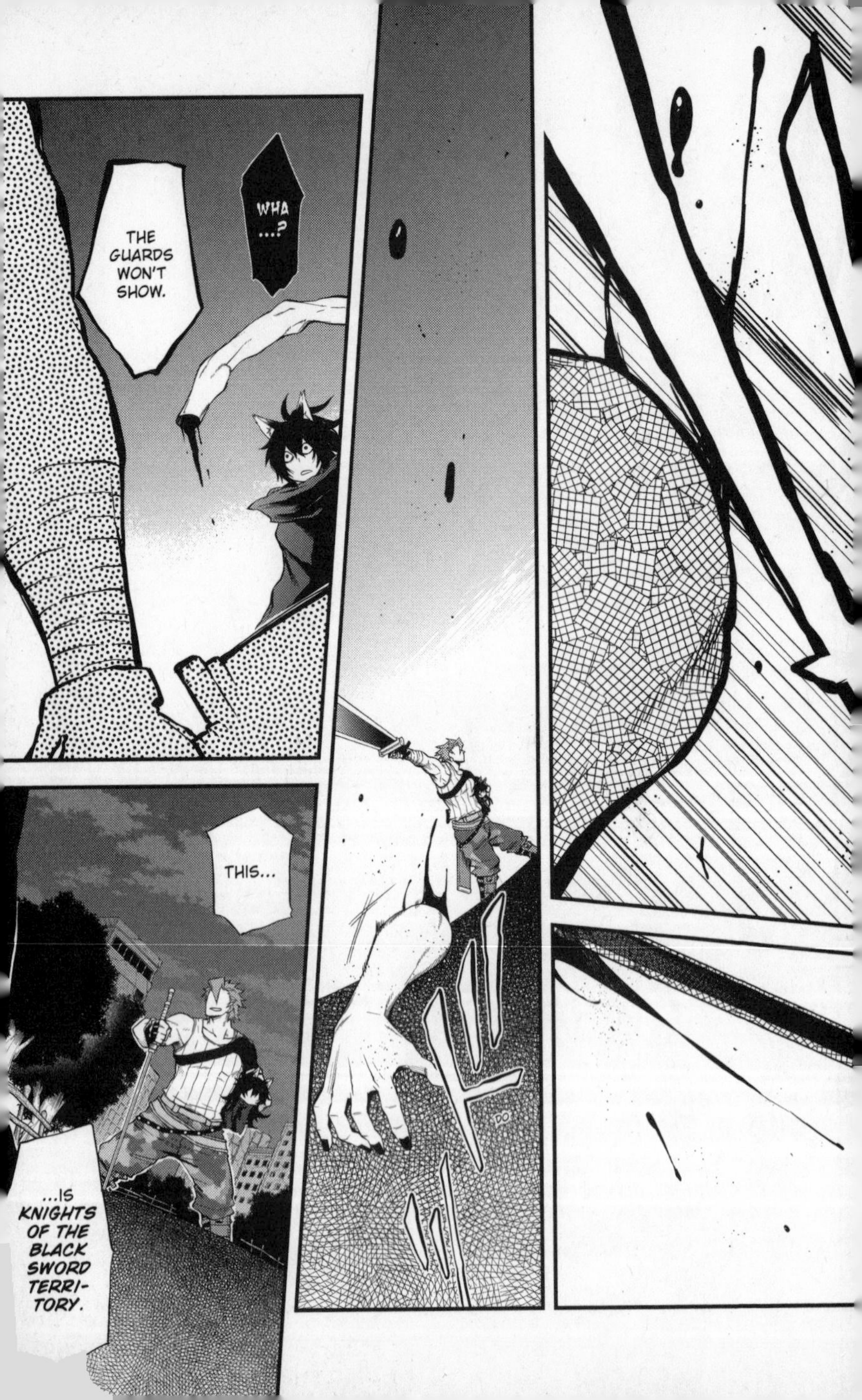
DO
WHA ...?
THE GUARDS WON'T SHOW.
THIS...
...IS KNIGHTS OF THE BLACK SWORD TERRI-TORY.

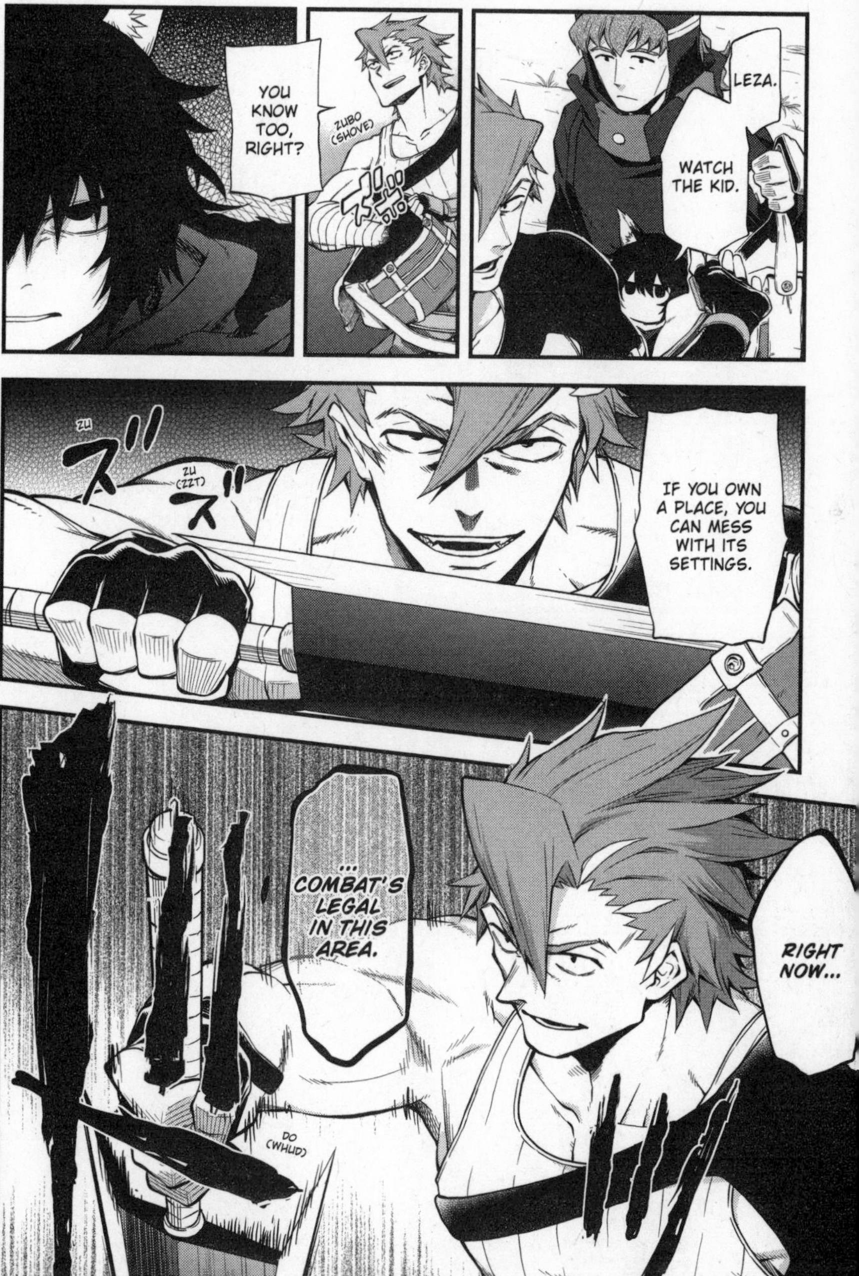
LEZA.
WATCH THE KID.
YOU KNOW TOO, RIGHT?
ZUBO (SHOVE)
IF YOU OWN A PLACE, YOU CAN MESS WITH ITS SETTINGS.
ZU
ZU (ZZT)
RIGHT NOW...
...COMBAT'S LEGAL IN THIS AREA.
DO (WHUD)

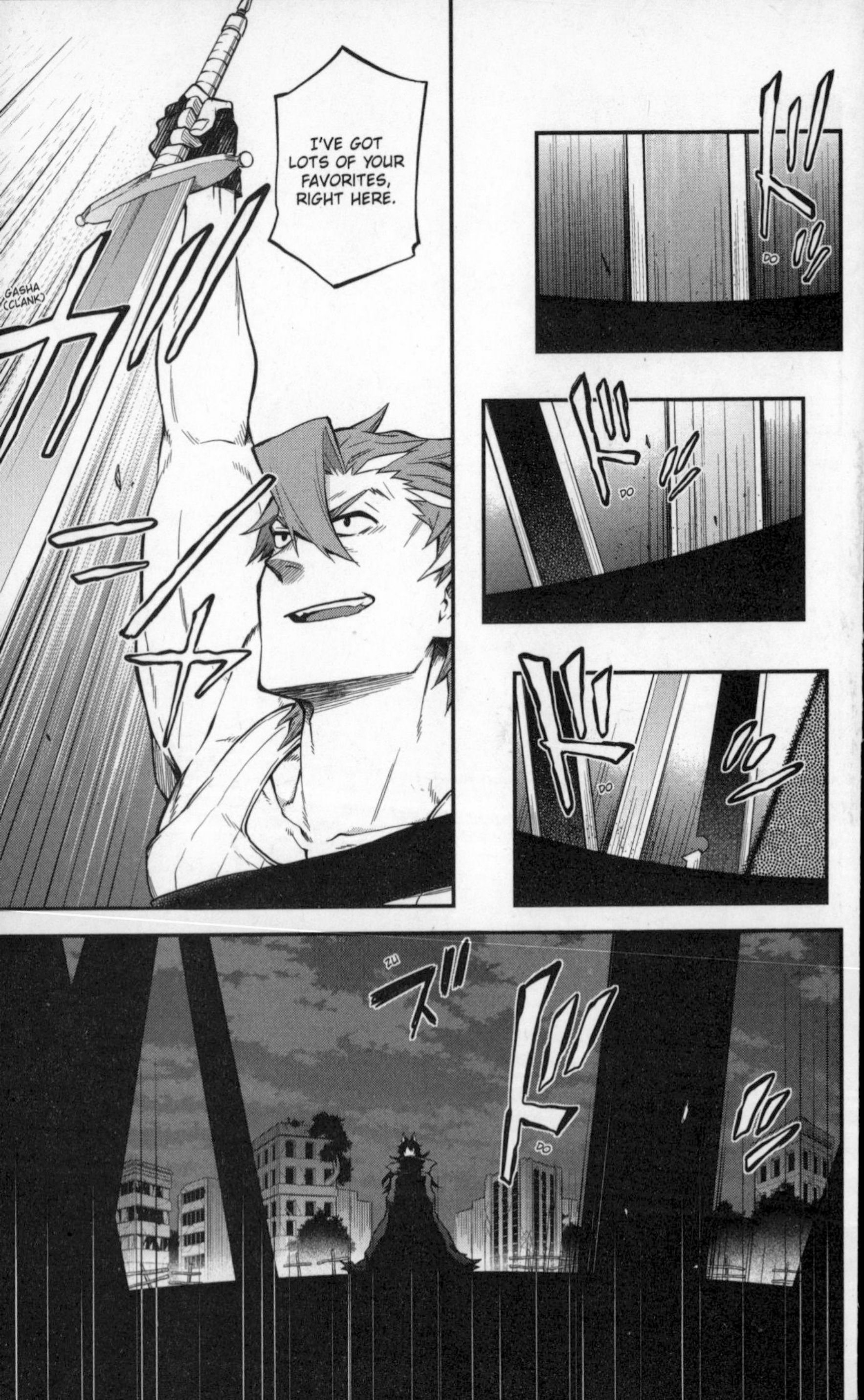
DO
DO
DO
I'VE GOT LOTS OF YOUR FAVORITES, RIGHT HERE.
GASHA (CLANK)
ZU
DO

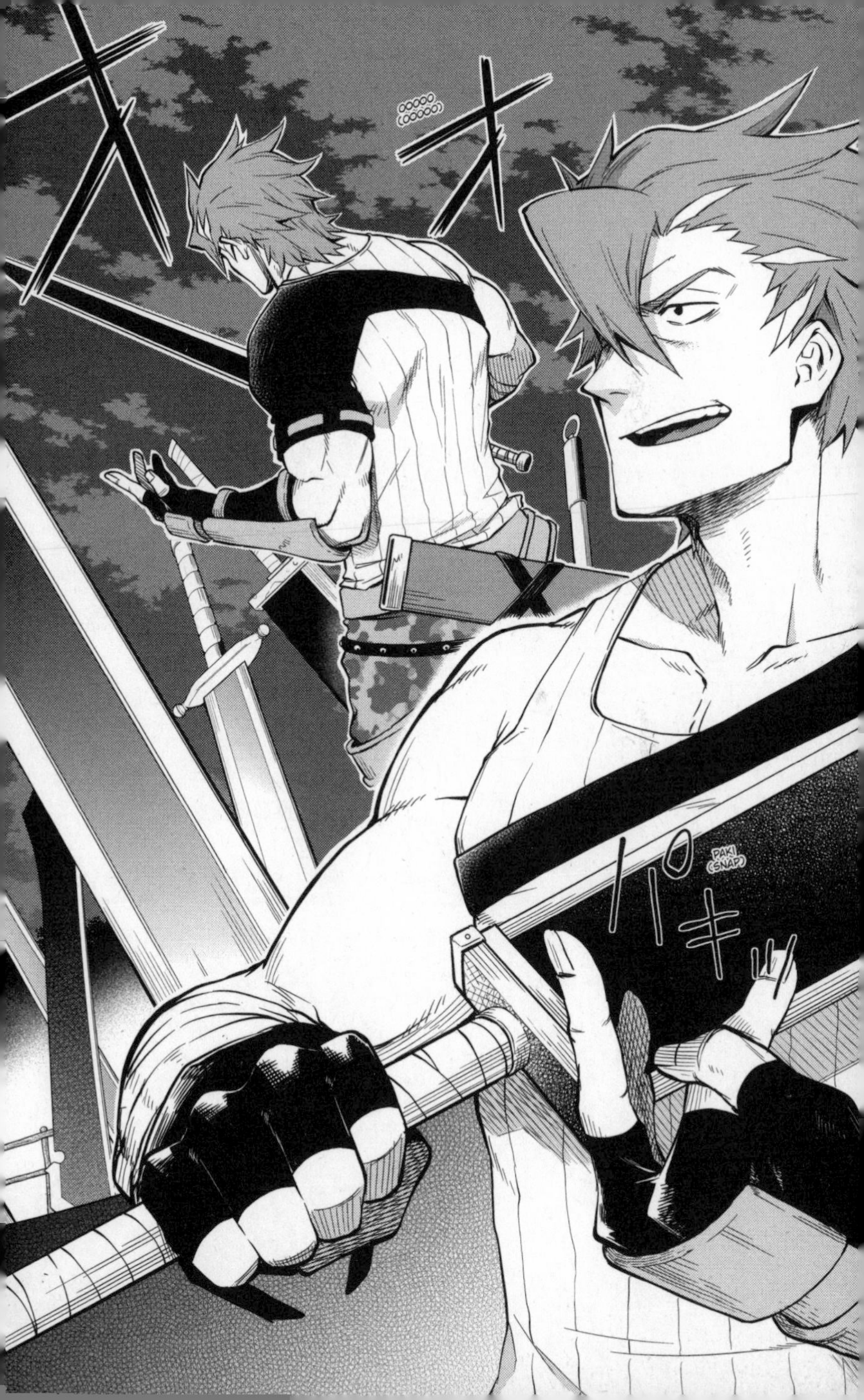
OOOOO (OOOOOO)
PAKI (SNAP)

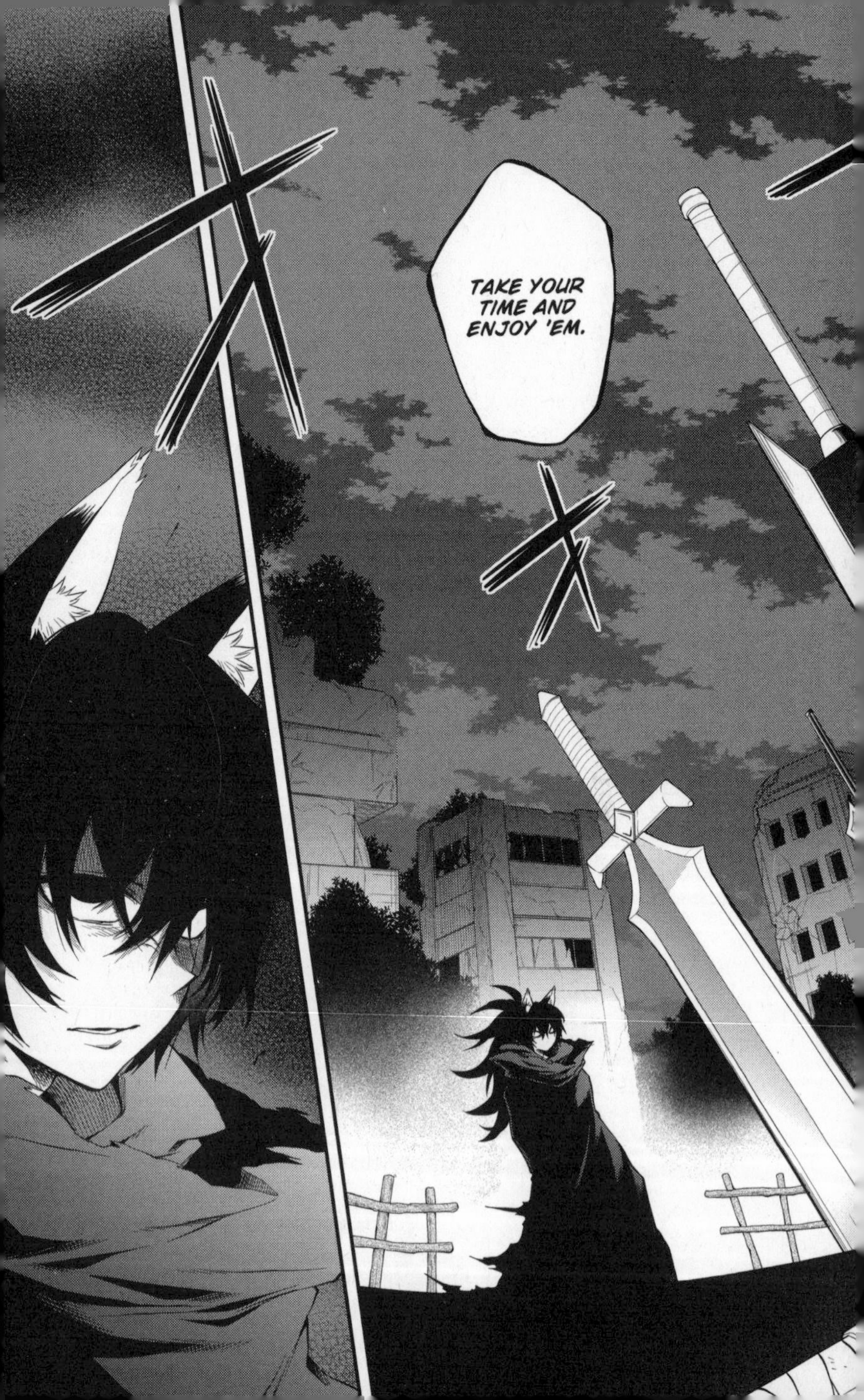
TAKE YOUR TIME AND ENJOY 'EM.

LOG HORIZON

THE WEST WIND BRIGADE

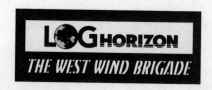

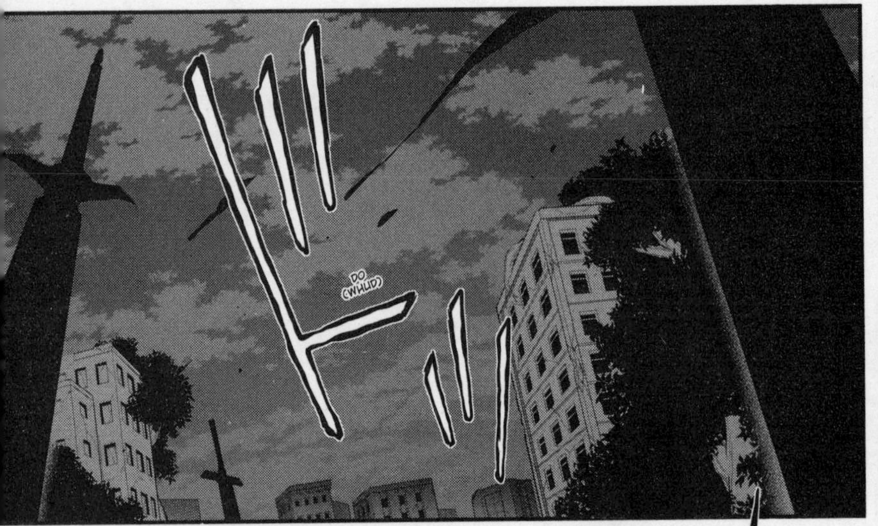
DO
(WHUD)

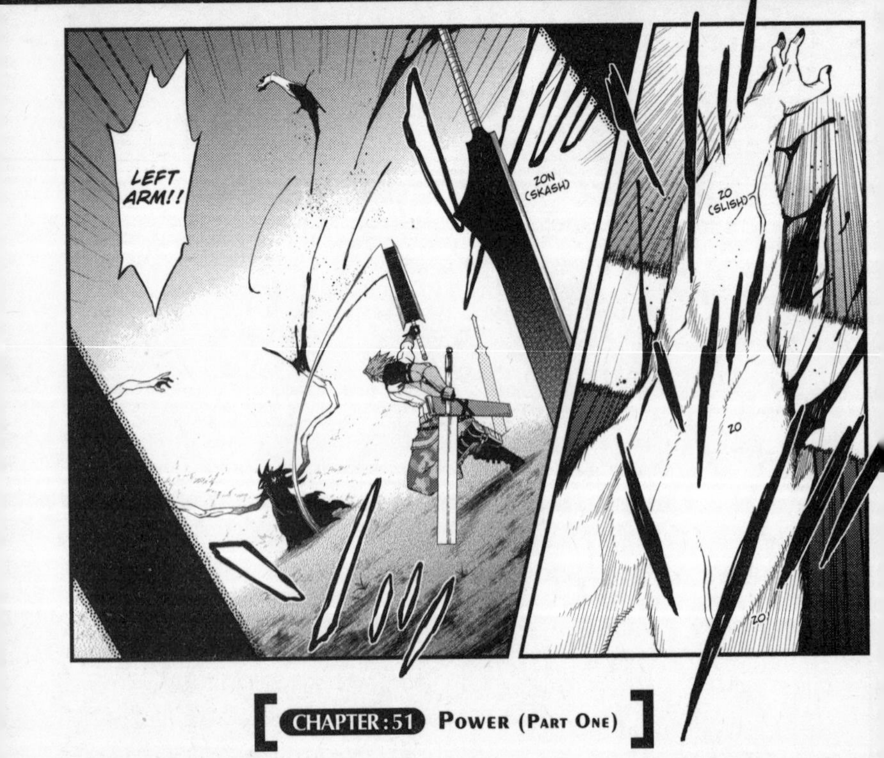
ZO
(SLISH)
ZO
ZO
LEFT ARM!!
ZON
(SKASH)

[CHAPTER: 51 Power (Part One)]

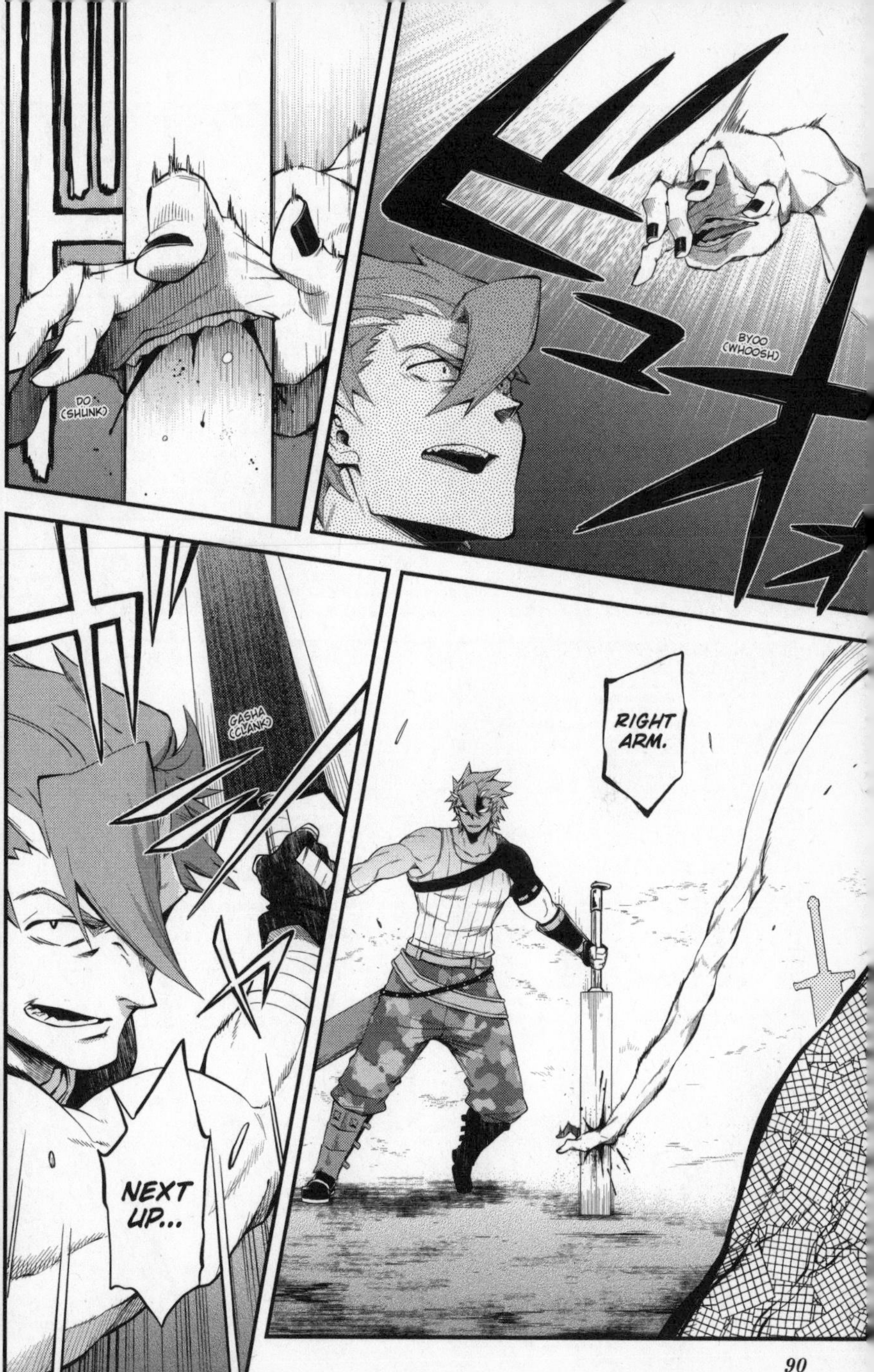
BYOO (WHOOSH)
DO (SHUNK)
RIGHT ARM.
GASHA (CLANK)
NEXT UP...

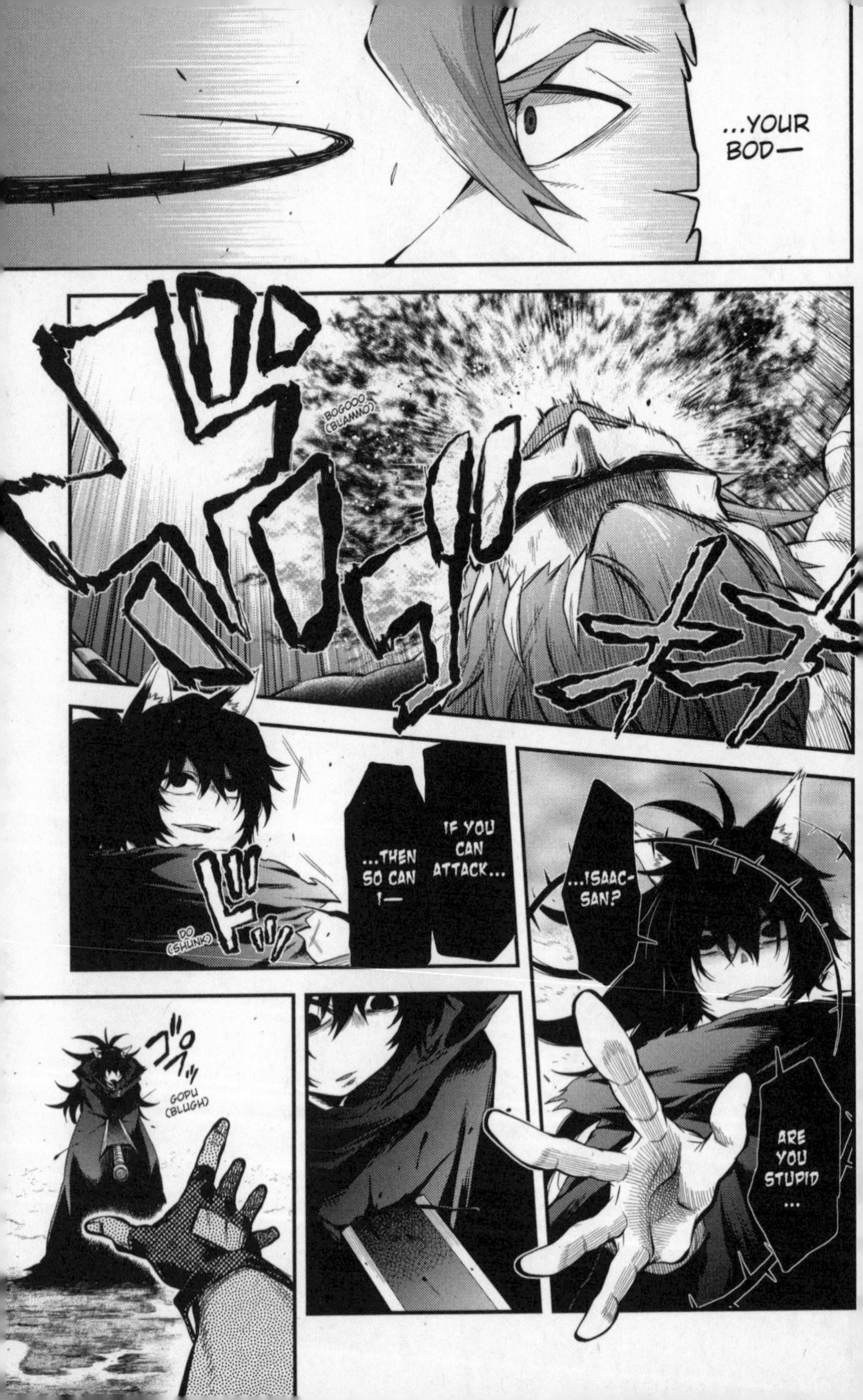
...YOUR BOD—
BOGOOO (BLAMMO)
...ISAAC-SAN?
ARE YOU STUPID ...
IF YOU CAN ATTACK...
...THEN SO CAN I—
DO (SHUNK)
GOPU (BLUGH)

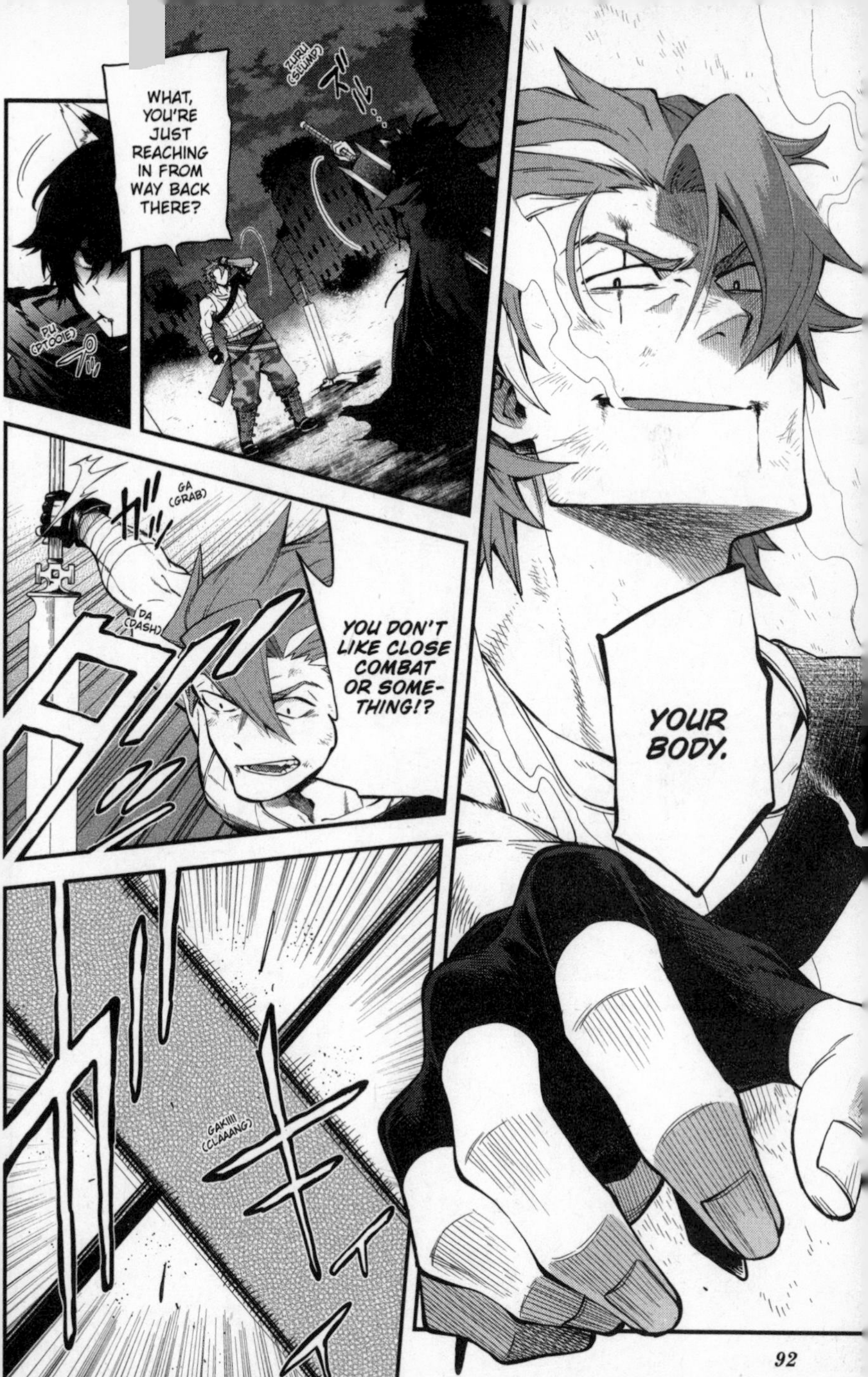
YOUR BODY.
ZURU (SLUMP)
WHAT, YOU'RE JUST REACHING IN FROM WAY BACK THERE?
PU (PTOOIE)
GA (GRAB)
DA (DASH)
YOU DON'T LIKE CLOSE COMBAT OR SOME-THING!?
GAKIIII (CLAAANG)

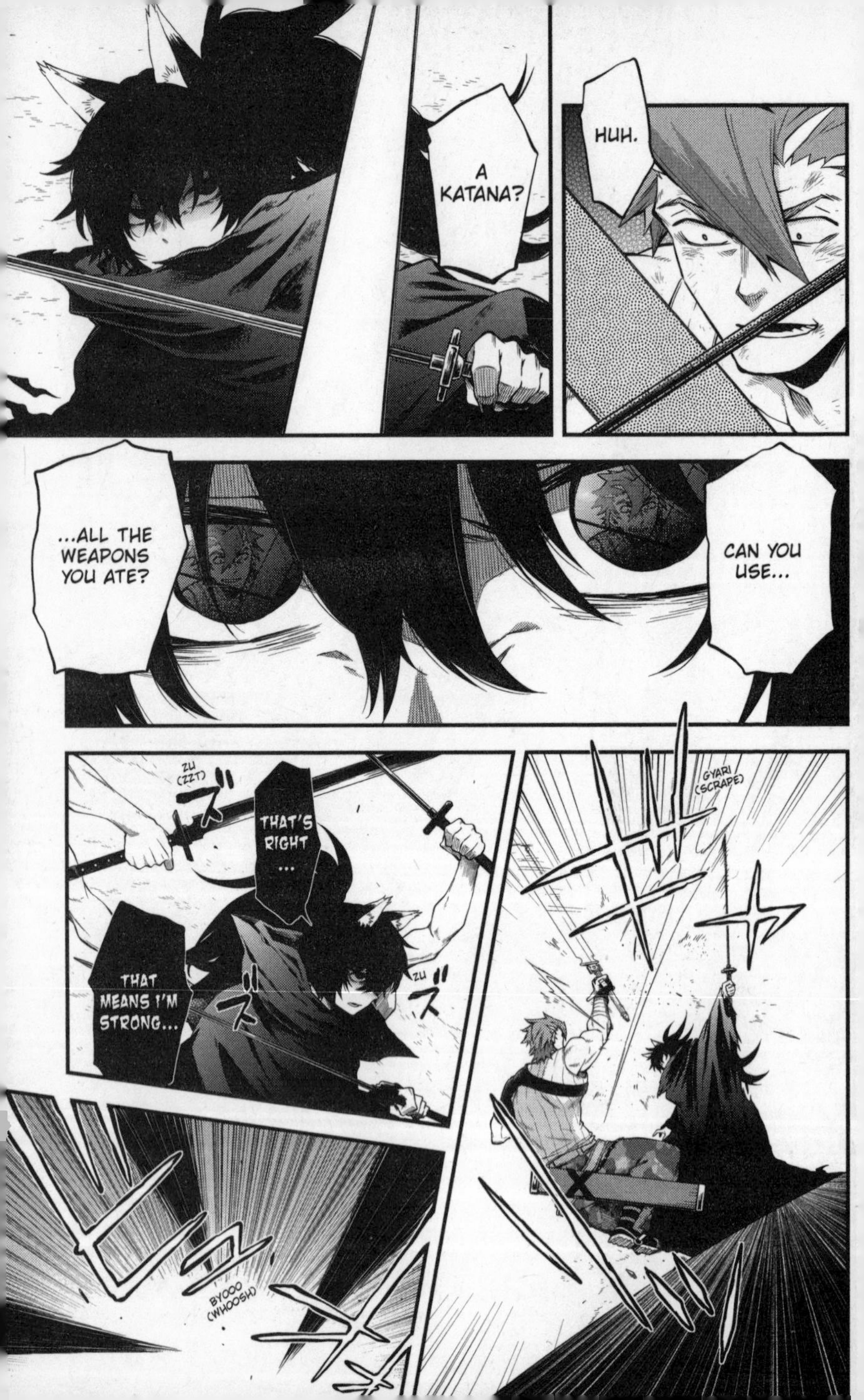
HUH.
A KATANA?
CAN YOU USE...
...ALL THE WEAPONS YOU ATE?
GYARI (SCRAPE)
ZU (ZZZT)
THAT'S RIGHT...
THAT MEANS I'M STRONG...
ZU
BYOOO (WHOOSH)

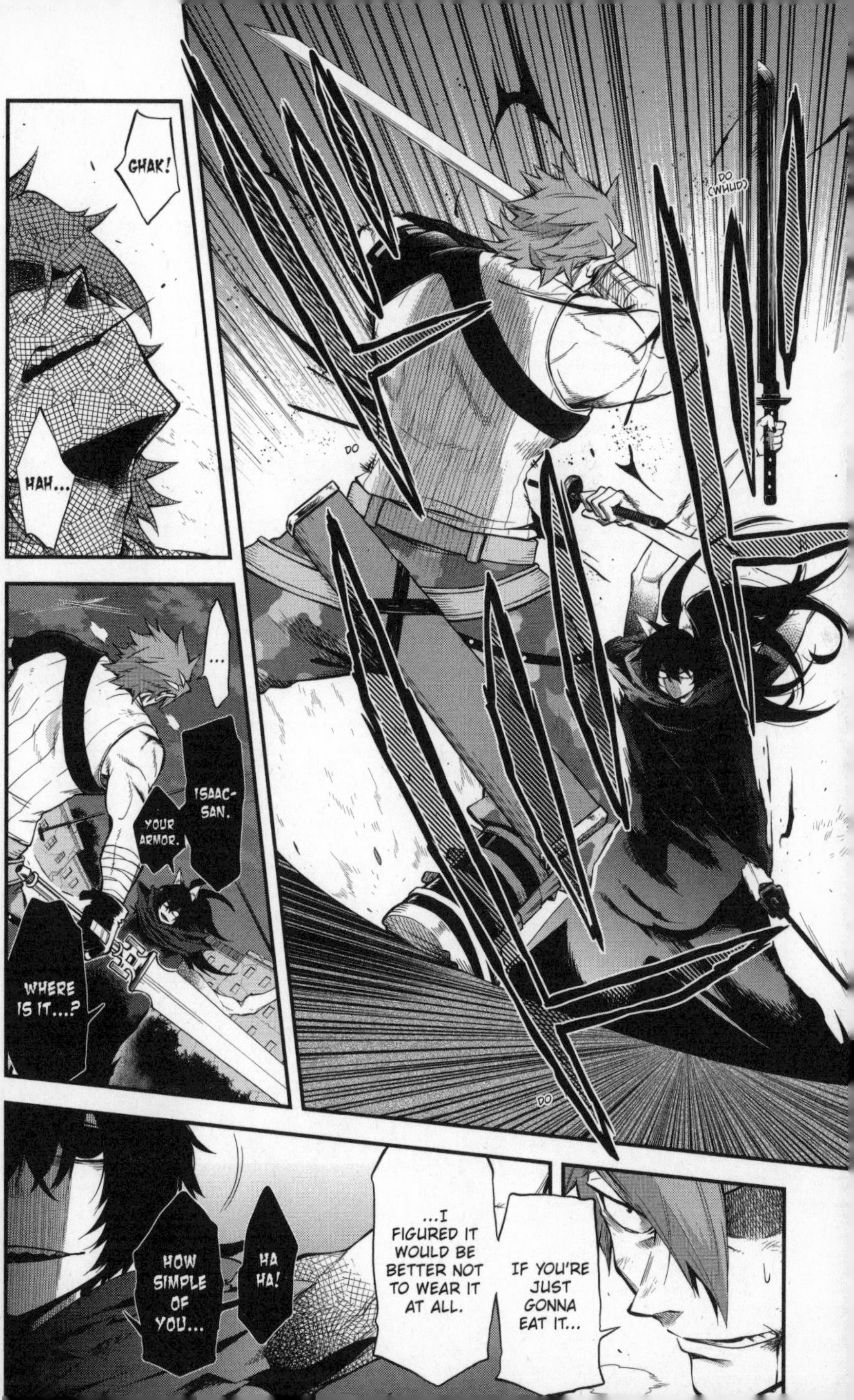
DO (WHUD)
DO
DO
GHAK!
HAH...
...
ISAAC-SAN.
YOUR ARMOR.
WHERE IS IT...?
IF YOU'RE JUST GONNA EAT IT...
...I FIGURED IT WOULD BE BETTER NOT TO WEAR IT AT ALL.
HA HA!
HOW SIMPLE OF YOU...

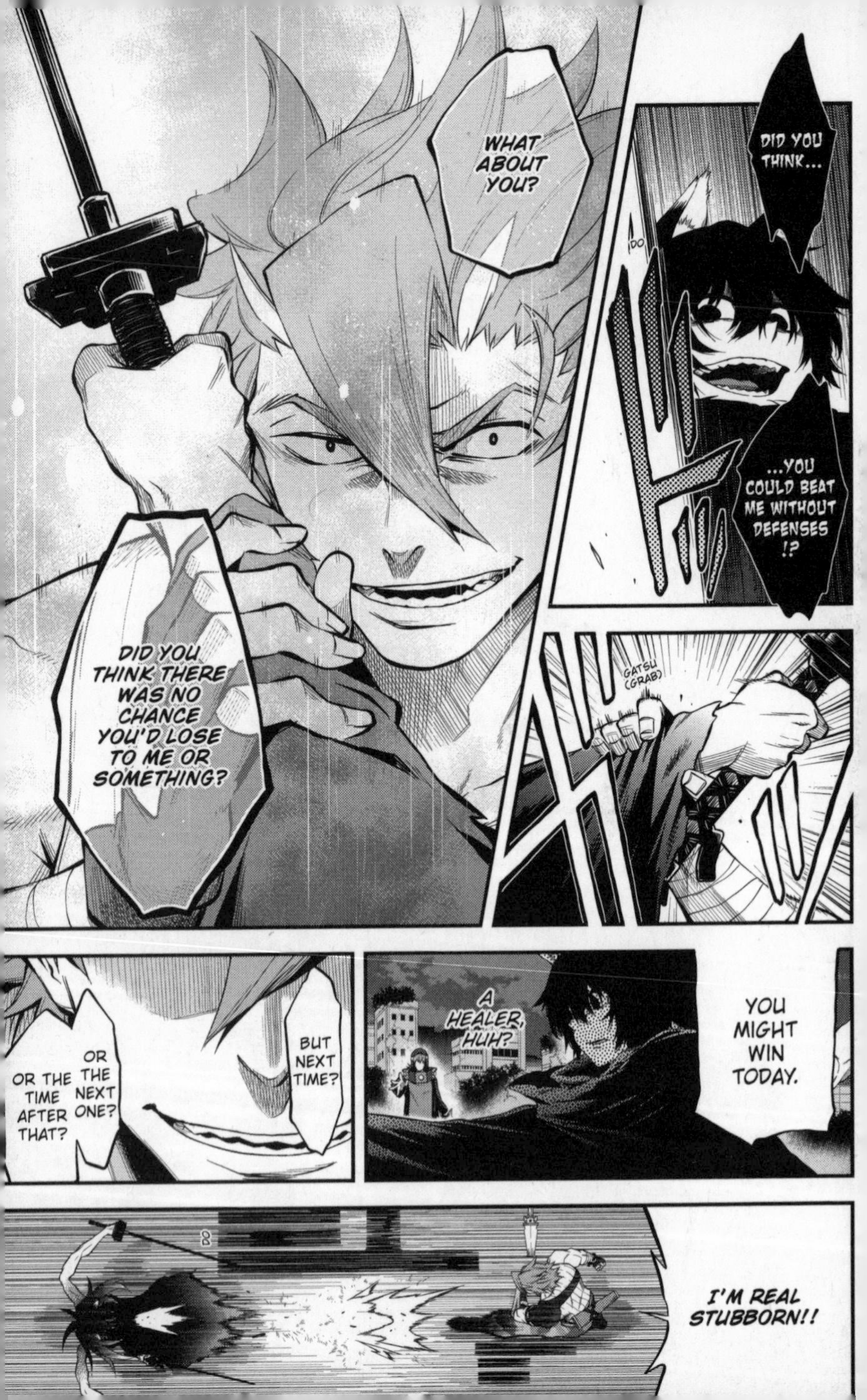
DID YOU THINK...
...YOU COULD BEAT ME WITHOUT DEFENSES!?
GATSU (GRAB)
WHAT ABOUT YOU?
DID YOU THINK THERE WAS NO CHANCE YOU'D LOSE TO ME OR SOMETHING?
YOU MIGHT WIN TODAY.
A HEALER, HUH?
BUT NEXT TIME?
OR THE NEXT ONE?
OR THE TIME AFTER THAT?
I'M REAL STUBBORN!!

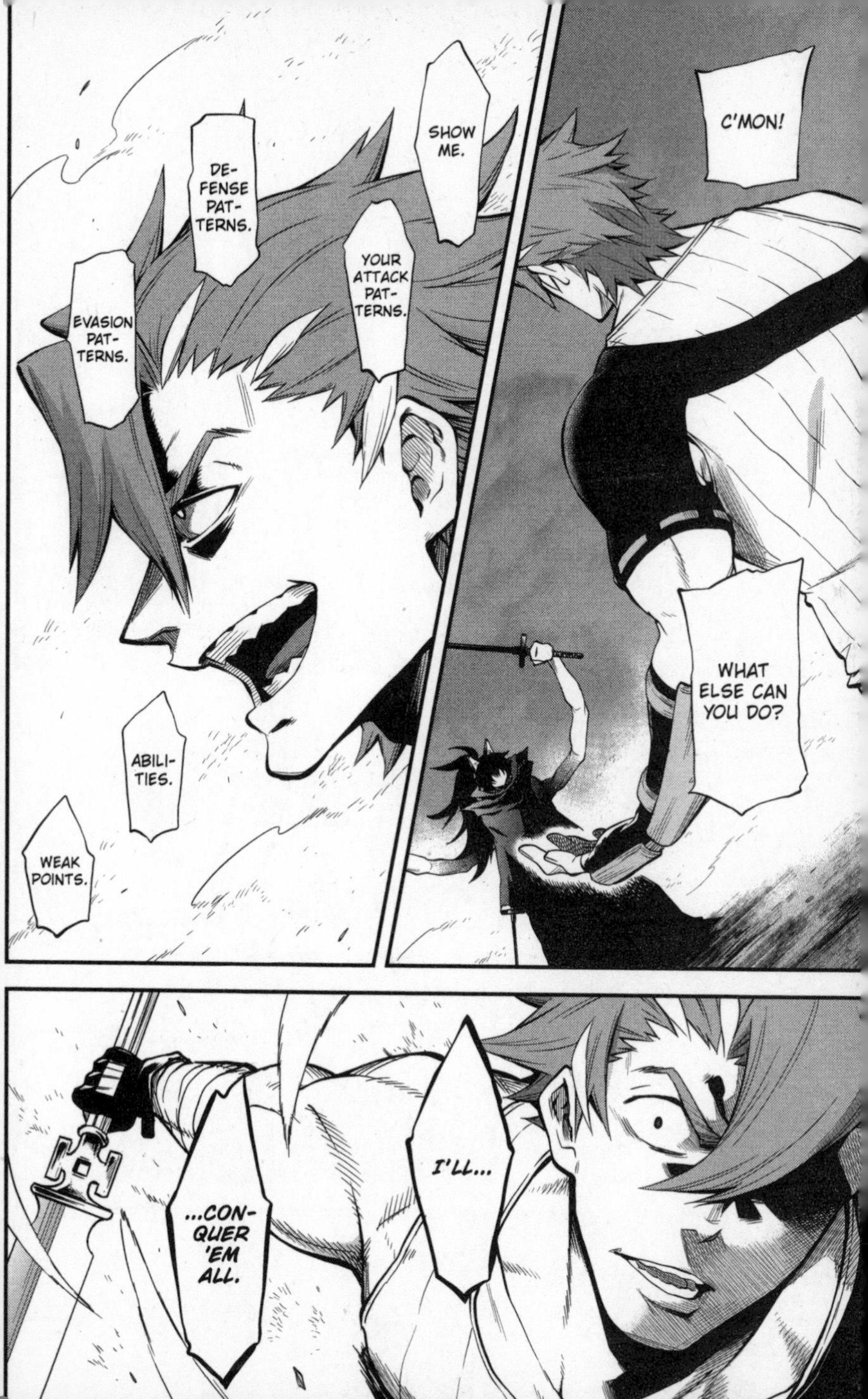
C'MON!
WHAT ELSE CAN YOU DO?
SHOW ME.
YOUR ATTACK PAT-TERNS.
DE-FENSE PAT-TERNS.
EVASION PAT-TERNS.
ABILI-TIES.
WEAK POINTS.
I'LL...
...CON-QUER 'EM ALL.

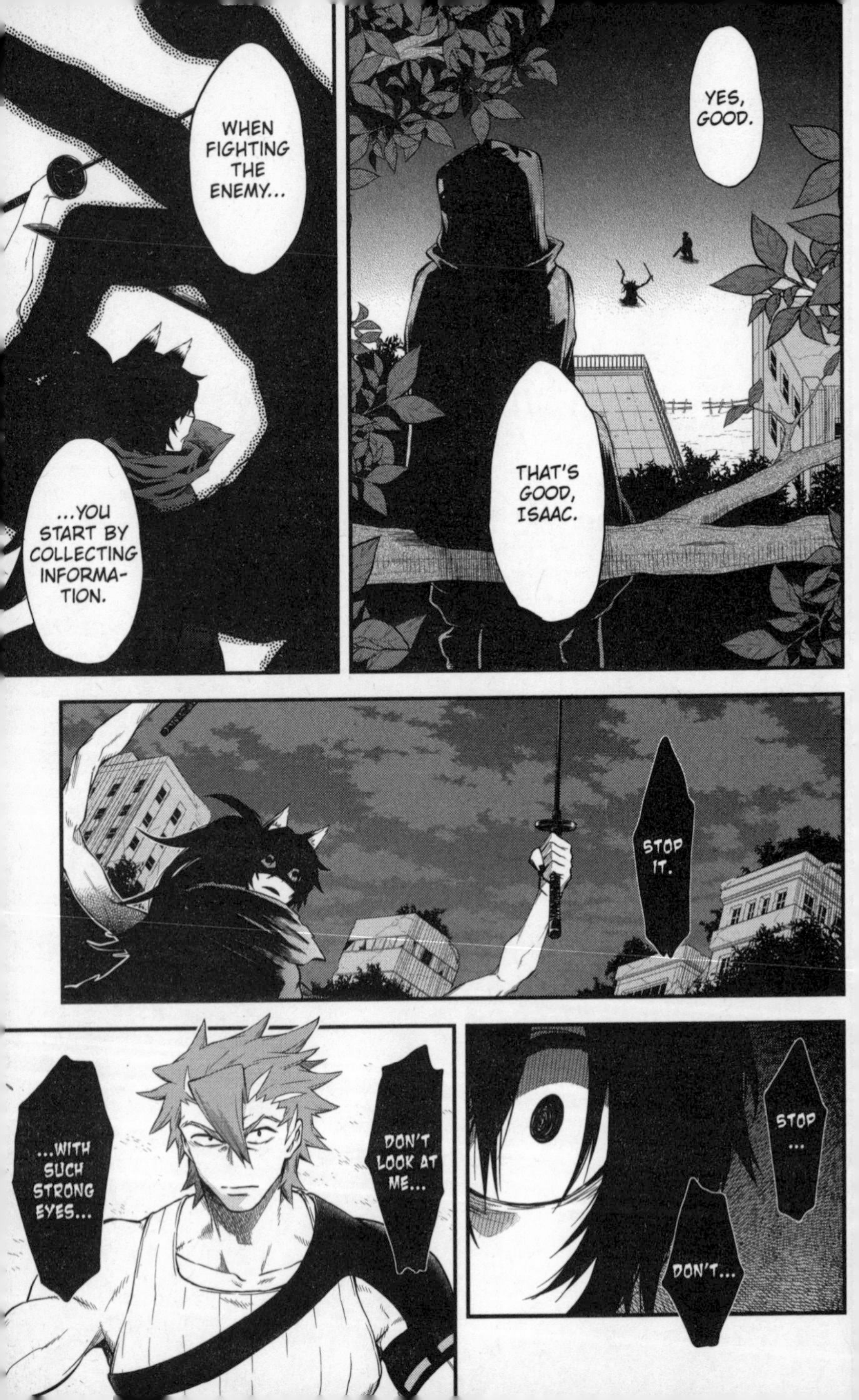
YES, GOOD.
THAT'S GOOD, ISAAC.
WHEN FIGHTING THE ENEMY...
...YOU START BY COLLECTING INFORMATION.
STOP IT.
STOP...
DON'T...
DON'T LOOK AT ME...
...WITH SUCH STRONG EYES...

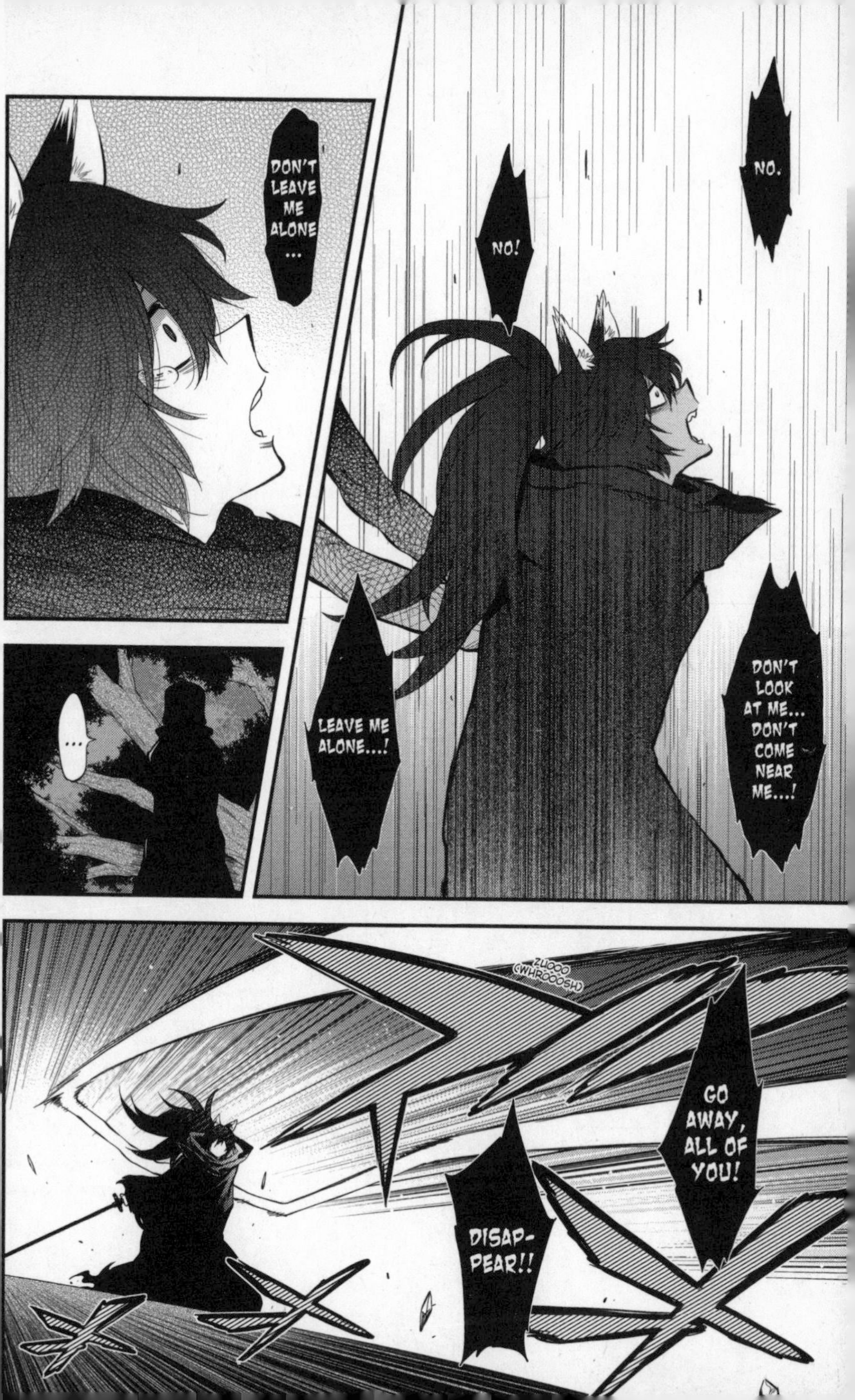
NO.
NO!
DON'T LOOK AT ME... DON'T COME NEAR ME...!
LEAVE ME ALONE...!
DON'T LEAVE ME ALONE...
...
ZUOOO (WHROOOSH)
GO AWAY, ALL OF YOU!
DISAP-PEAR!!

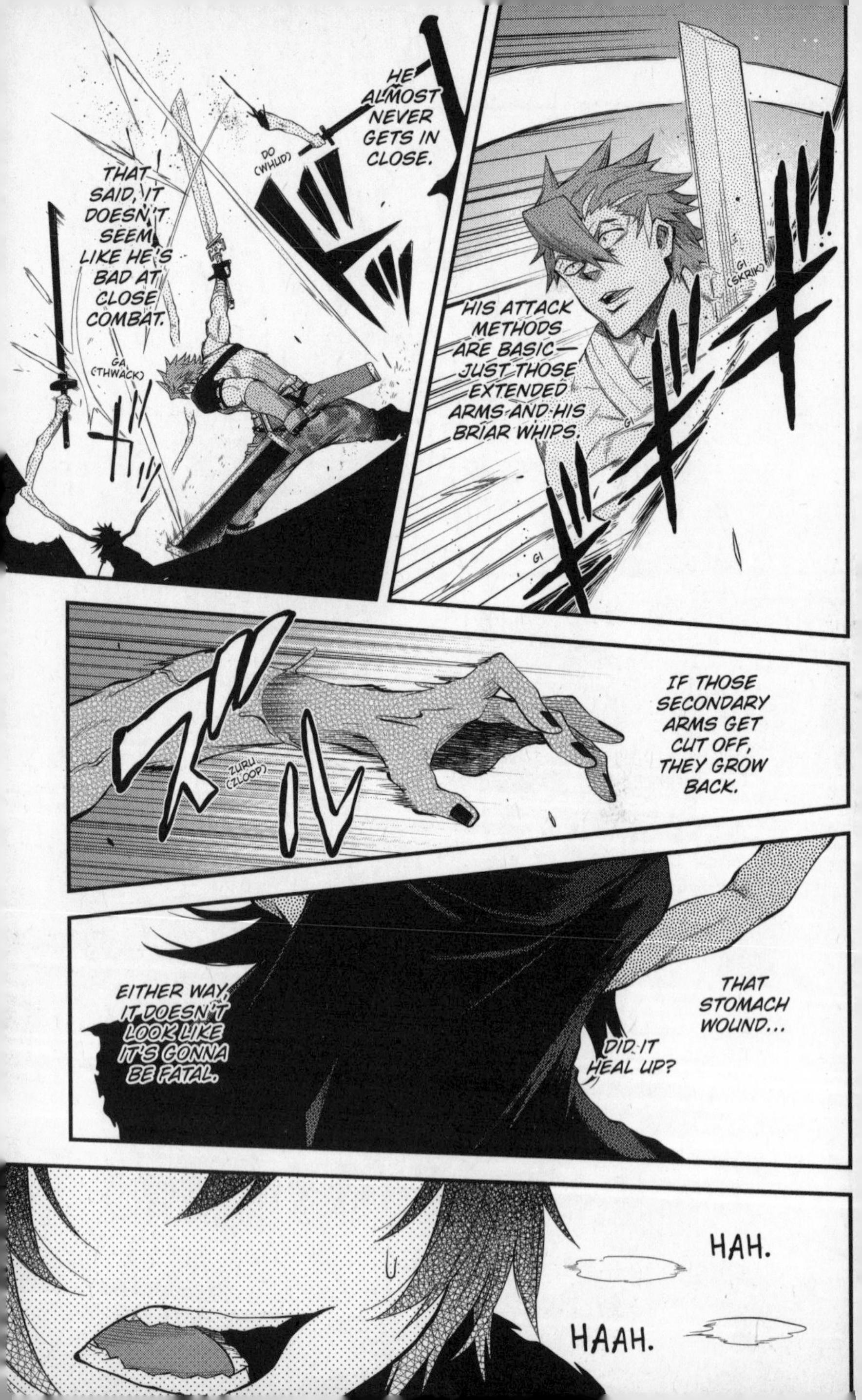
HIS ATTACK METHODS ARE BASIC—JUST THOSE EXTENDED ARMS AND HIS BRIAR WHIPS.
GI (SKRIK)
GI
GI
HE ALMOST NEVER GETS IN CLOSE.
DO (WHUD)
THAT SAID, IT DOESN'T SEEM LIKE HE'S BAD AT CLOSE COMBAT.
GA (THWACK)
IF THOSE SECONDARY ARMS GET CUT OFF, THEY GROW BACK.
ZURU (ZLOOP)
THAT STOMACH WOUND...
DID IT HEAL UP?
EITHER WAY, IT DOESN'T LOOK LIKE IT'S GONNA BE FATAL.
HAH.
HAAH.

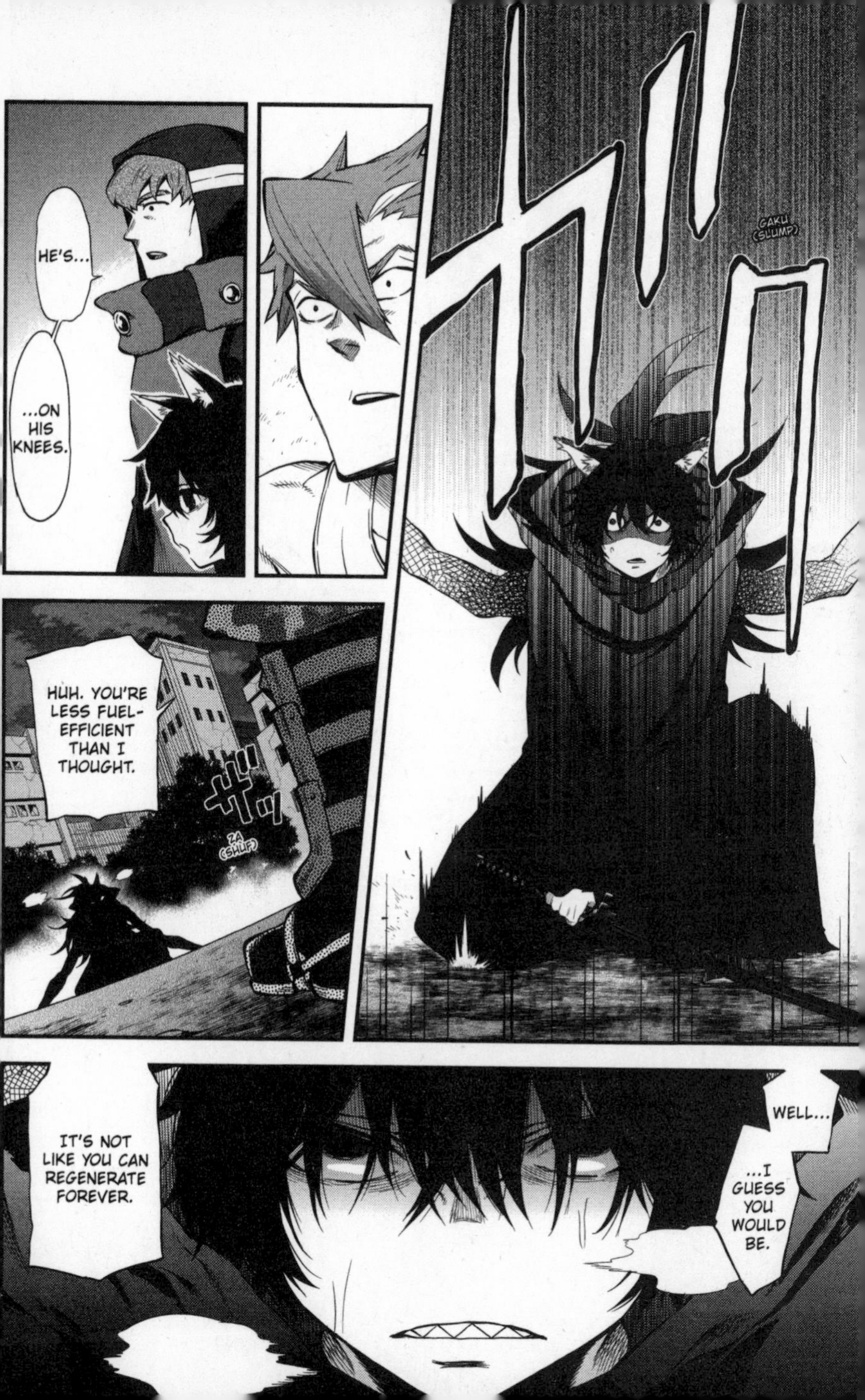
GAKU (SLUMP)
HE'S...
...ON HIS KNEES.
HUH. YOU'RE LESS FUEL-EFFICIENT THAN I THOUGHT.
ZA (SHUF)
WELL...
...I GUESS YOU WOULD BE.
IT'S NOT LIKE YOU CAN REGENERATE FOREVER.

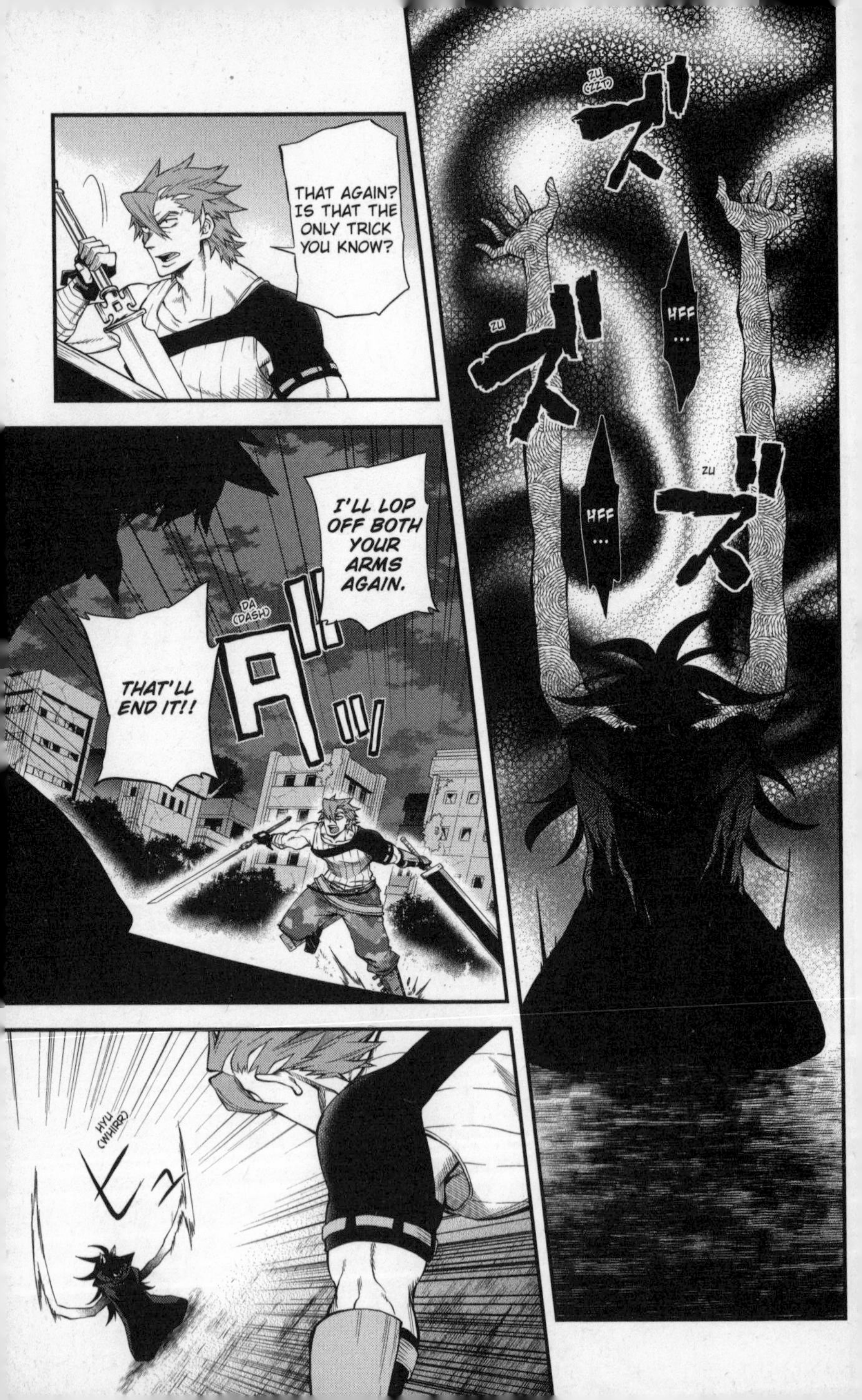
ZU (ZZZT)
HFF...
ZU
ZU
HFF...
THAT AGAIN? IS THAT THE ONLY TRICK YOU KNOW?
I'LL LOP OFF BOTH YOUR ARMS AGAIN.
DA (DASH)
THAT'LL END IT!!
HYU (WHIRR)

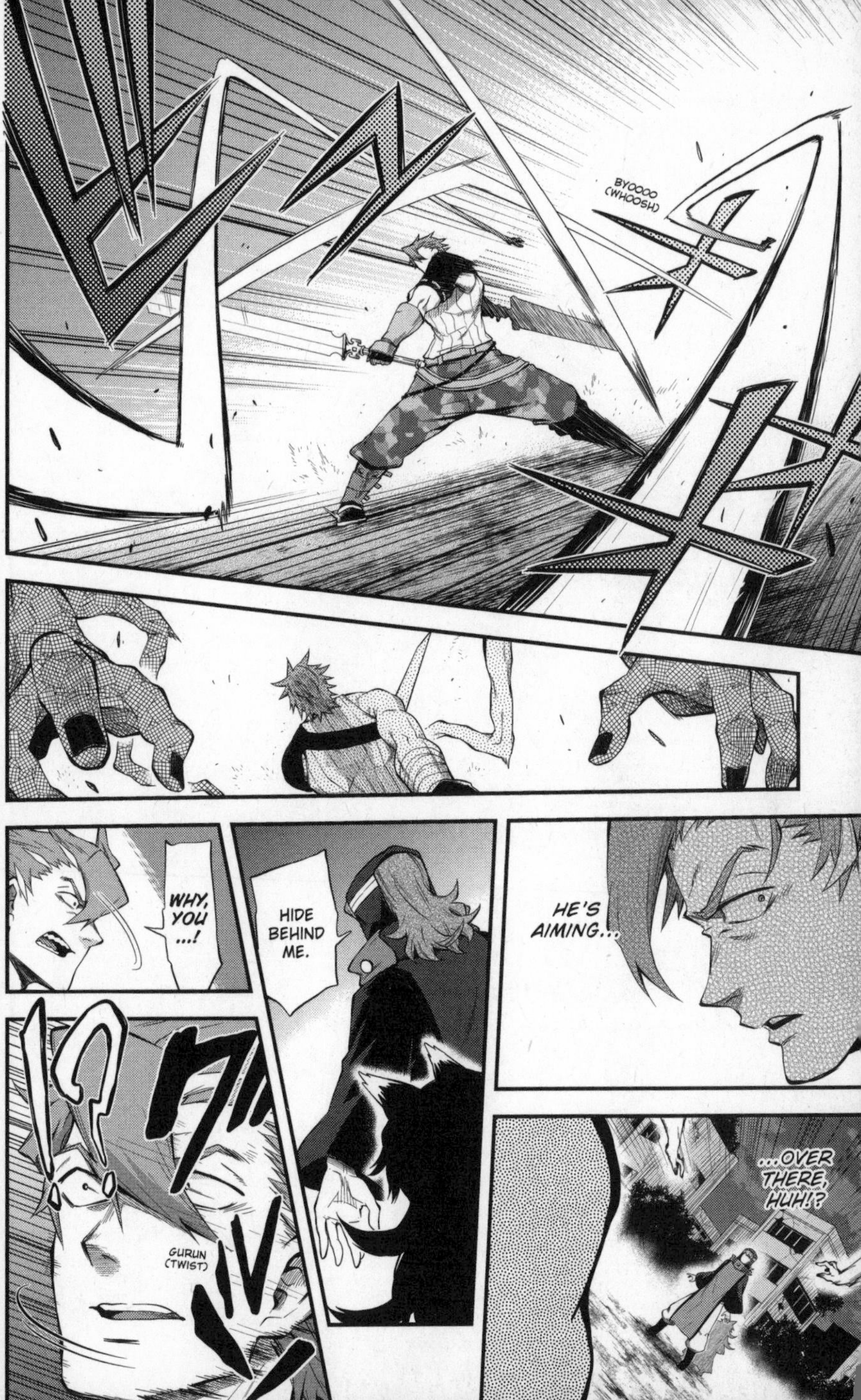
BYOOOO (WHOOSH)
HE'S AIMING...
HIDE BEHIND ME.
WHY, YOU ...!
...OVER THERE, HUH!?
GURUN (TWIST)

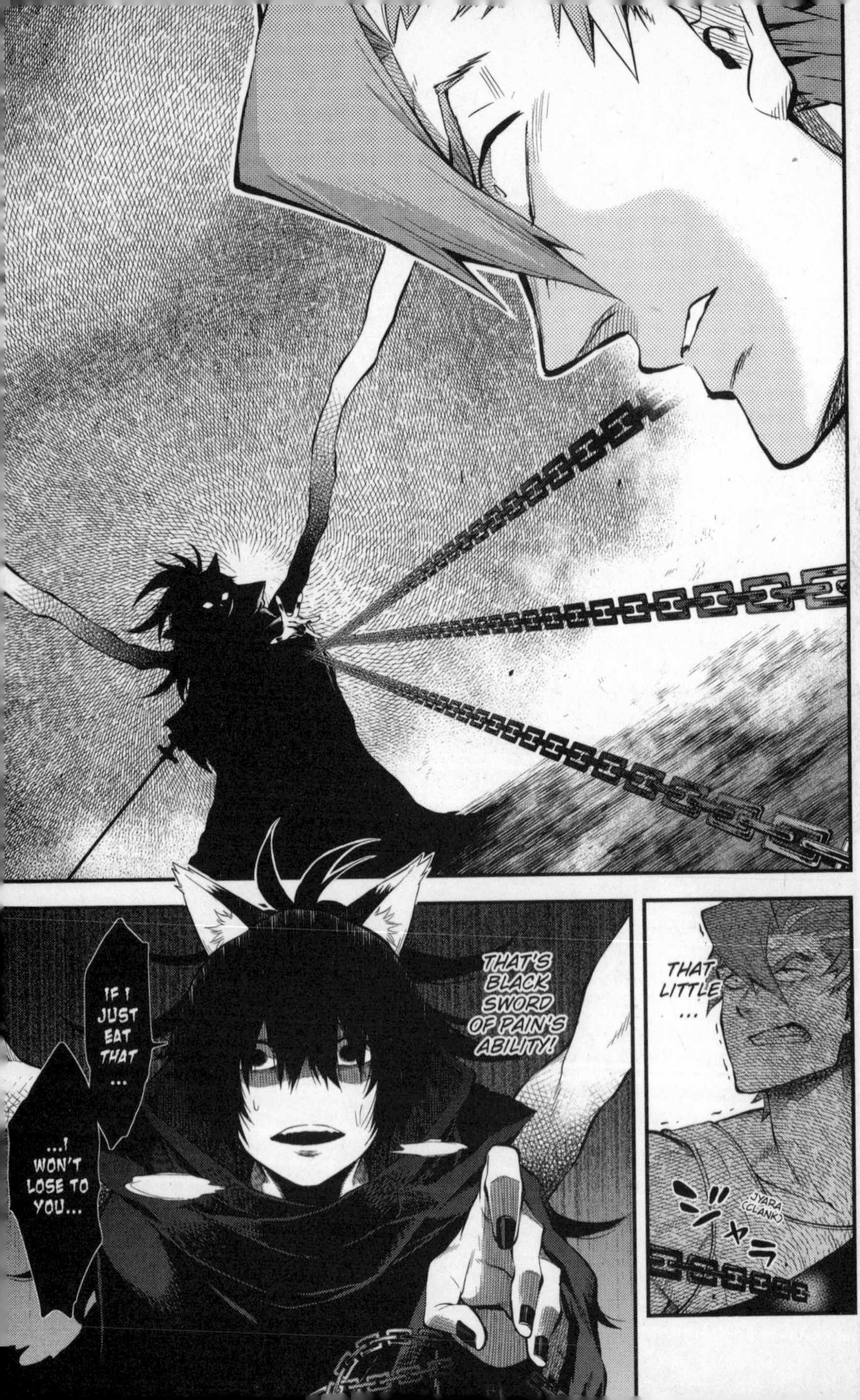
THAT LITTLE ...
ジャラ
JYARA (CLANK)
THAT'S BLACK SWORD OF PAIN'S ABILITY!
IF I JUST EAT THAT ...
...I WON'T LOSE TO YOU...

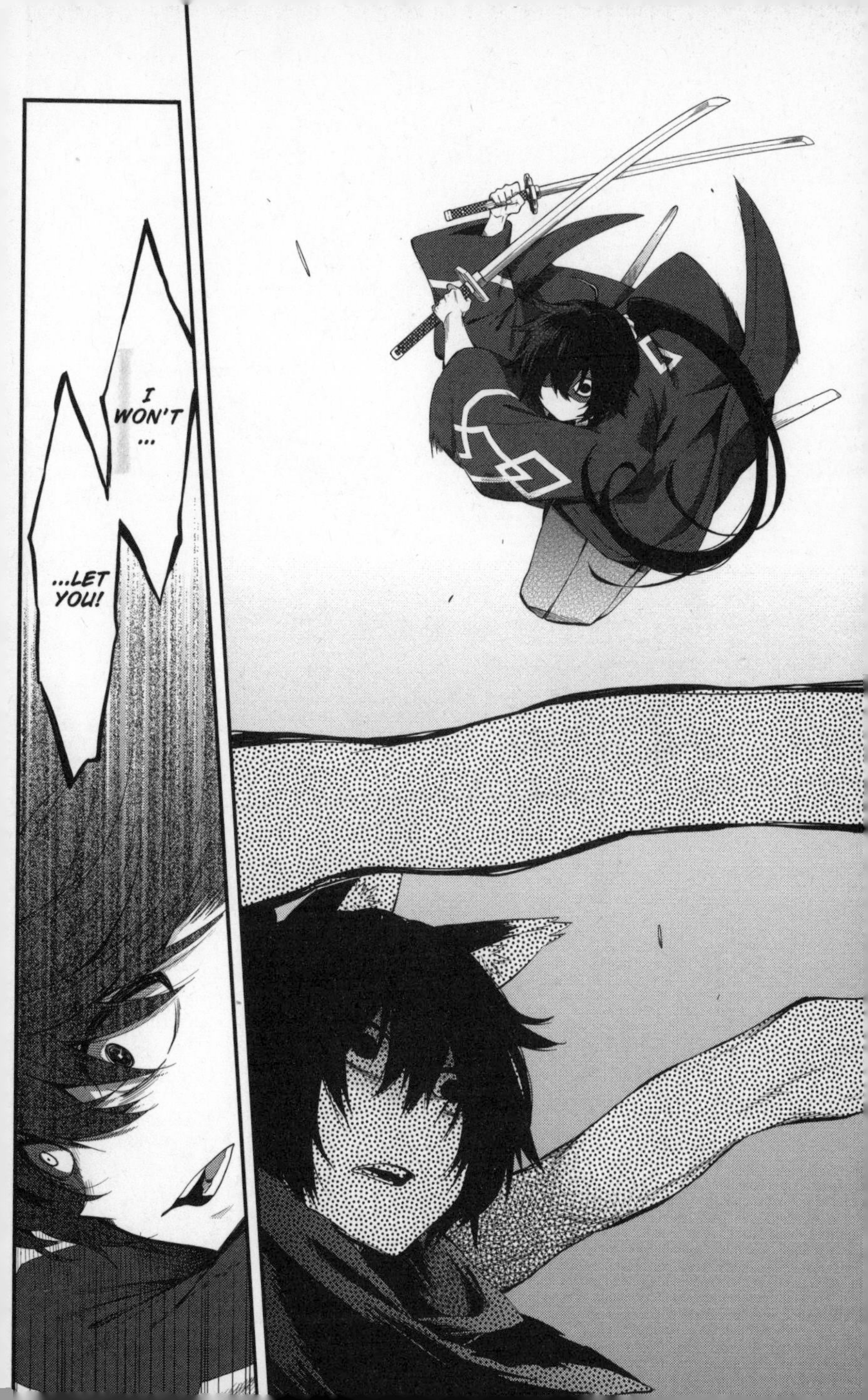
I WON'T ...
...LET YOU!

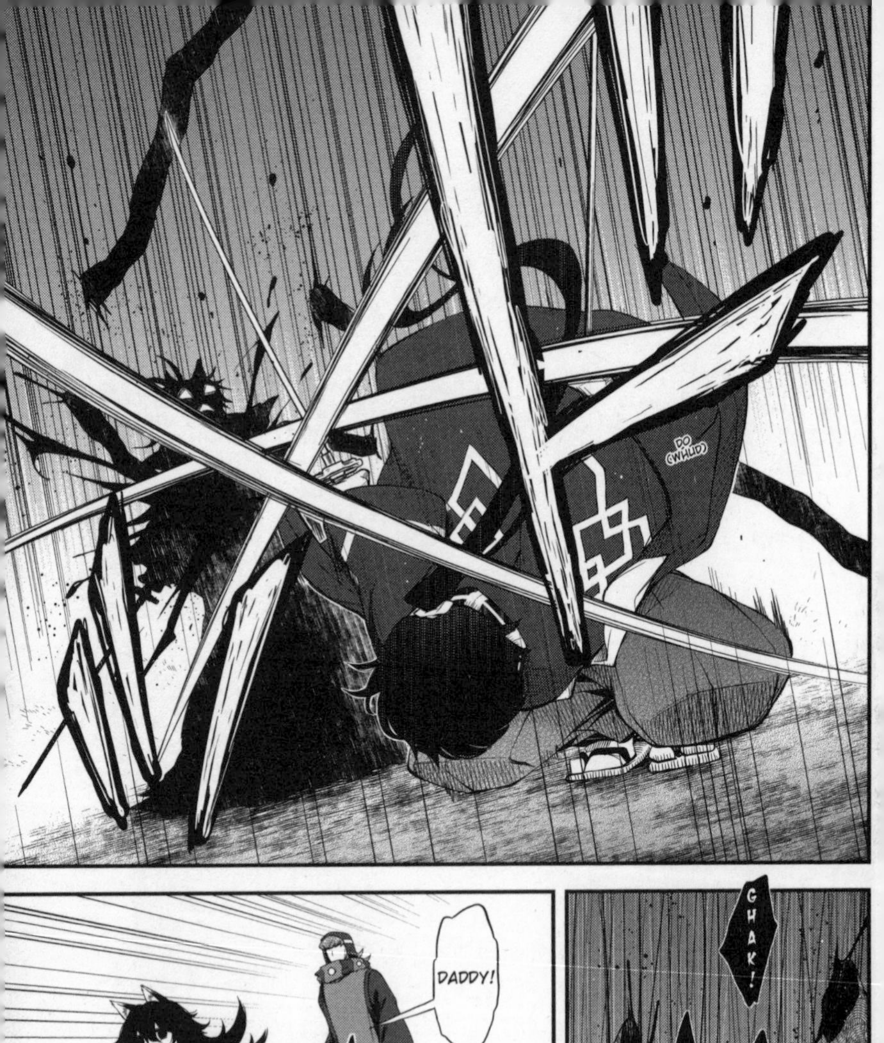
DO
(WHUD)

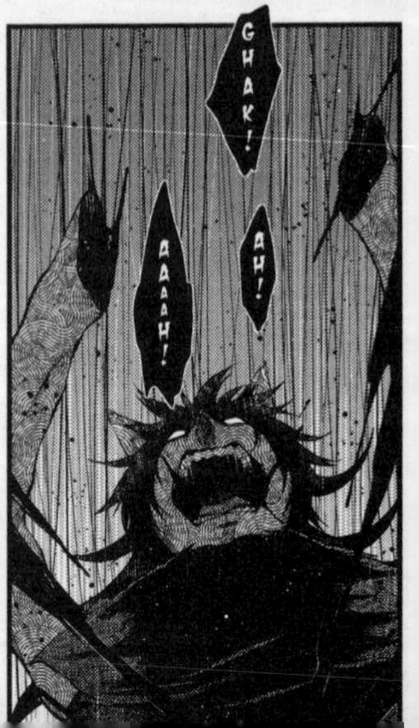
GHAK!
AH!
AAAAH!

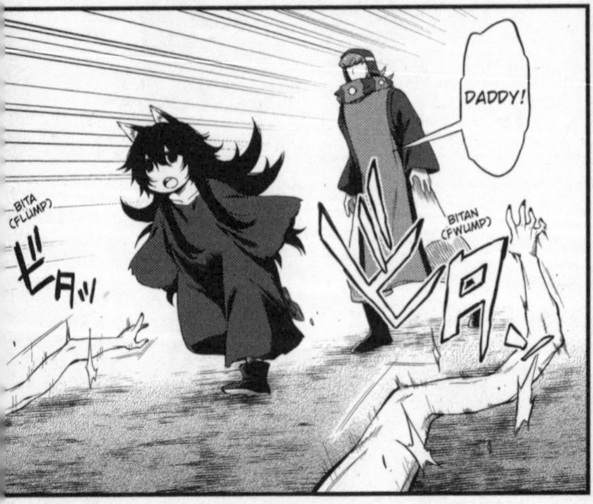
DADDY!
BITAN
(FWUMP)
BITA
(FLUMP)
ビタッ

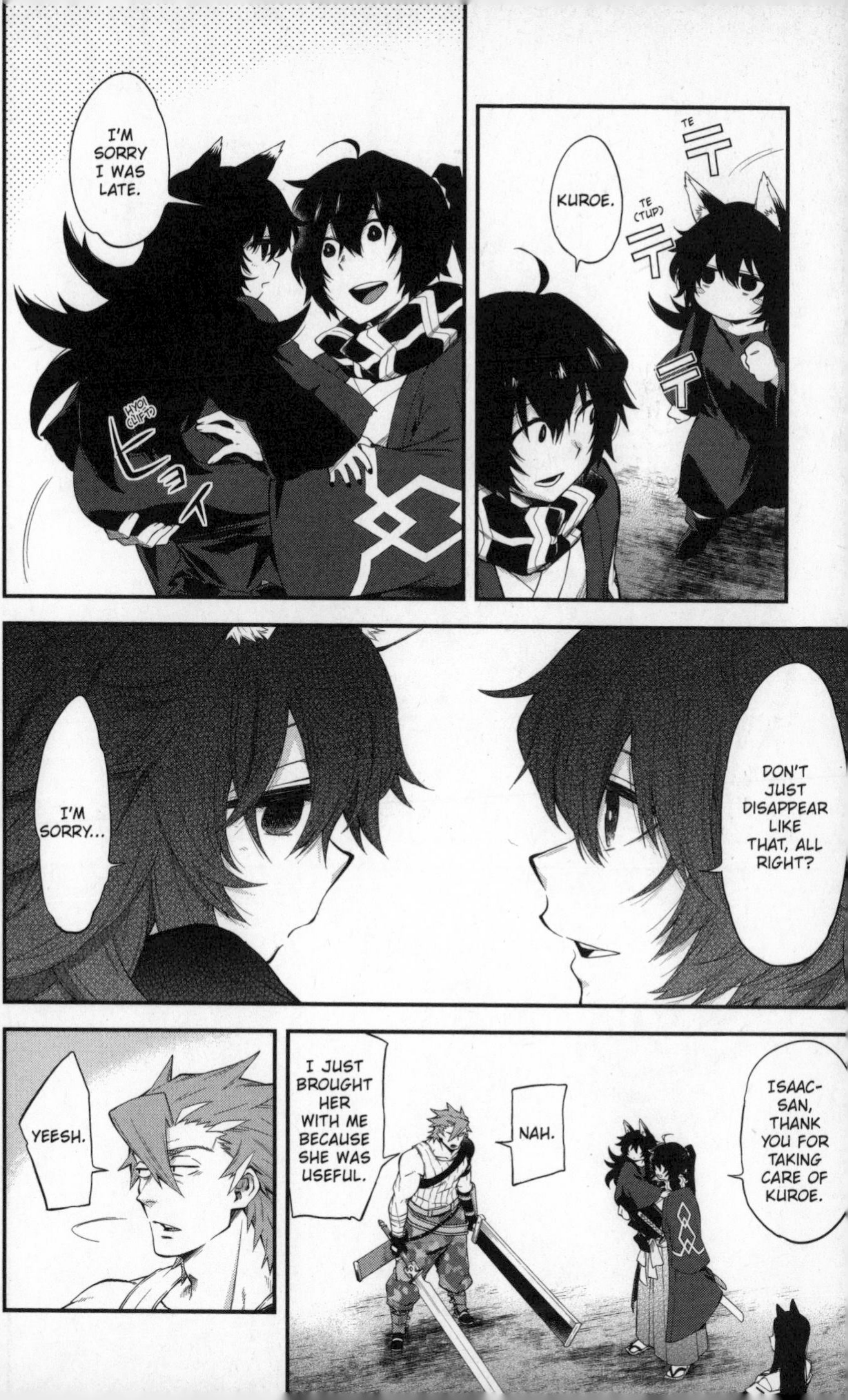

TE
KUROE.
TE (TUP)
I'M SORRY I WAS LATE.
HYOI (LIFT)
DON'T JUST DISAPPEAR LIKE THAT, ALL RIGHT?
I'M SORRY...
ISAAC-SAN, THANK YOU FOR TAKING CARE OF KUROE.
NAH.
I JUST BROUGHT HER WITH ME BECAUSE SHE WAS USEFUL.
YEESH.

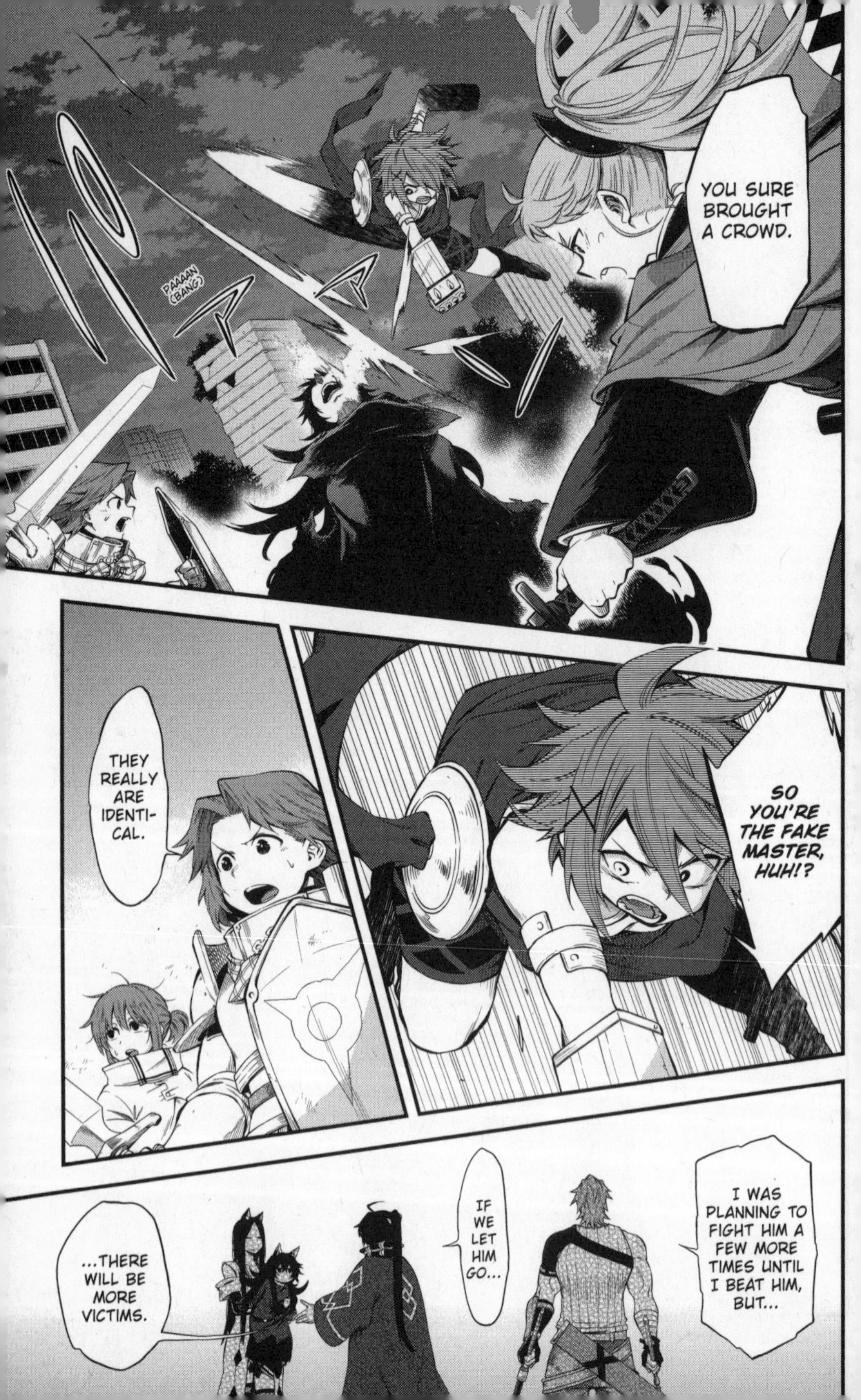
YOU SURE BROUGHT A CROWD.
PAAAAN (BANG)
SO YOU'RE THE FAKE MASTER, HUH!?
THEY REALLY ARE IDENTICAL.
I WAS PLANNING TO FIGHT HIM A FEW MORE TIMES UNTIL I BEAT HIM, BUT...
IF WE LET HIM GO...
...THERE WILL BE MORE VICTIMS.

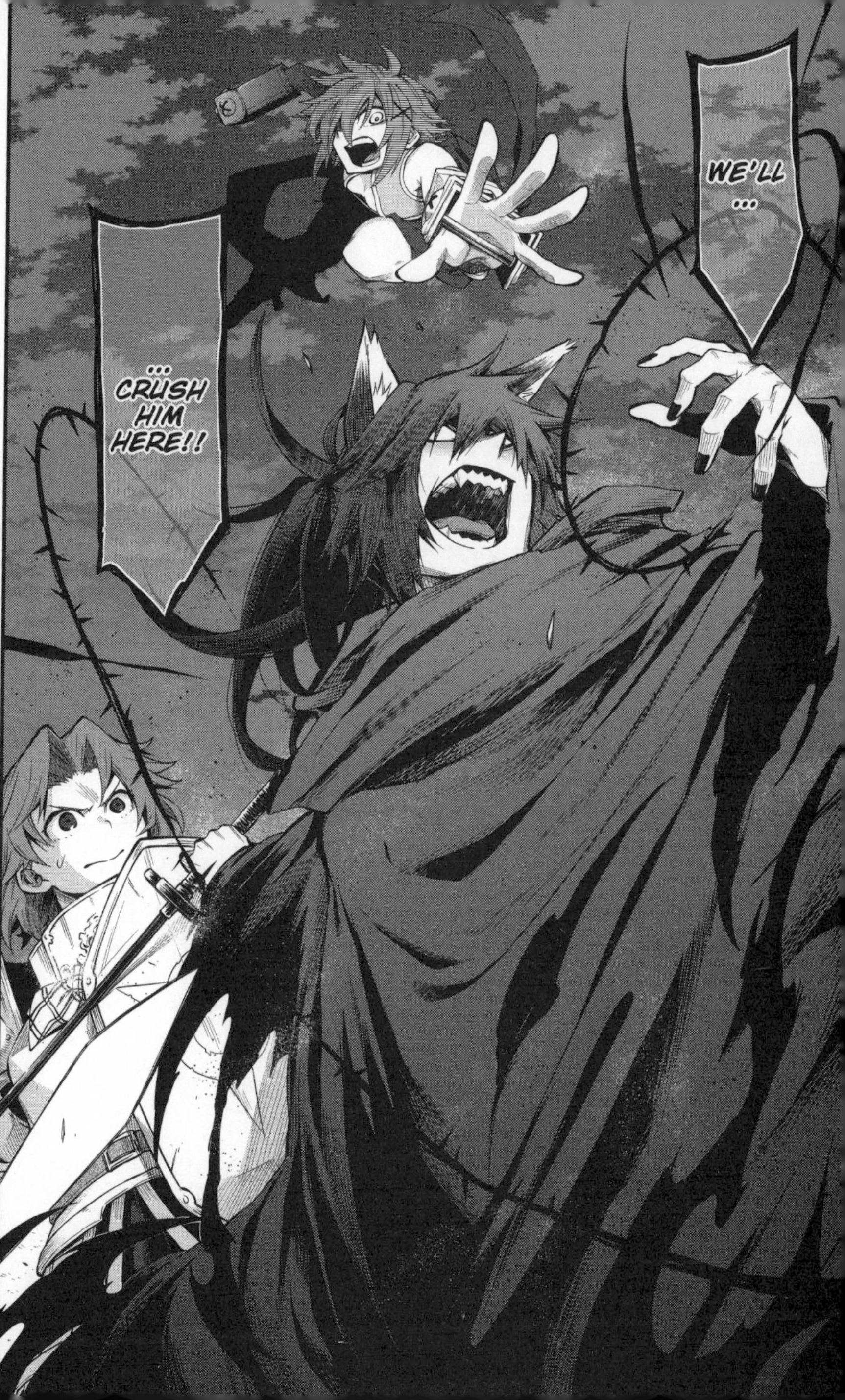
WE'LL ...
... CRUSH HIM HERE!!

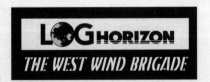

LOG HORIZON

THE WEST WIND BRIGADE

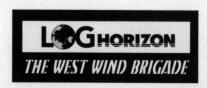

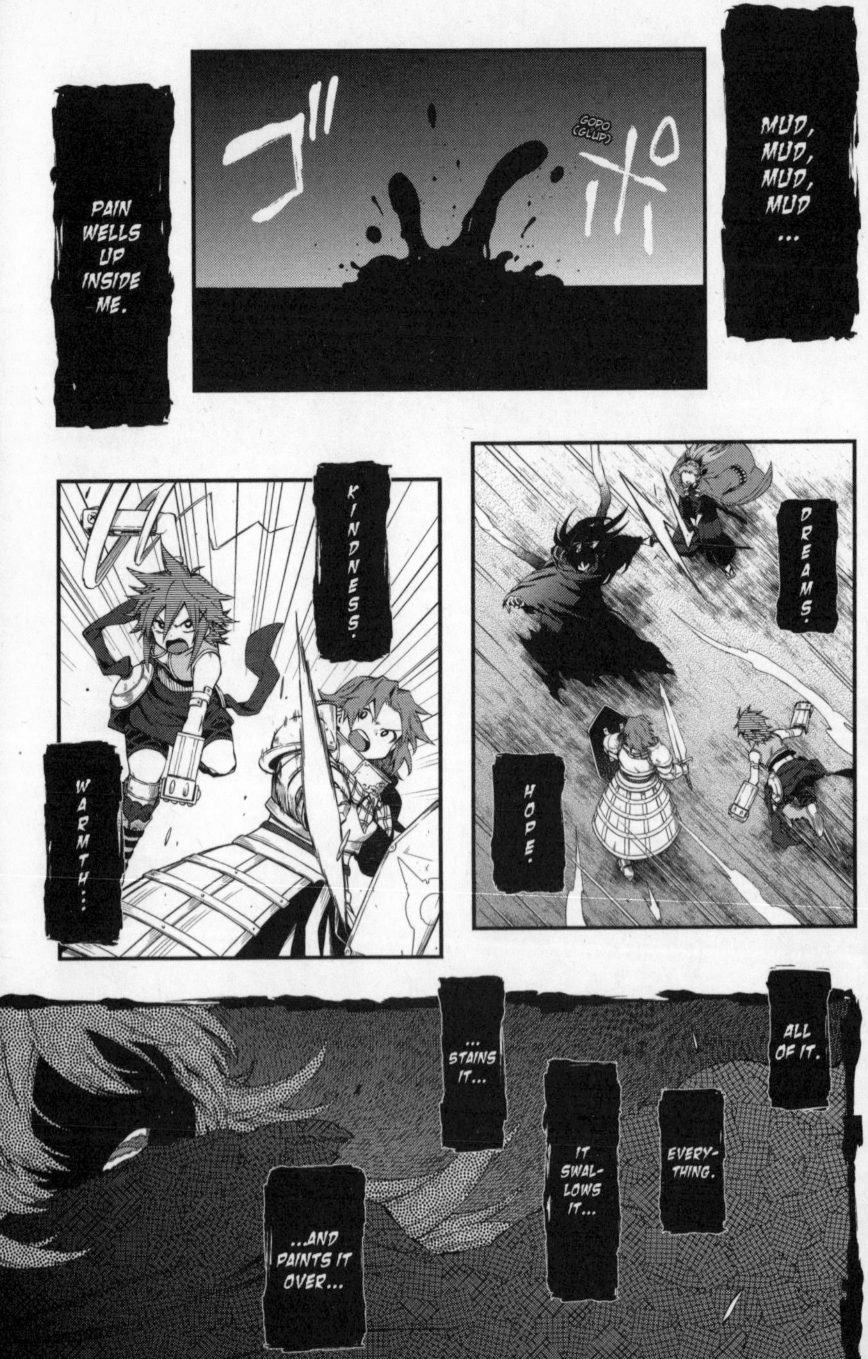
MUD, MUD, MUD, MUD ...
ゴポ
GOPO (GLUP)
PAIN WELLS UP INSIDE ME.
DREAMS.
HOPE.
KINDNESS.
WARMTH...
ALL OF IT.
EVERY-THING.
IT SWAL-LOWS IT...
...STAINS IT...
...AND PAINTS IT OVER...

...IN PITCH-BLACK.

CHAPTER: 52 Power (Part Two)

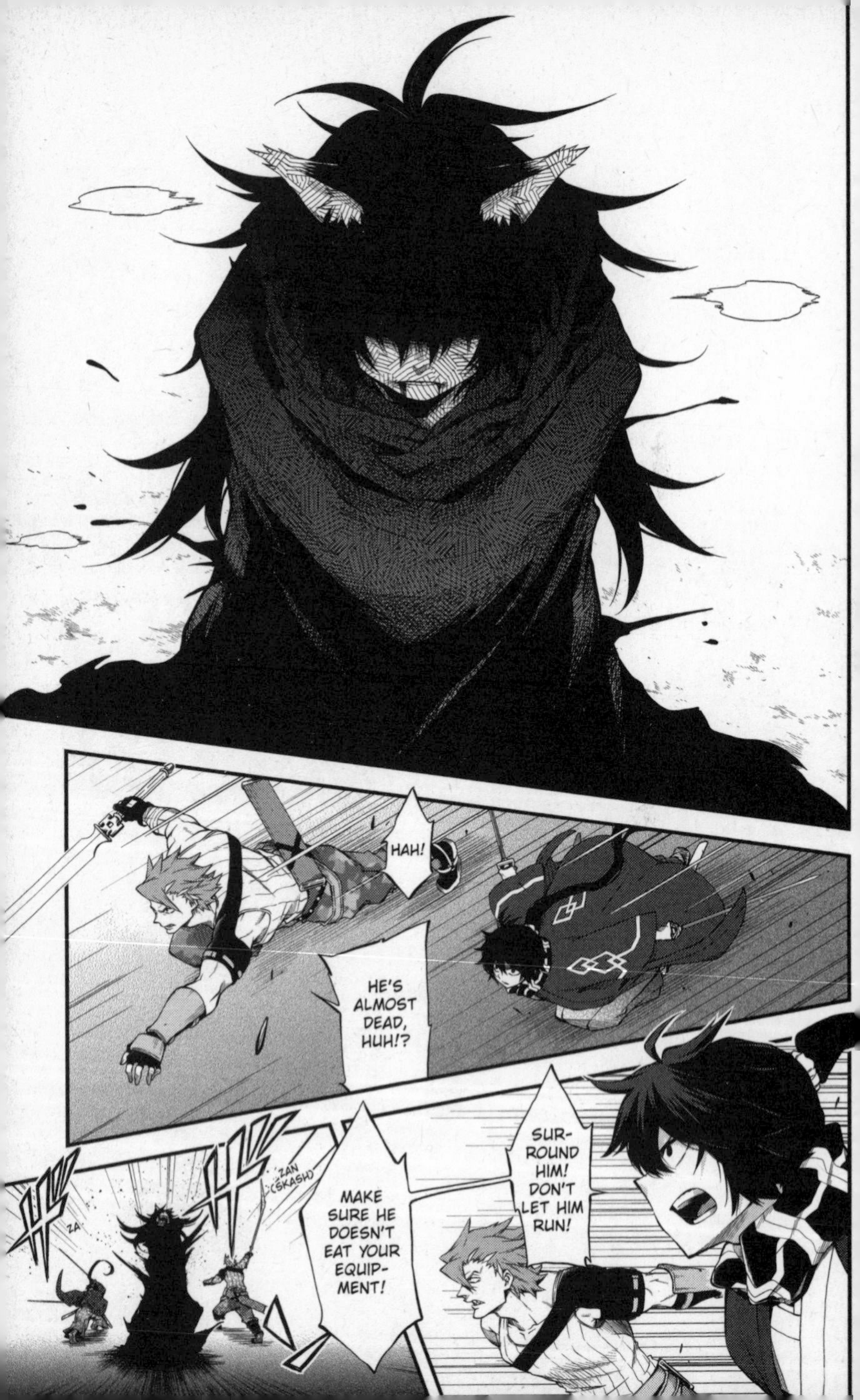
HAH!
HE'S ALMOST DEAD, HUH!?
SUR-ROUND HIM! DON'T LET HIM RUN!
MAKE SURE HE DOESN'T EAT YOUR EQUIP-MENT!
ZAN (SKASH)
ZA

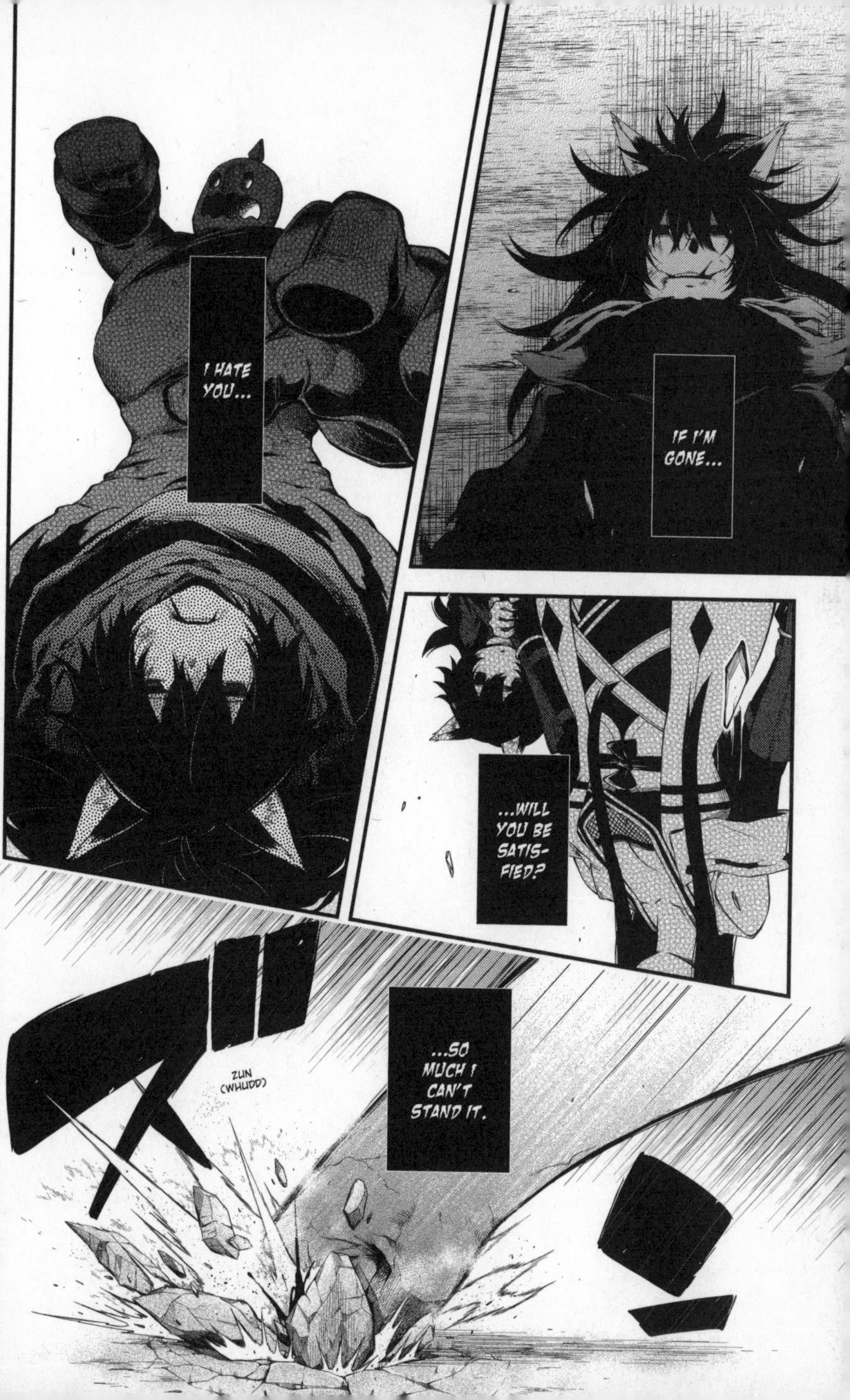
IF I'M GONE...
...WILL YOU BE SATIS-FIED?
I HATE YOU...
...SO MUCH I CAN'T STAND IT.
ZUN (WHUDD)

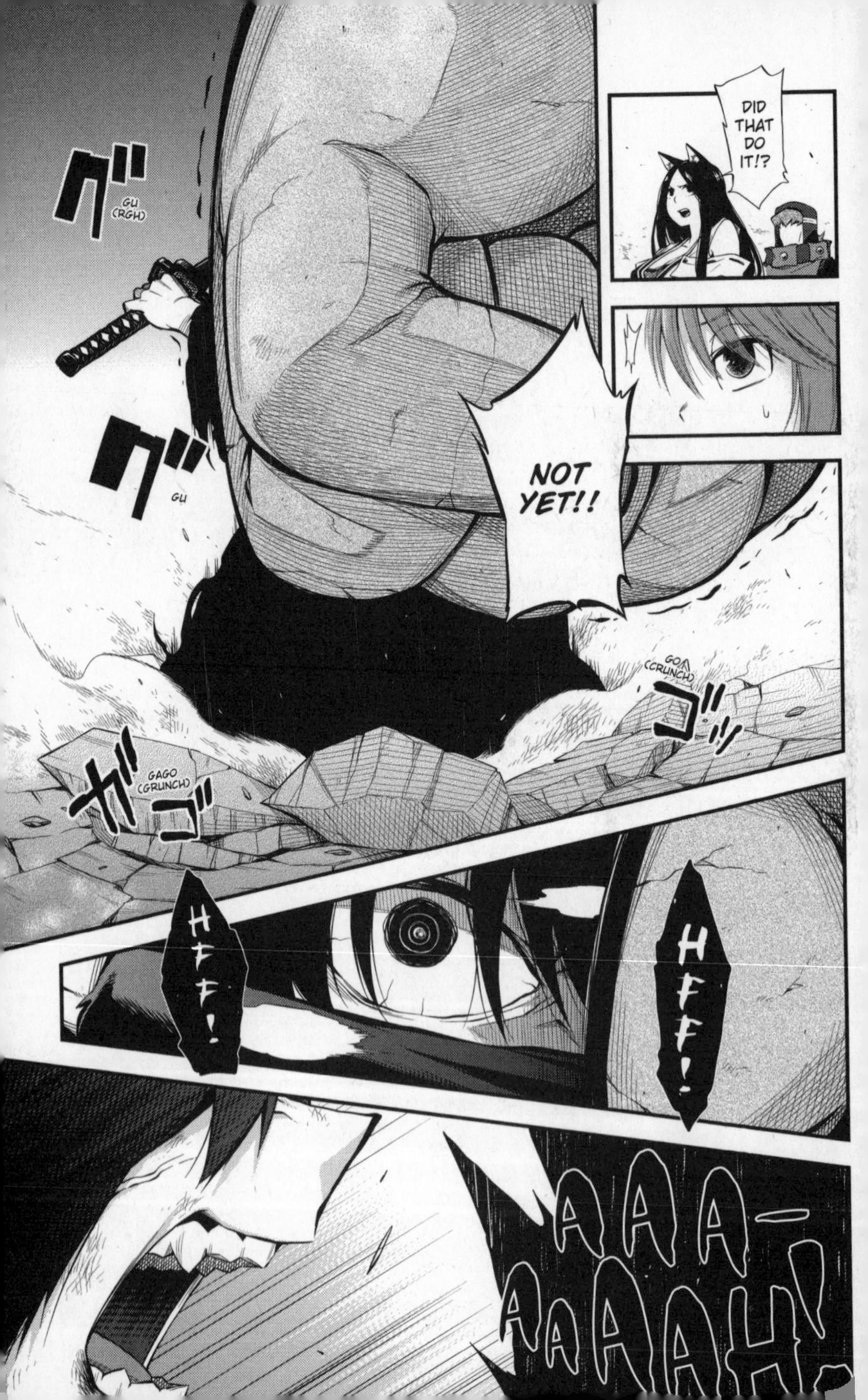
DID THAT DO IT!?
GU (RGH)
NOT YET!!
GU
GO (CRUNCH)
GAGO (CRUNCH)
HFF!
HFF!
AAA-AAAAAH!

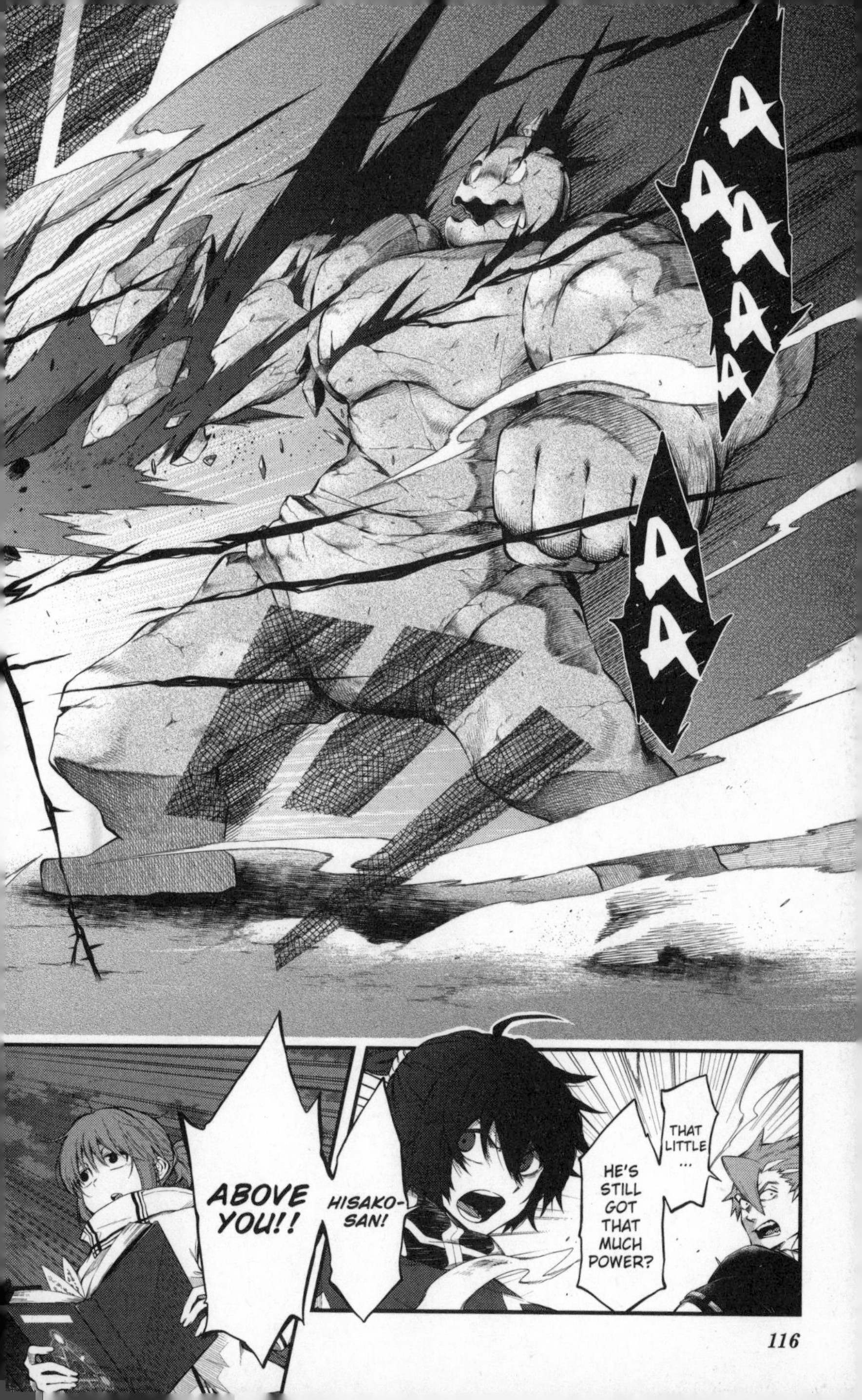
AAAAA
AA
THAT LITTLE ...
HE'S STILL GOT THAT MUCH POWER?
HISAKO-SAN!
ABOVE YOU!!

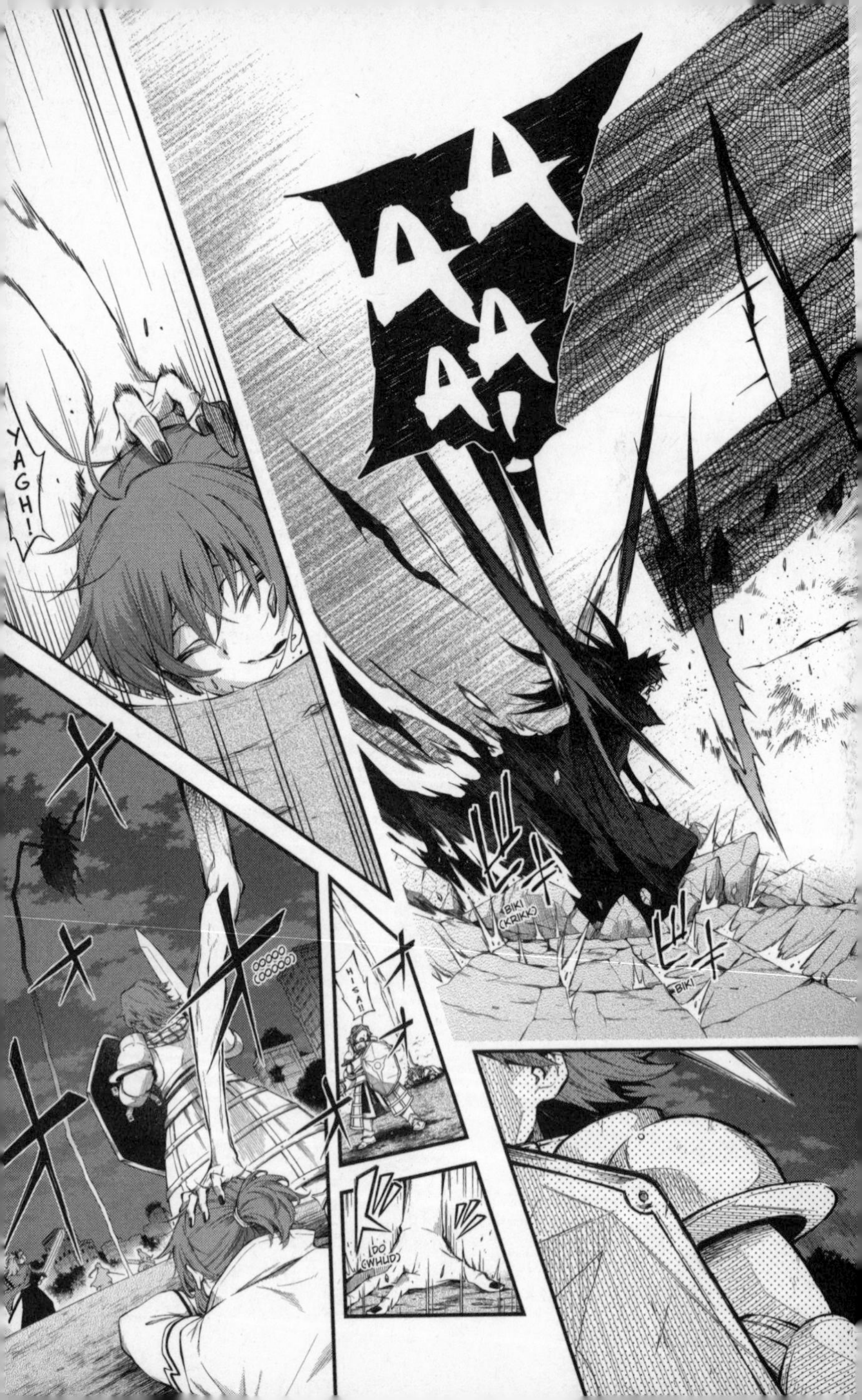
AAAA!
BIKI (KRIKK)
BIKI
YAGH!
HISA!!
DO (WHUD)
OOOOO (OOOOO)

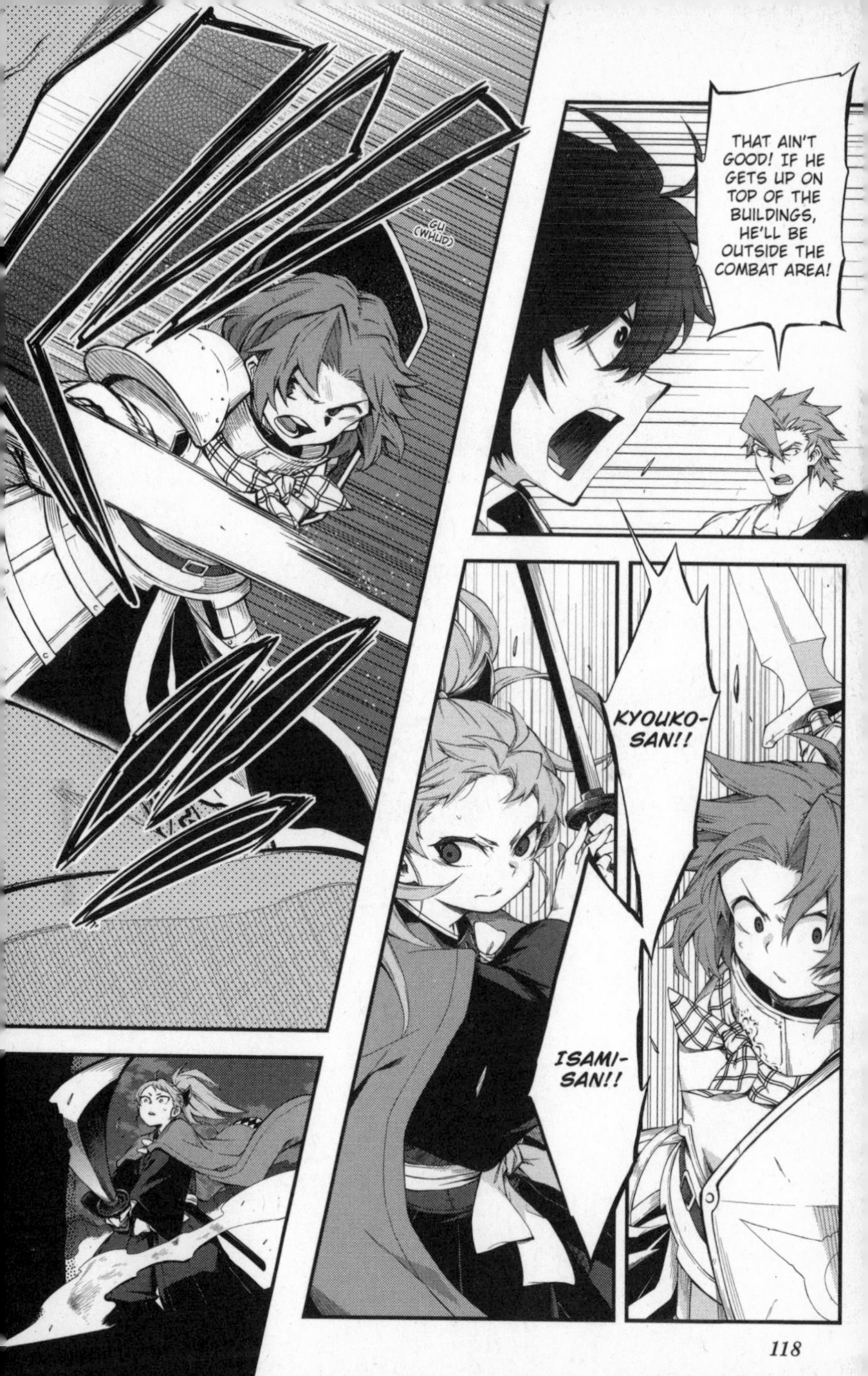
THAT AIN'T GOOD! IF HE GETS UP ON TOP OF THE BUILDINGS, HE'LL BE OUTSIDE THE COMBAT AREA!
KYOUKO-SAN!!
ISAMI-SAN!!
GU (WHUD)

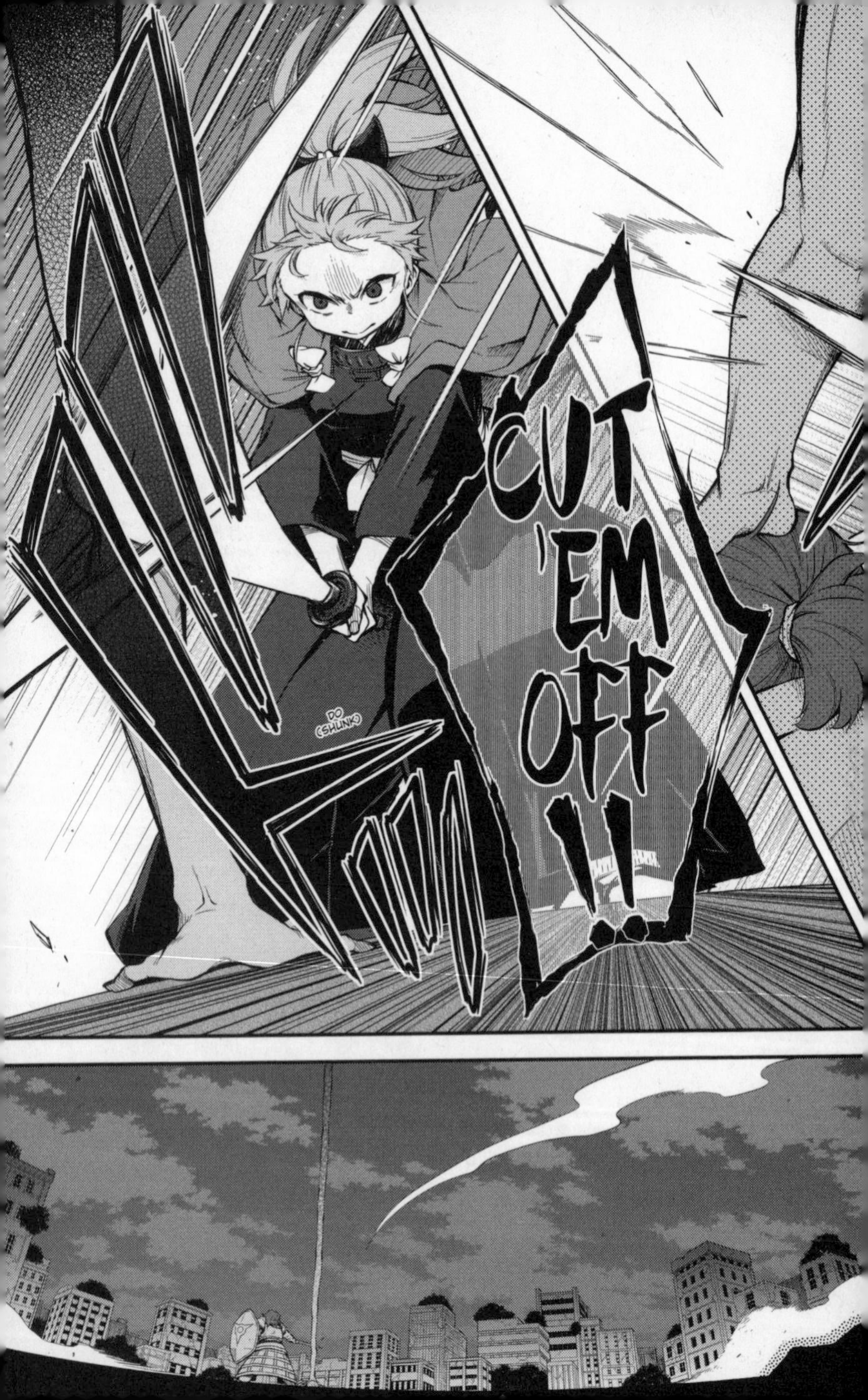
CUT 'EM OFF!!
DO (SHUNK)

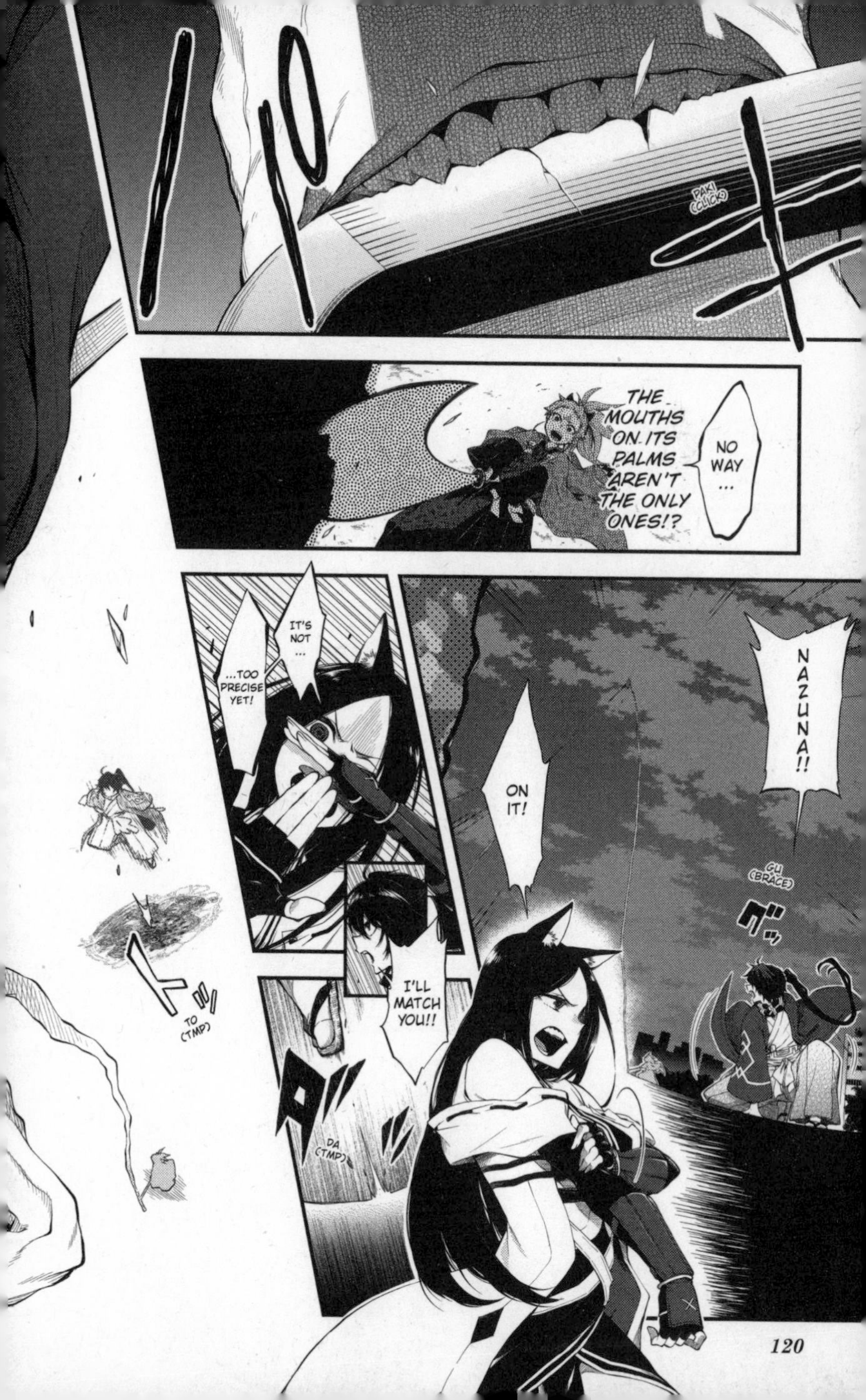
PAKI (CLICK)
NO WAY ...
THE MOUTHS ON ITS PALMS AREN'T THE ONLY ONES!?
NAZUNA!!
GU (BRACE)
ON IT!
IT'S NOT ...
...TOO PRECISE YET!
I'LL MATCH YOU!!
DA (TMP)
TO (TMP)

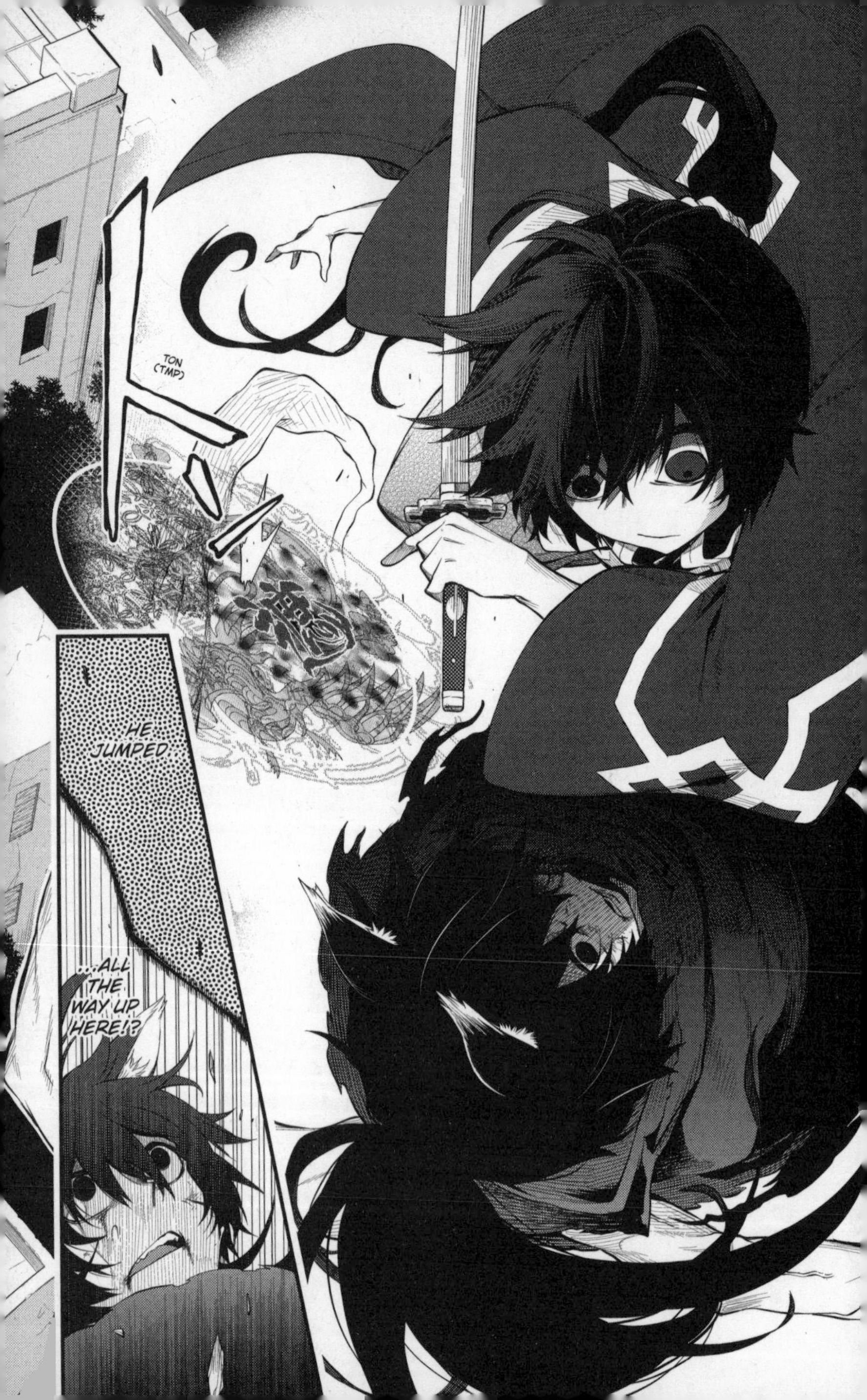
TON (TMP)
HE JUMPED
...ALL THE WAY UP HERE!?

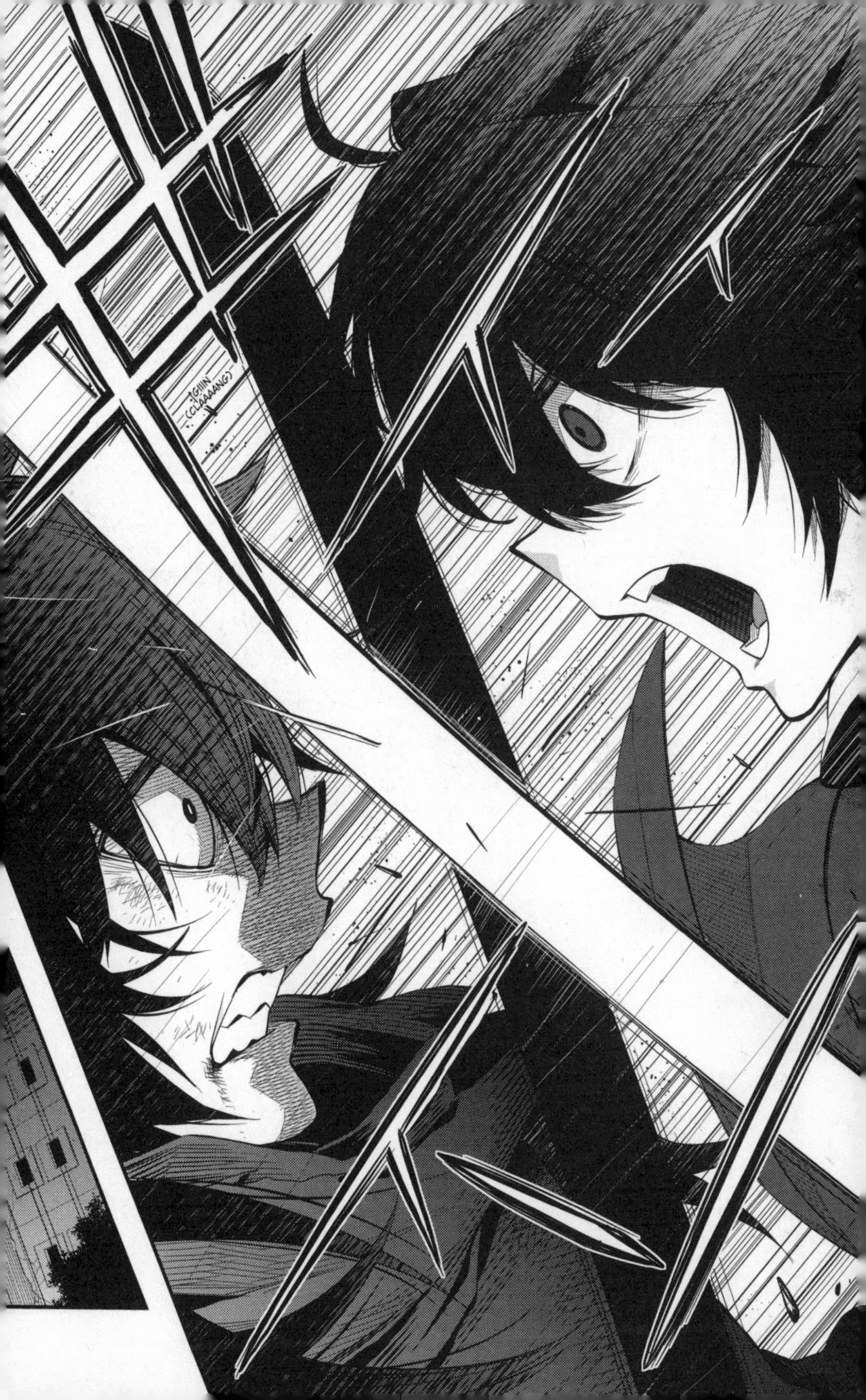
GIIIN
(CLAAAANG)

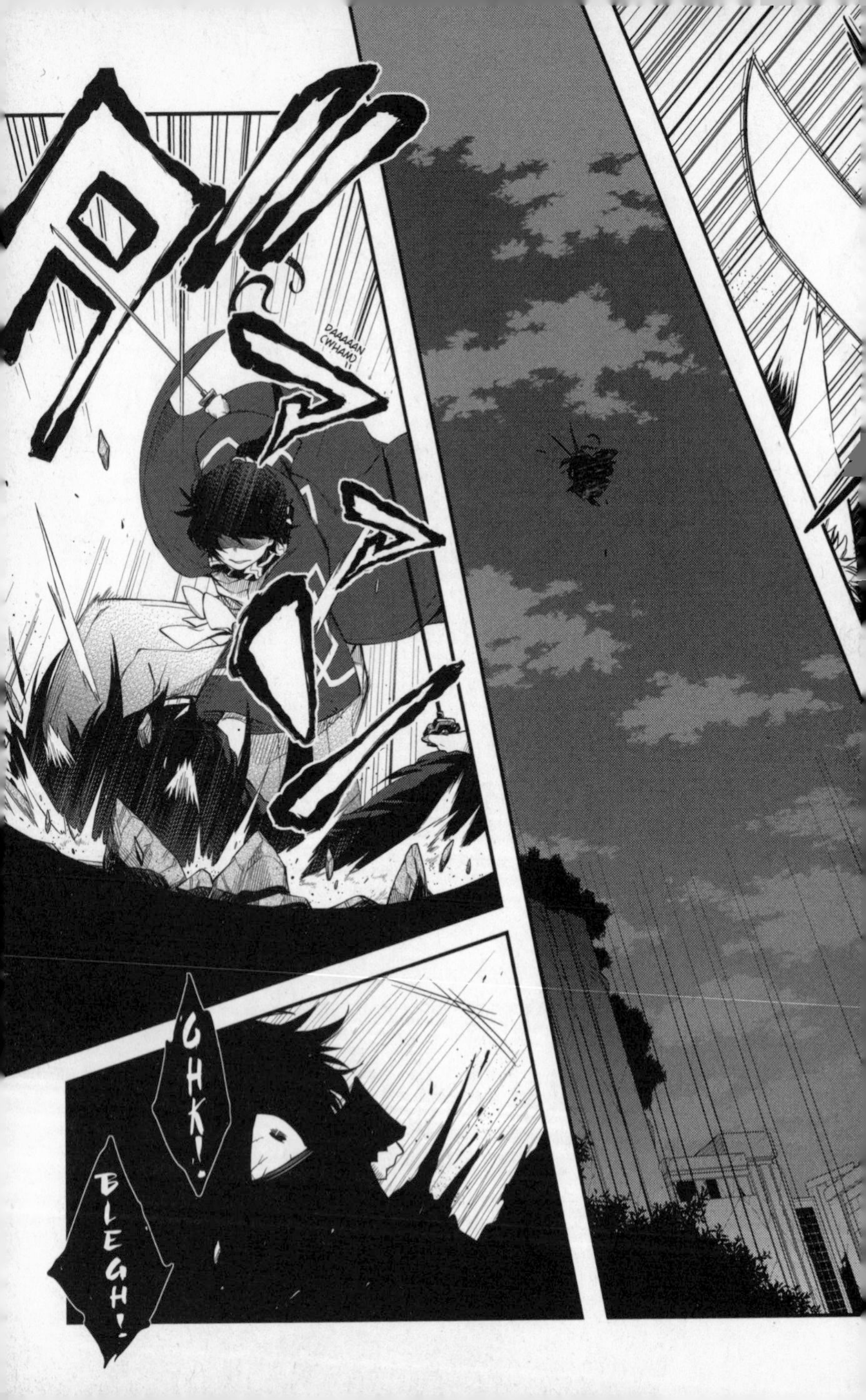
DAAAAAN
(WHAM)
GHK!
BLEGH!

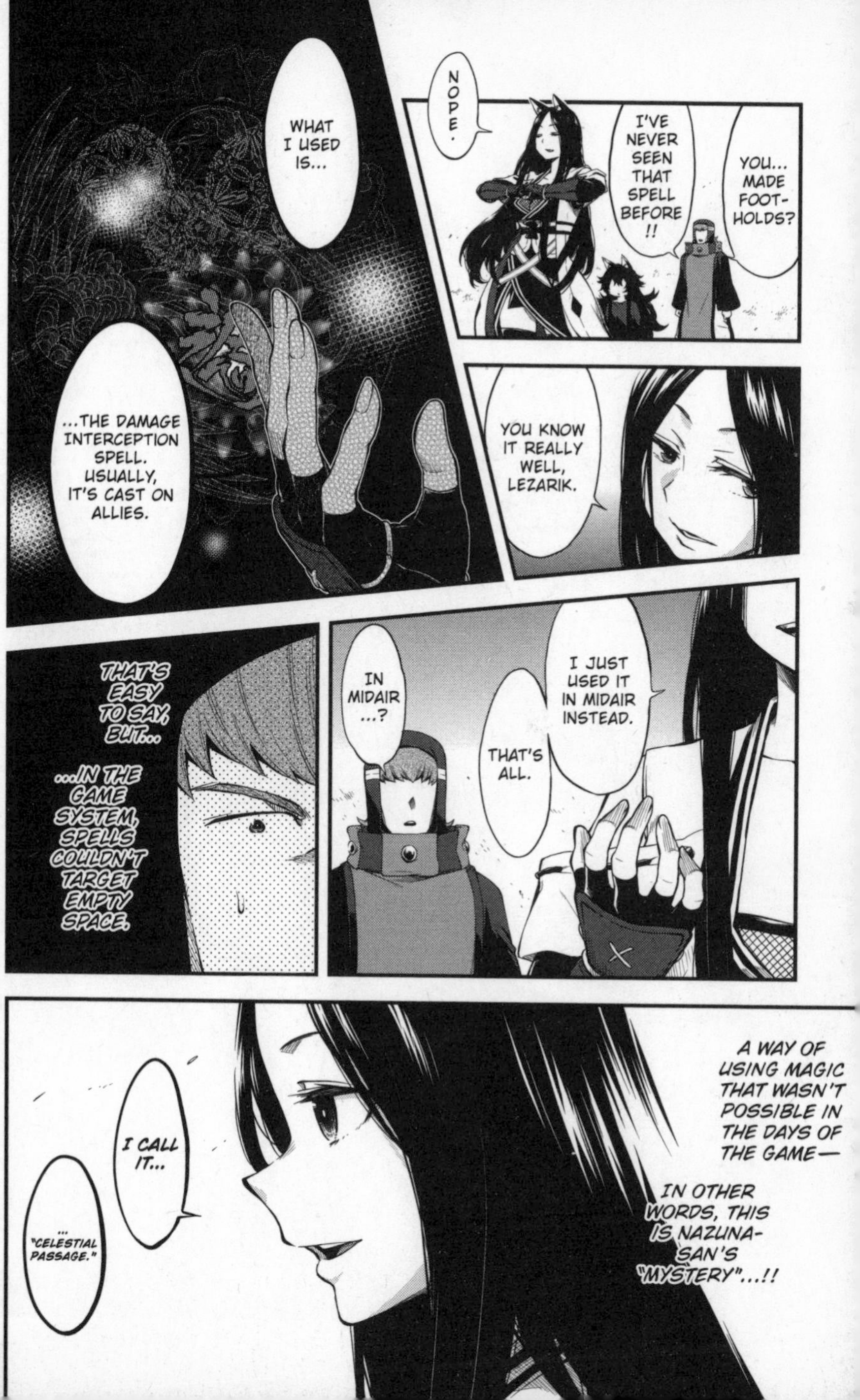
YOU... MADE FOOT-HOLDS?
I'VE NEVER SEEN THAT SPELL BEFORE!!
NOPE.
YOU KNOW IT REALLY WELL, LEZARIK.
WHAT I USED IS...
...THE DAMAGE INTERCEPTION SPELL. USUALLY, IT'S CAST ON ALLIES.
I JUST USED IT IN MIDAIR INSTEAD.
THAT'S ALL.
IN MIDAIR ...?
THAT'S EASY TO SAY, BUT...
...IN THE GAME SYSTEM, SPELLS COULDN'T TARGET EMPTY SPACE.
A WAY OF USING MAGIC THAT WASN'T POSSIBLE IN THE DAYS OF THE GAME—
IN OTHER WORDS, THIS IS NAZUNA-SAN'S "MYSTERY"...!!
I CALL IT...
..."CELESTIAL PASSAGE."

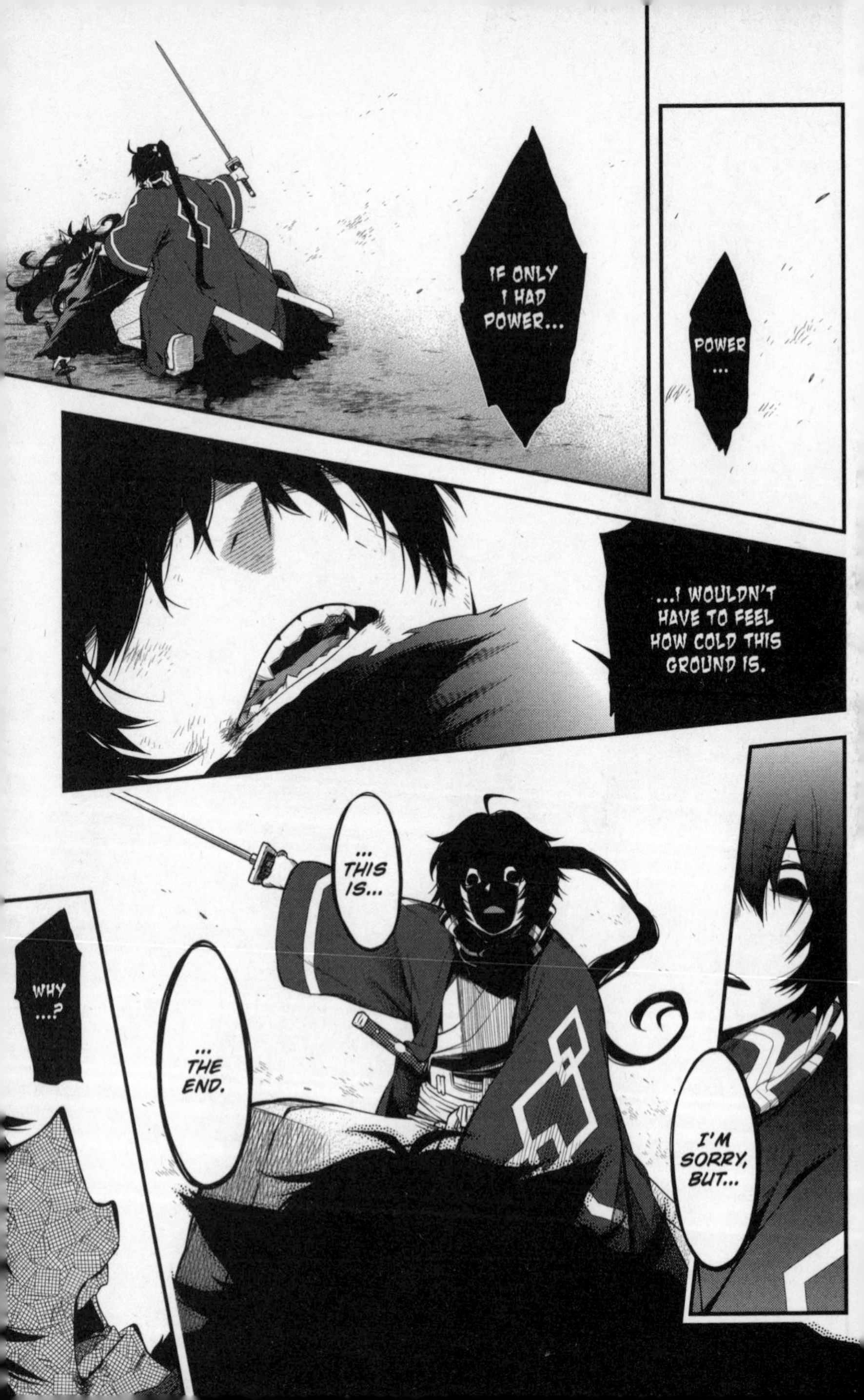
POWER...
IF ONLY I HAD POWER...
...I WOULDN'T HAVE TO FEEL HOW COLD THIS GROUND IS.
I'M SORRY, BUT...
...THIS IS...
...THE END.
WHY...?

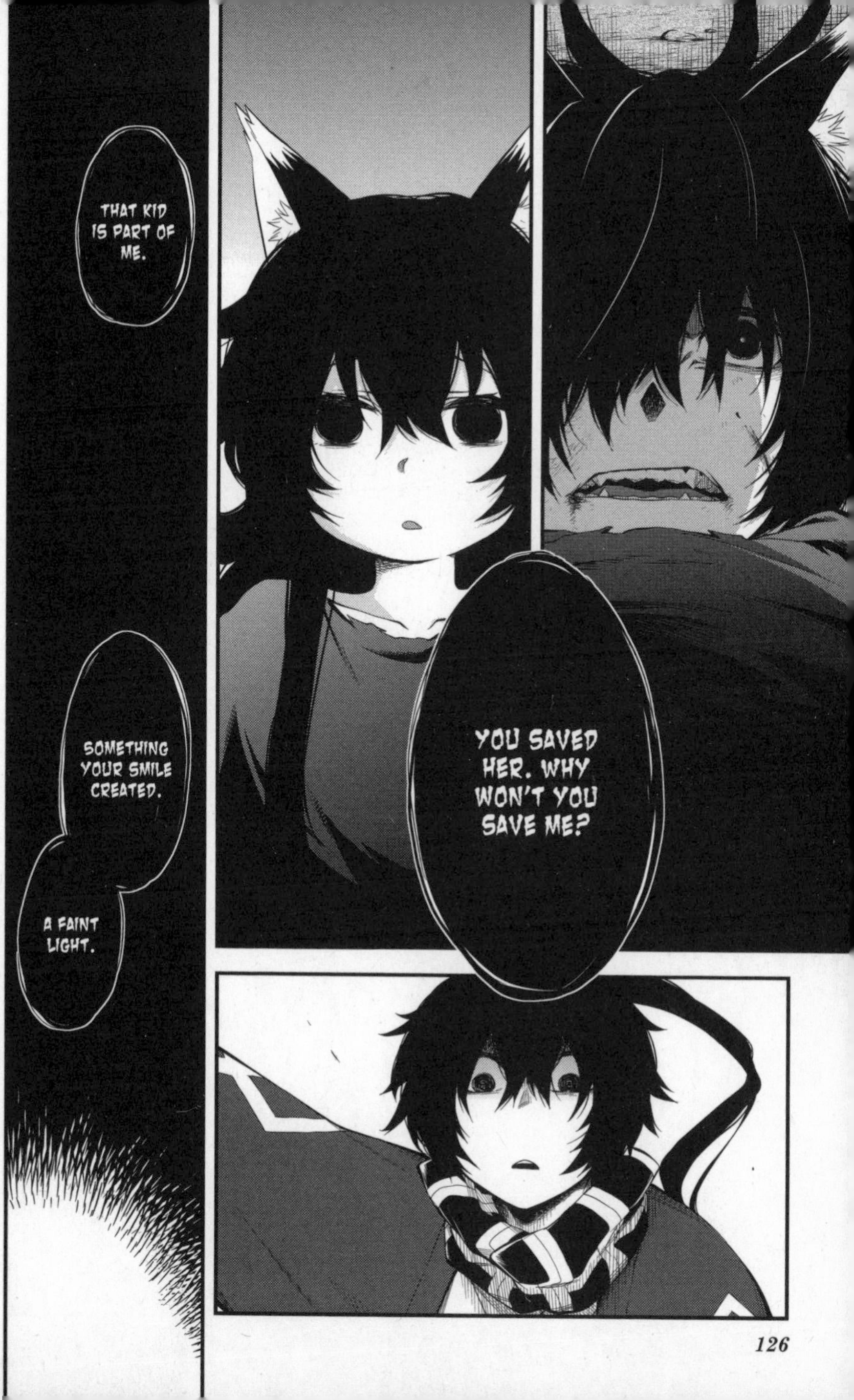
YOU SAVED HER. WHY WON'T YOU SAVE ME?
THAT KID IS PART OF ME.
SOMETHING YOUR SMILE CREATED.
A FAINT LIGHT.

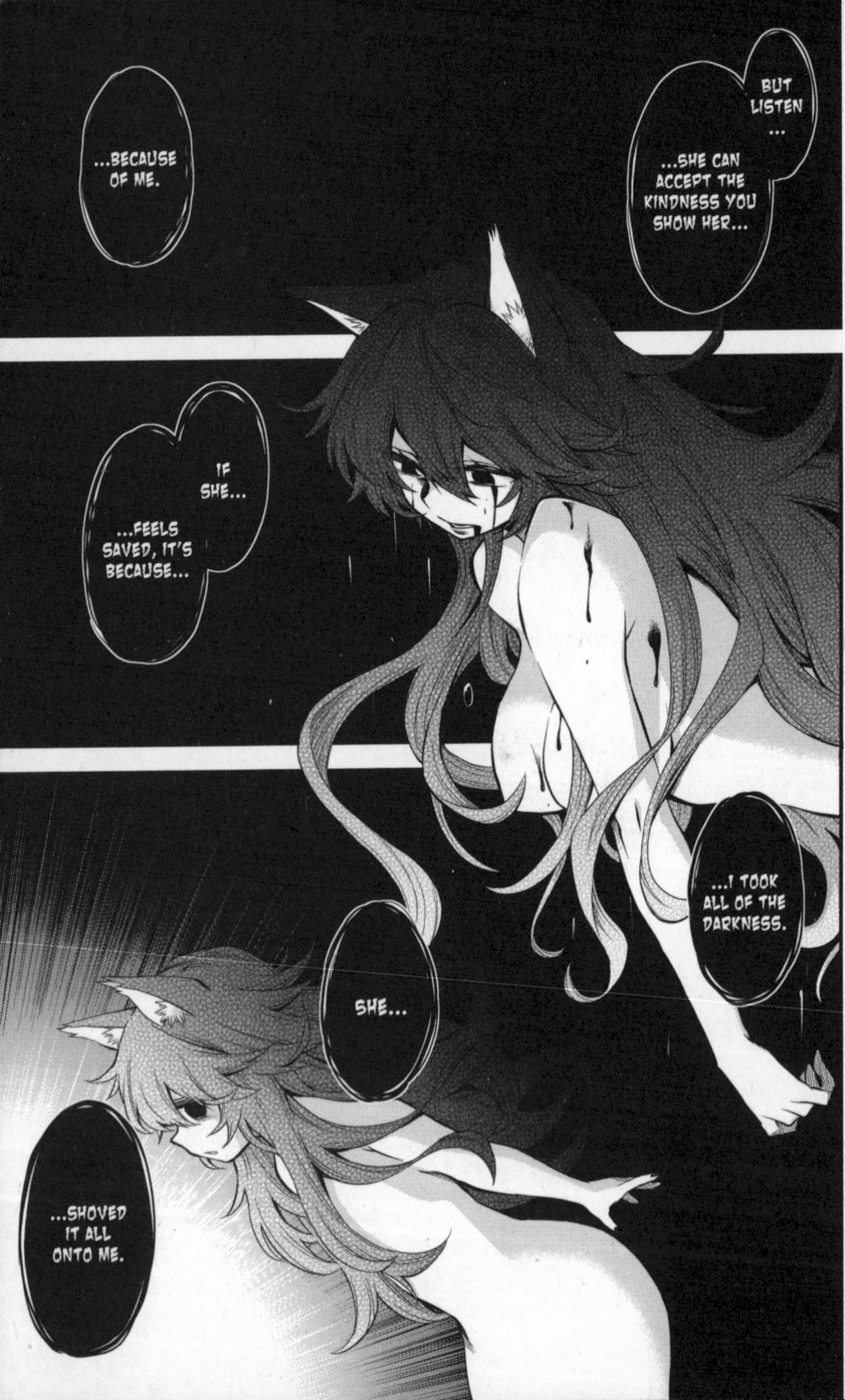
BUT LISTEN...
...SHE CAN ACCEPT THE KINDNESS YOU SHOW HER...
...BECAUSE OF ME.
IF SHE...
...FEELS SAVED, IT'S BECAUSE...
...I TOOK ALL OF THE DARKNESS.
SHE...
...SHOVED IT ALL ONTO ME.

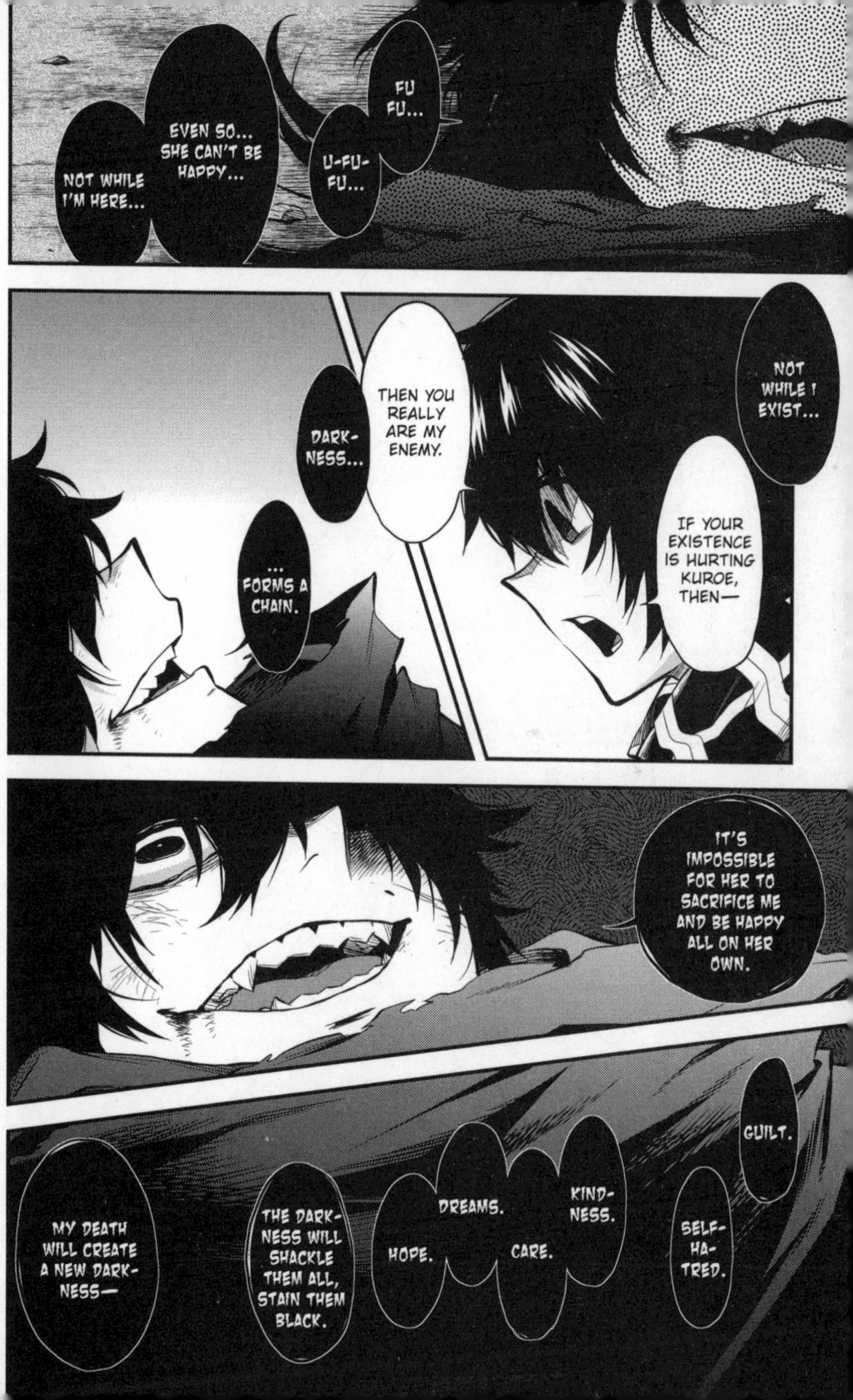
FU FU...
U-FU-FU...
EVEN SO... SHE CAN'T BE HAPPY...
NOT WHILE I'M HERE...
NOT WHILE I EXIST...
IF YOUR EXISTENCE IS HURTING KUROE, THEN—
THEN YOU REALLY ARE MY ENEMY.
DARKNESS...
...FORMS A CHAIN.
IT'S IMPOSSIBLE FOR HER TO SACRIFICE ME AND BE HAPPY ALL ON HER OWN.
GUILT.
SELF-HATRED.
KINDNESS.
CARE.
DREAMS.
HOPE.
THE DARKNESS WILL SHACKLE THEM ALL, STAIN THEM BLACK.
MY DEATH WILL CREATE A NEW DARKNESS—

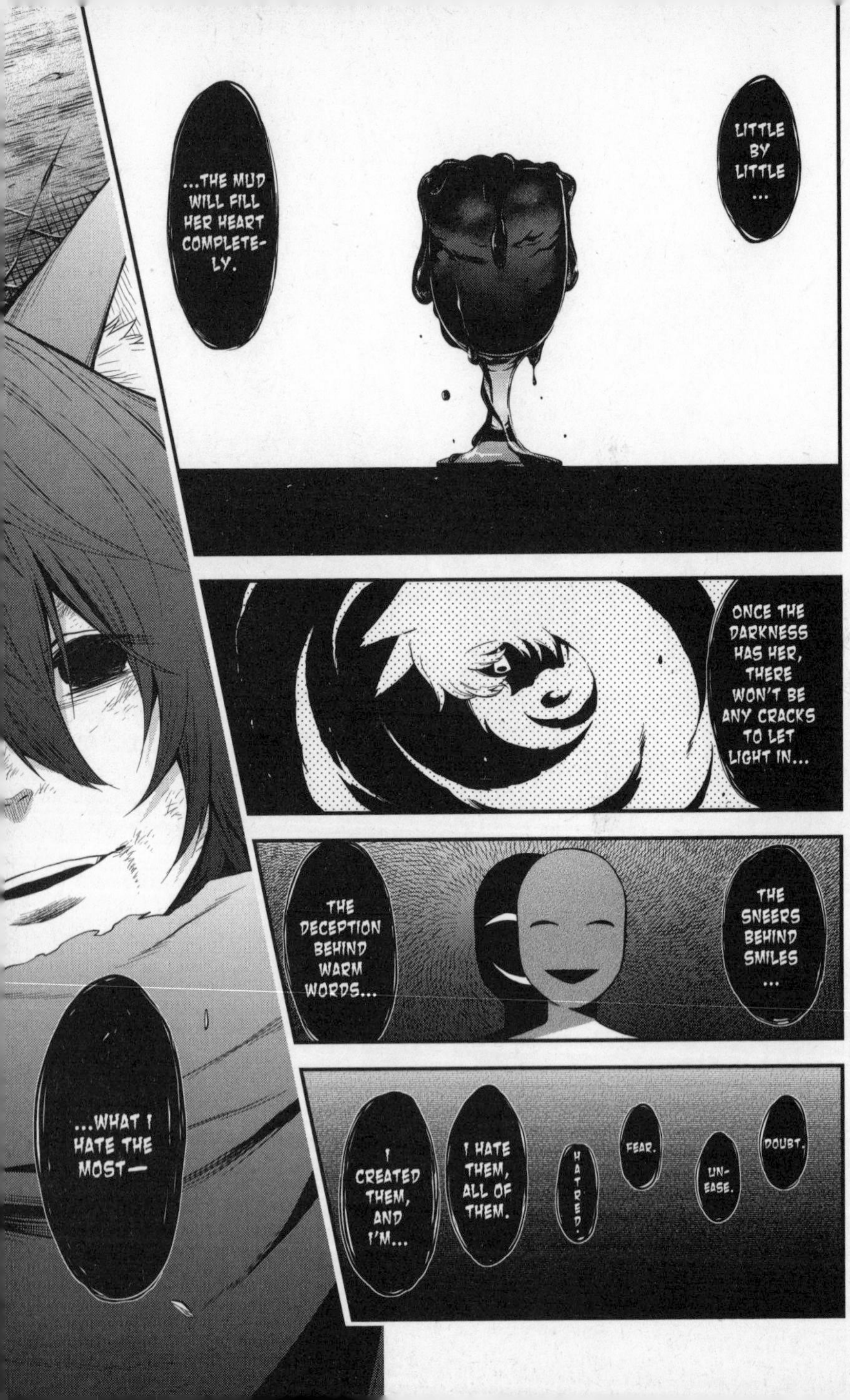
LITTLE BY LITTLE...
...THE MUD WILL FILL HER HEART COMPLETE-LY.
ONCE THE DARKNESS HAS HER, THERE WON'T BE ANY CRACKS TO LET LIGHT IN...
THE SNEERS BEHIND SMILES...
THE DECEPTION BEHIND WARM WORDS...
DOUBT.
FEAR.
UN-EASE.
HATRED.
I HATE THEM, ALL OF THEM.
I CREATED THEM, AND I'M...
...WHAT I HATE THE MOST—

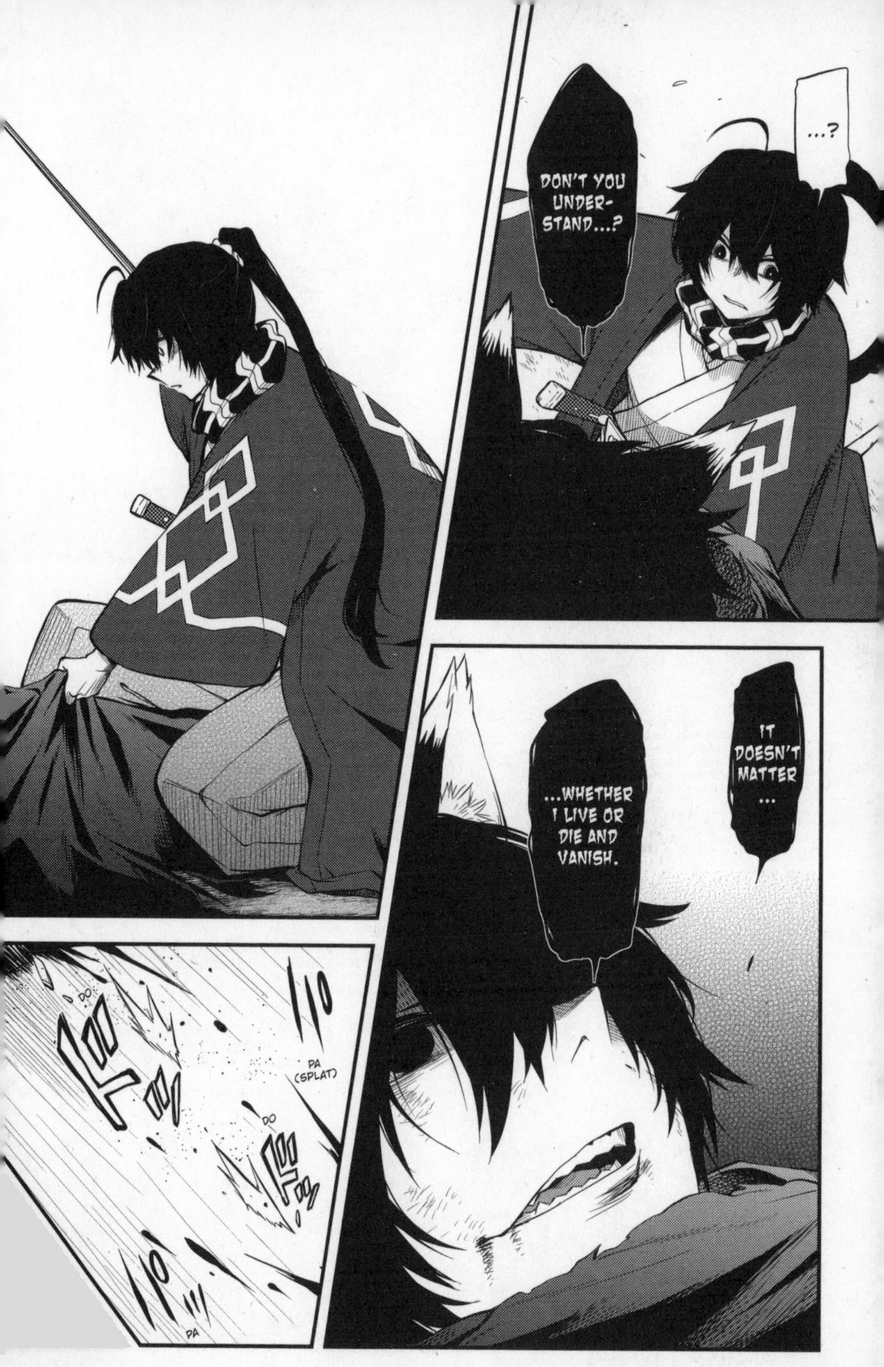
...?
DON'T YOU UNDER-STAND...?
IT DOESN'T MATTER...
...WHETHER I LIVE OR DIE AND VANISH.
DO
PA (SPLAT)
DO
PA

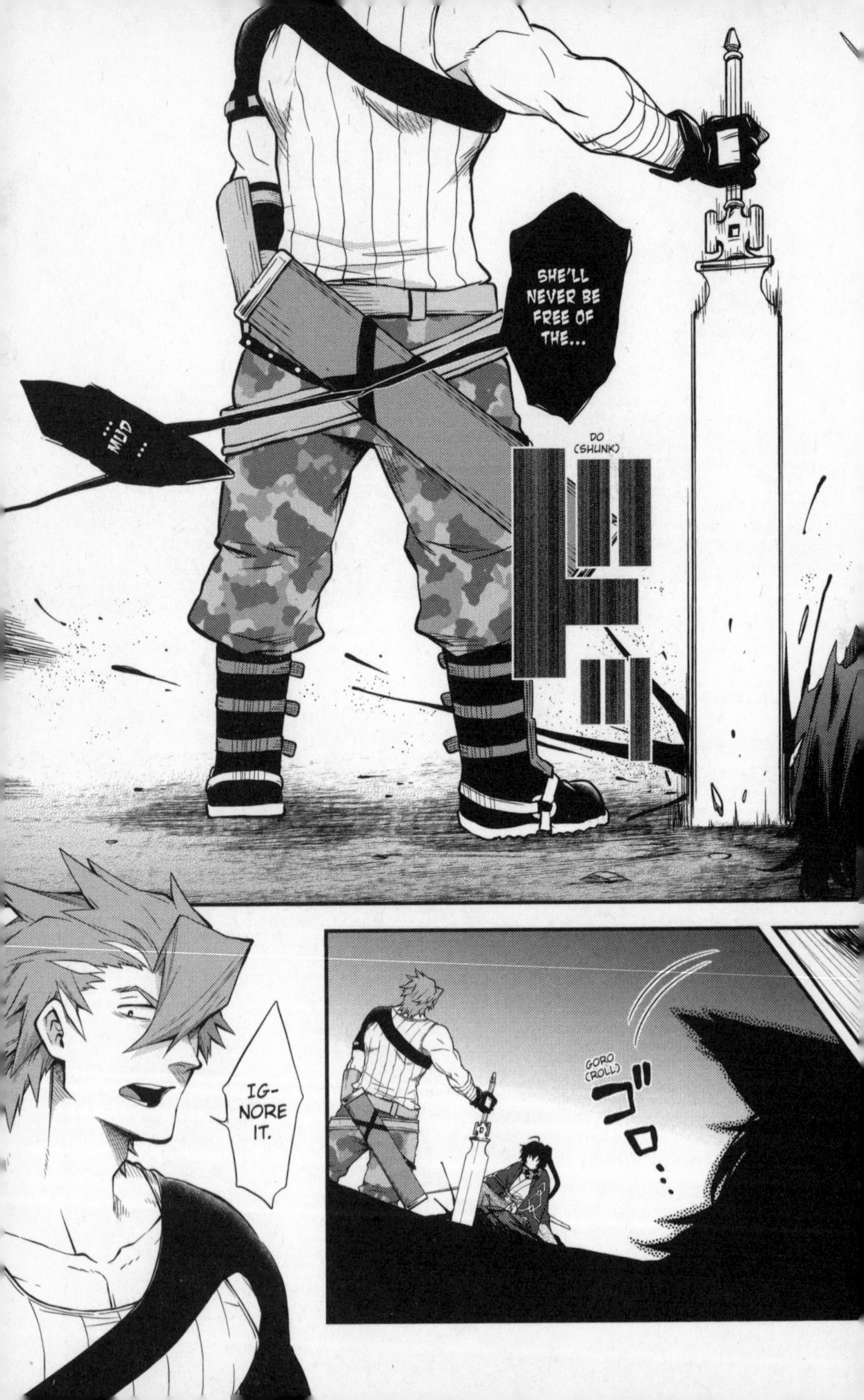
SHE'LL NEVER BE FREE OF THE...
...MUD...
DO (SHUNK)
ドッ
GORO (ROLL)
ゴロ...
IG-NORE IT.

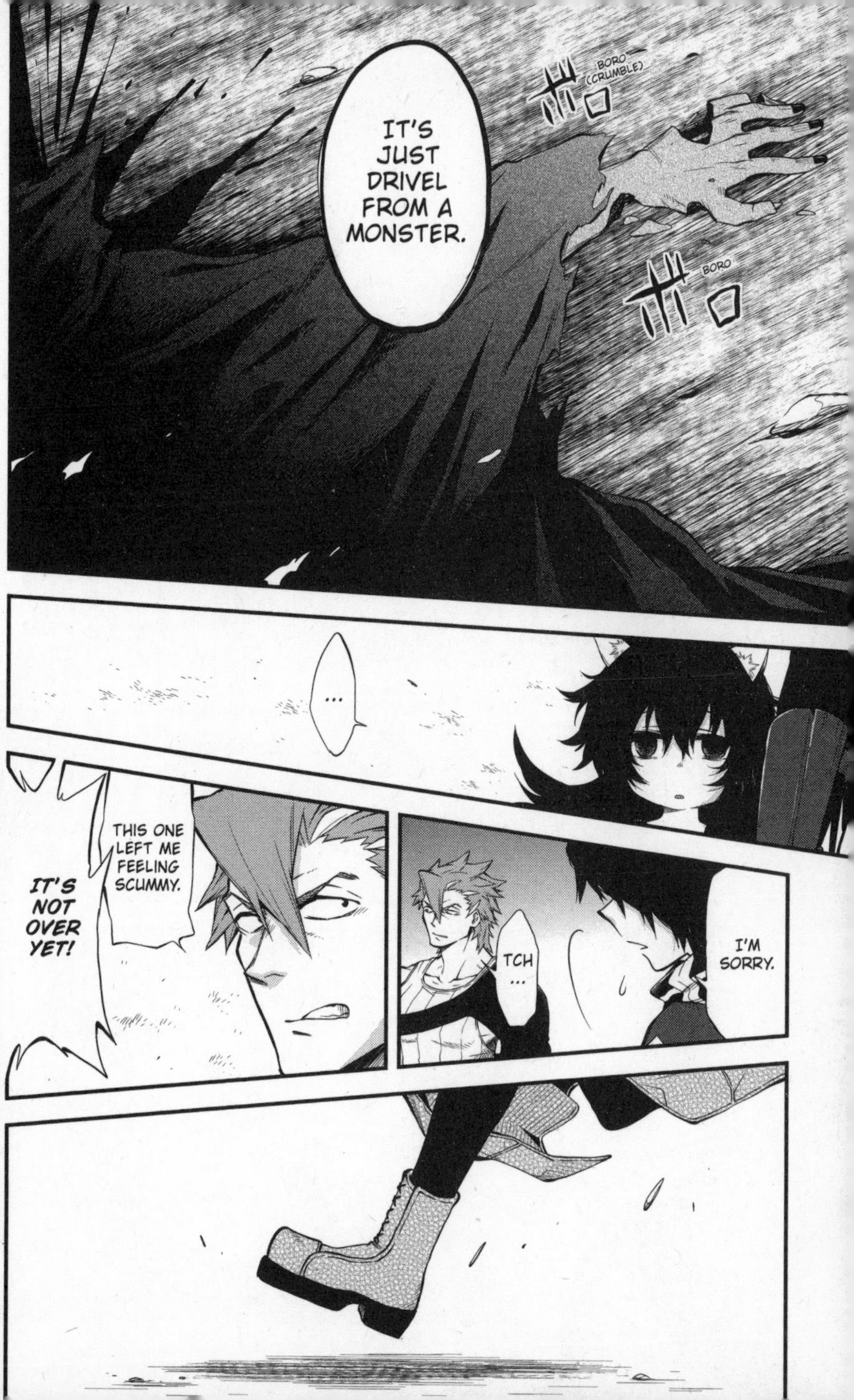

BORO (CRUMBLE)
IT'S JUST DRIVEL FROM A MONSTER.
BORO
...
I'M SORRY.
TCH...
THIS ONE LEFT ME FEELING SCUMMY.
IT'S NOT OVER YET!

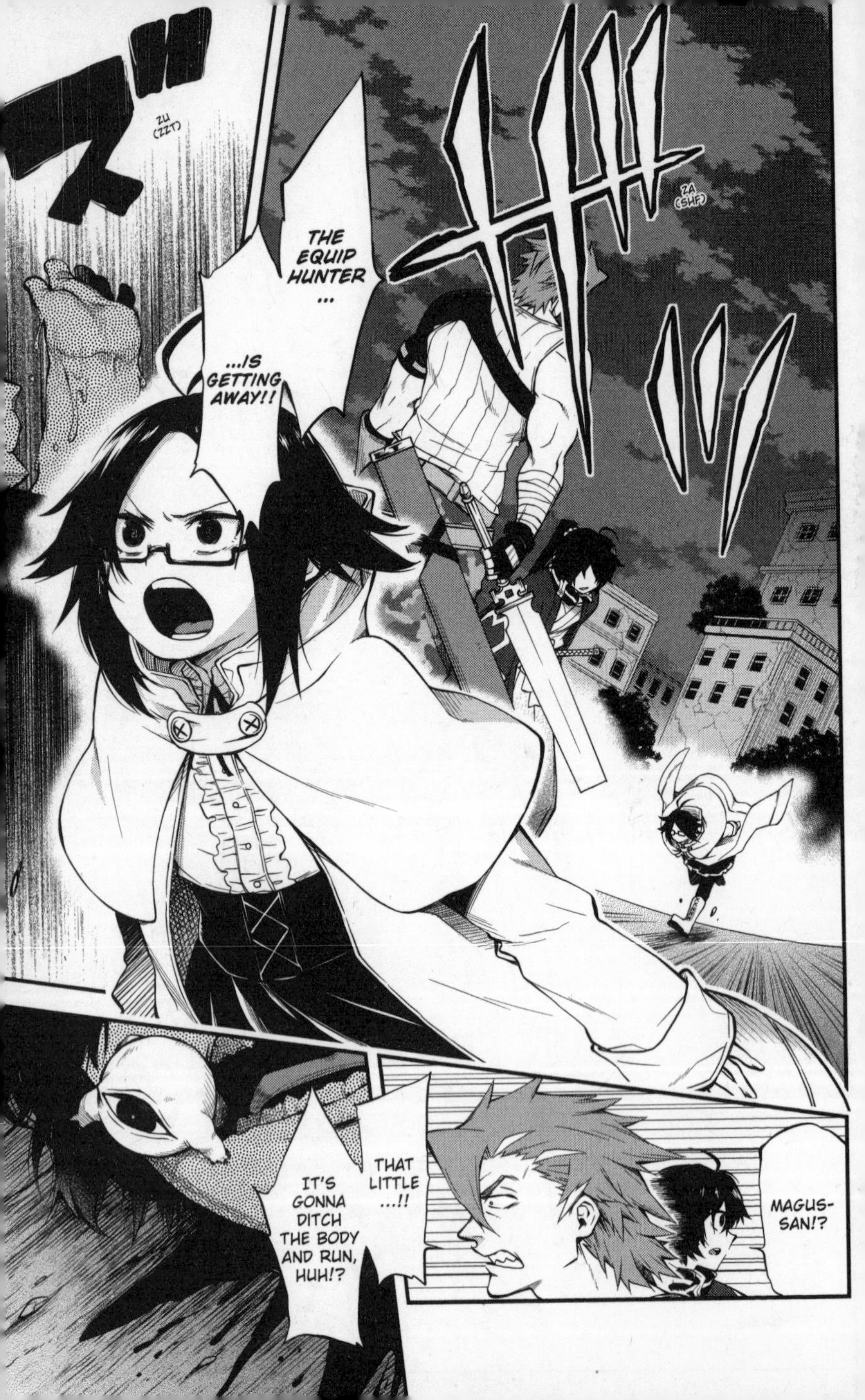
ZA (SHF)
THE EQUIP HUNTER ...
...IS GETTING AWAY!!
ZU (ZZT)
MAGUS-SAN!?
THAT LITTLE ...!!
IT'S GONNA DITCH THE BODY AND RUN, HUH!?

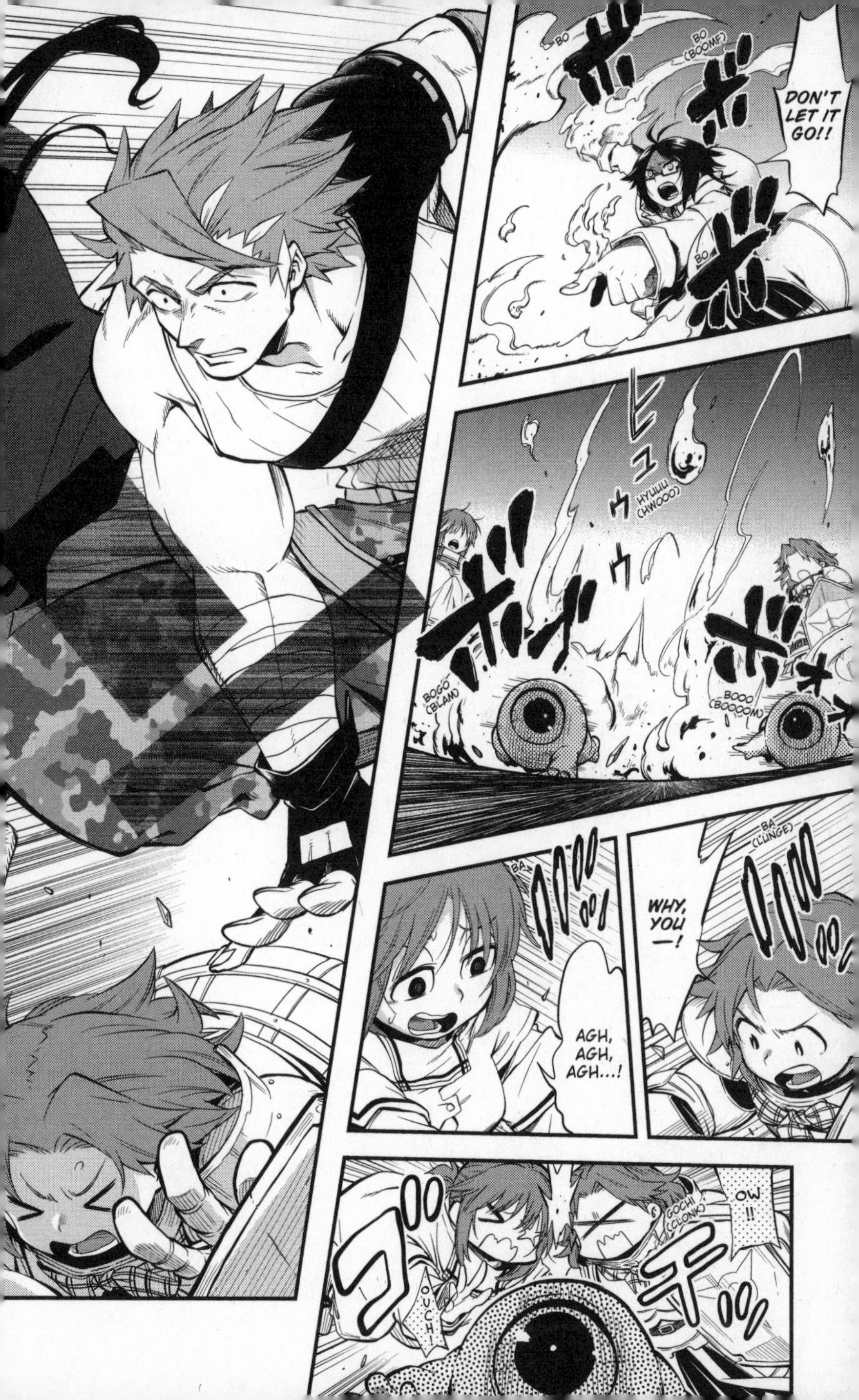
DON'T LET IT GO!!
BO
BO (BOOMF)
BO
HYUUU (HWOOO)
BOOO (BOOOOM)
BOGO (BLAM)
BA (LUNGE)
WHY, YOU—!
BA
AGH, AGH, AGH...!
OW!!
GOCHI (CLONK)
OUCH!

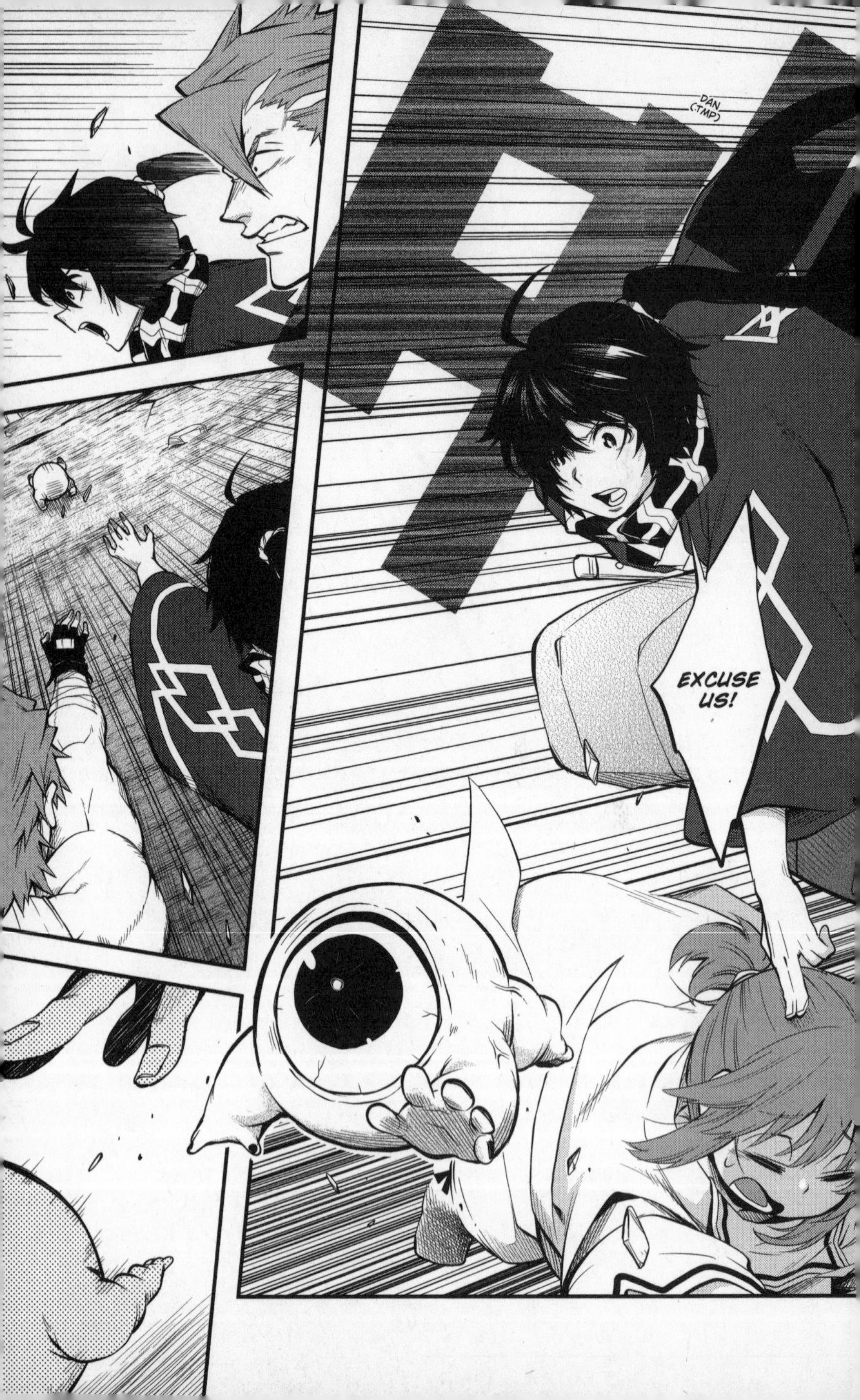
DAN (TMP)
EXCUSE US!

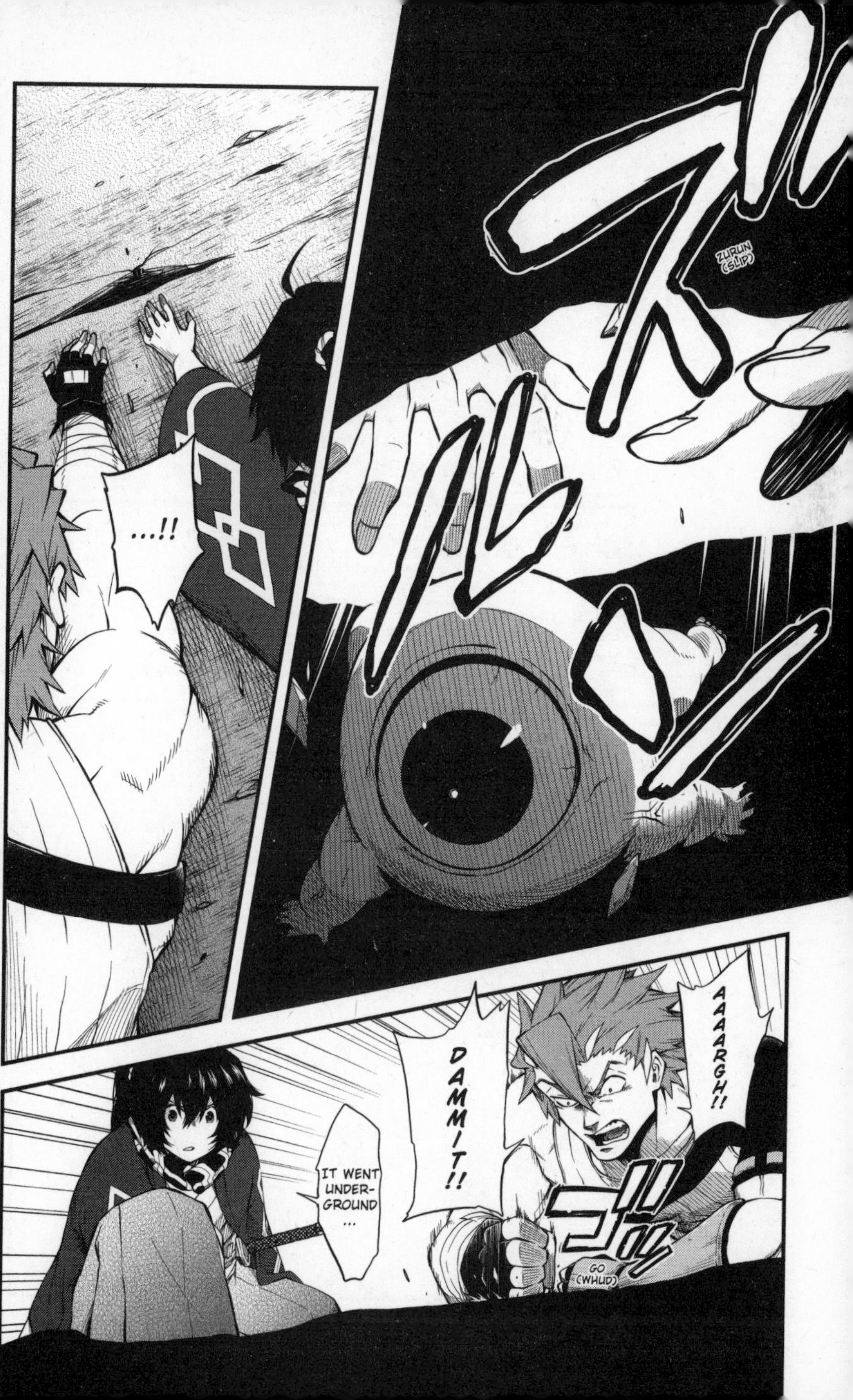
ZURUN (SLIP)
...!!
AAAARGH!!
DAMMIT!!
GO (WHUD)
IT WENT UNDER-GROUND...

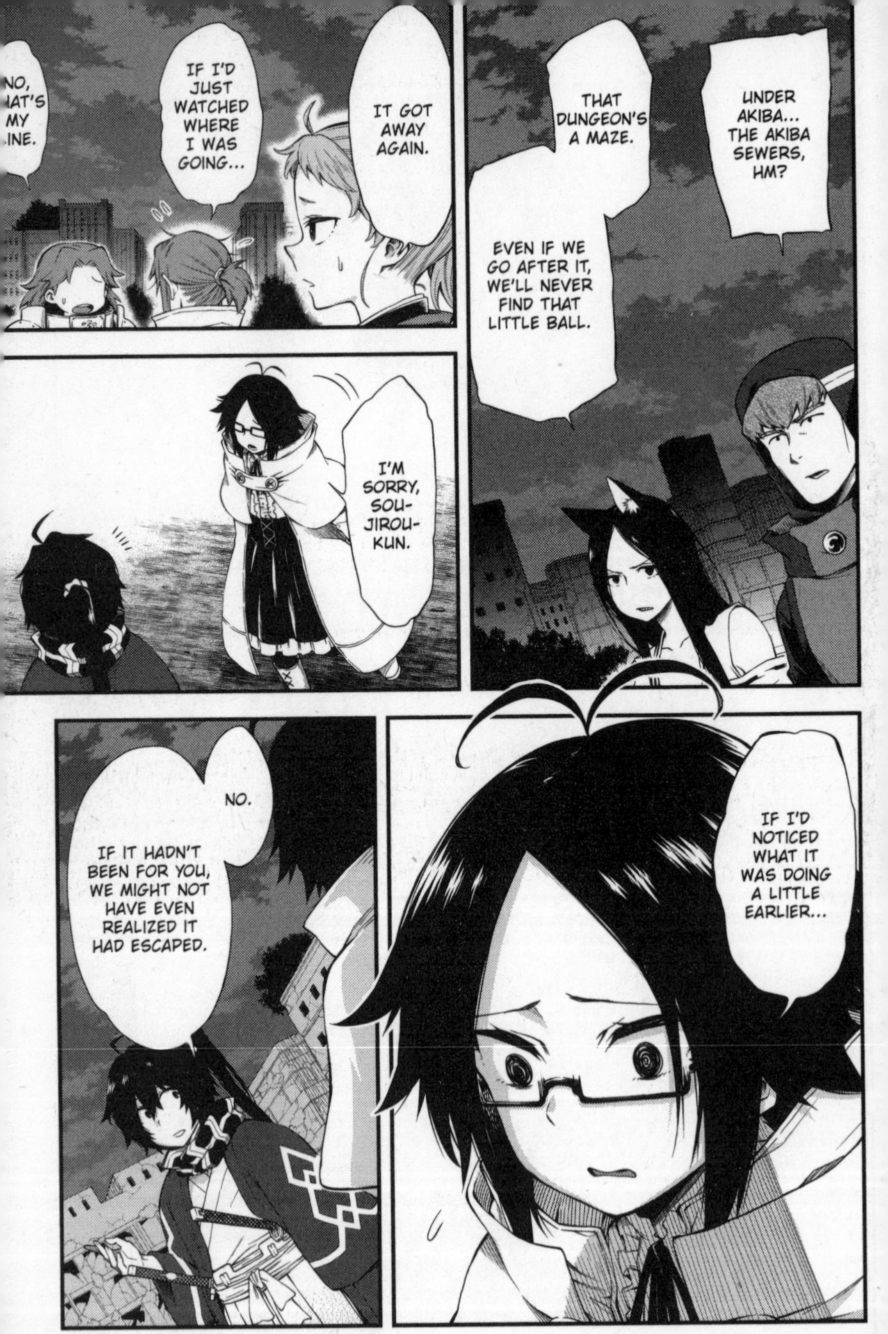
UNDER AKIBA... THE AKIBA SEWERS, HM?
THAT DUNGEON'S A MAZE.
EVEN IF WE GO AFTER IT, WE'LL NEVER FIND THAT LITTLE BALL.
IT GOT AWAY AGAIN.
IF I'D JUST WATCHED WHERE I WAS GOING...
NO, AT'S MY INE.
I'M SORRY, SOU-JIROU-KUN.
IF I'D NOTICED WHAT IT WAS DOING A LITTLE EARLIER...
NO.
IF IT HADN'T BEEN FOR YOU, WE MIGHT NOT HAVE EVEN REALIZED IT HAD ESCAPED.

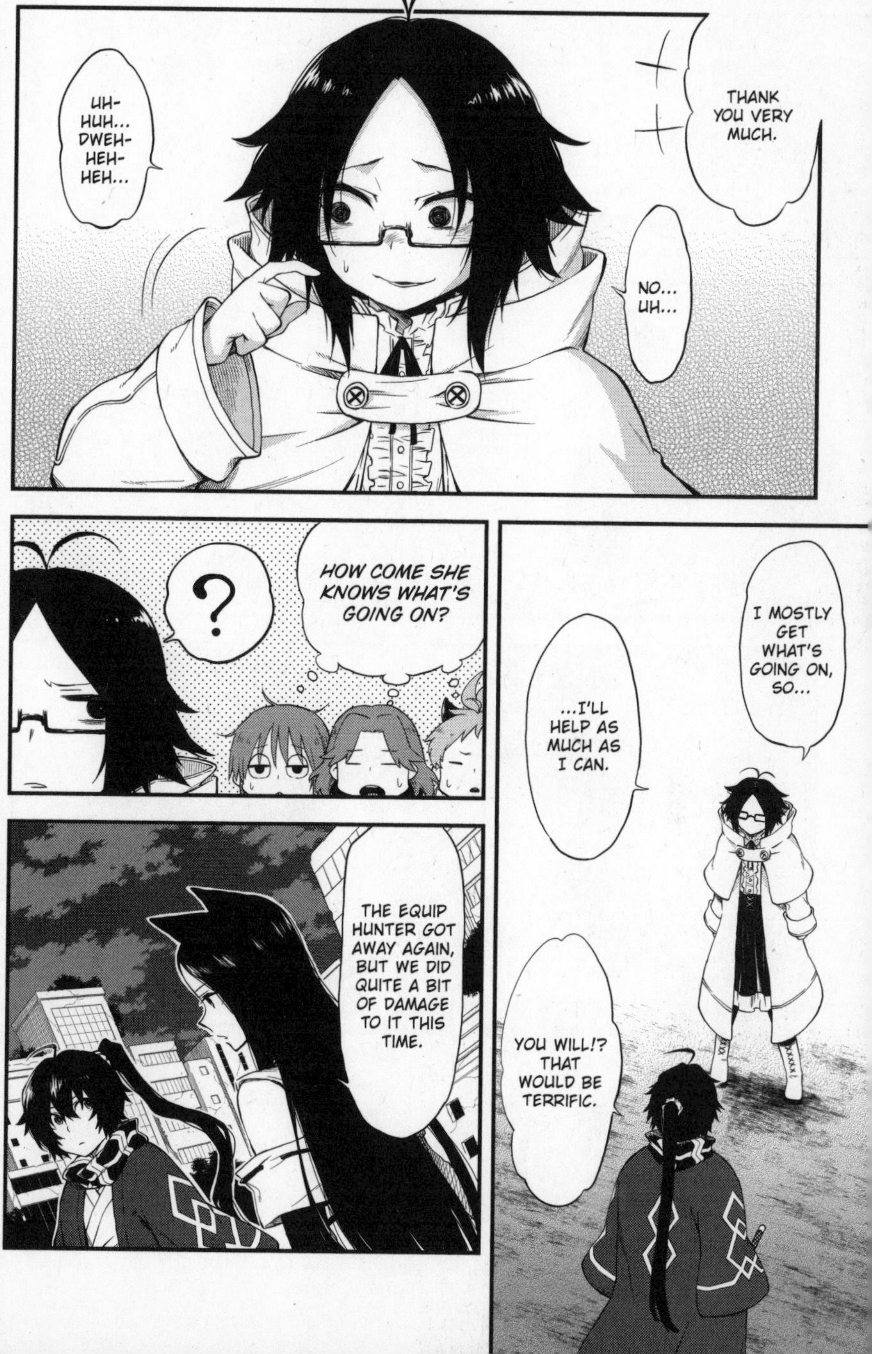
THANK YOU VERY MUCH.
NO... UH...
UH-HUH... DWEH-HEH-HEH...
I MOSTLY GET WHAT'S GOING ON, SO...
...I'LL HELP AS MUCH AS I CAN.
YOU WILL!? THAT WOULD BE TERRIFIC.
HOW COME SHE KNOWS WHAT'S GOING ON?
?
THE EQUIP HUNTER GOT AWAY AGAIN, BUT WE DID QUITE A BIT OF DAMAGE TO IT THIS TIME.

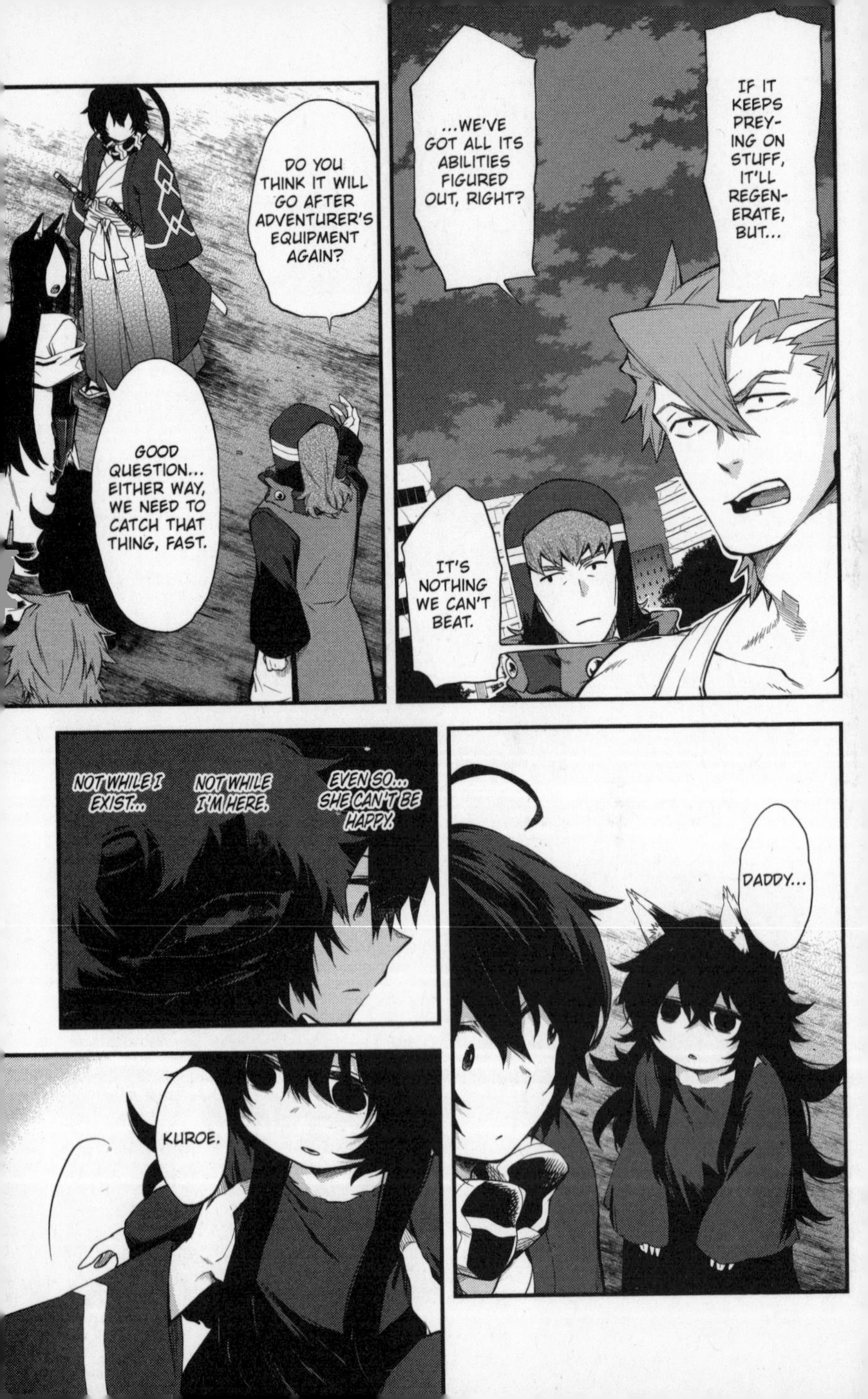
IF IT KEEPS PREY-ING ON STUFF, IT'LL REGEN-ERATE, BUT...
...WE'VE GOT ALL ITS ABILITIES FIGURED OUT, RIGHT?
IT'S NOTHING WE CAN'T BEAT.
DO YOU THINK IT WILL GO AFTER ADVENTURER'S EQUIPMENT AGAIN?
GOOD QUESTION... EITHER WAY, WE NEED TO CATCH THAT THING, FAST.
DADDY...
EVEN SO... SHE CAN'T BE HAPPY.
NOT WHILE I'M HERE.
NOT WHILE I EXIST...
KUROE.

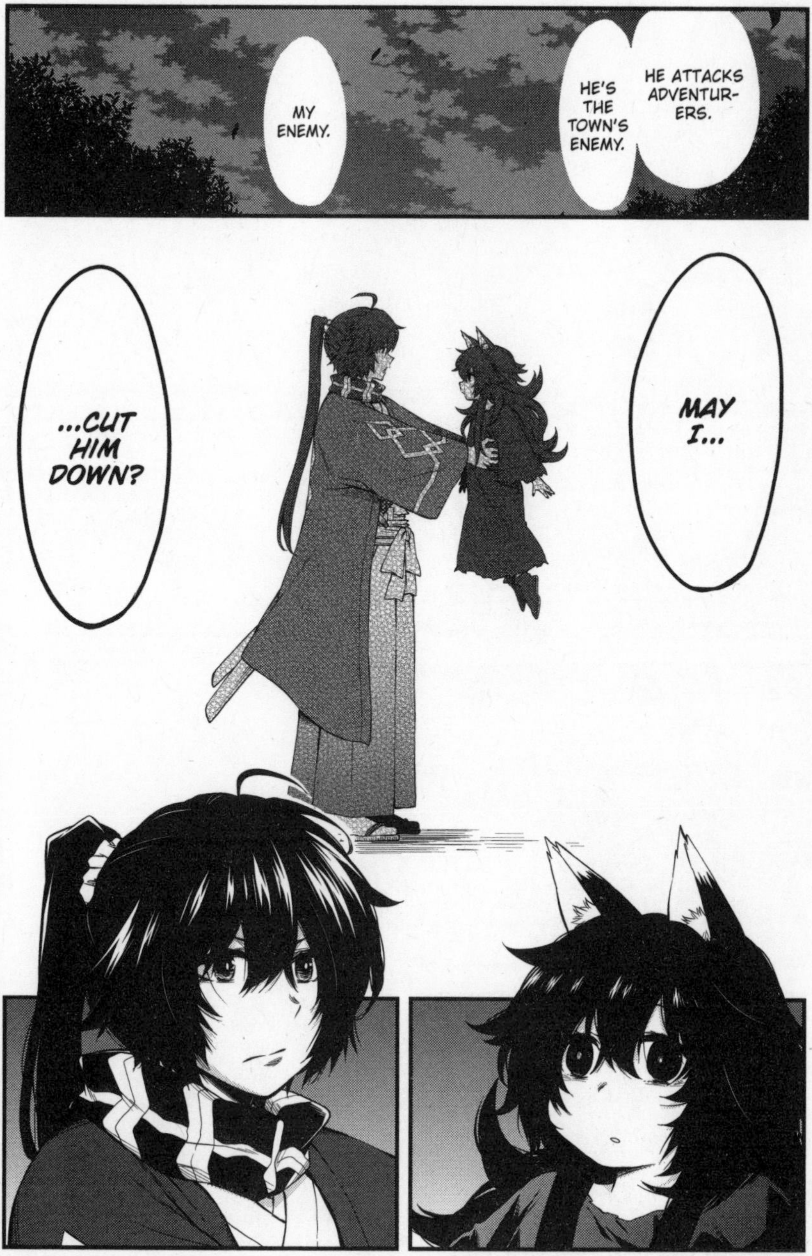
HE ATTACKS ADVENTUR- ERS.
HE'S THE TOWN'S ENEMY.
MY ENEMY.
MAY I...
...CUT HIM DOWN?

LOG HORIZON
THE WEST WIND BRIGADE

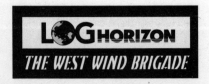

LOG HORIZON

THE WEST WIND BRIGADE

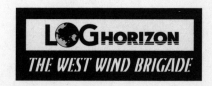

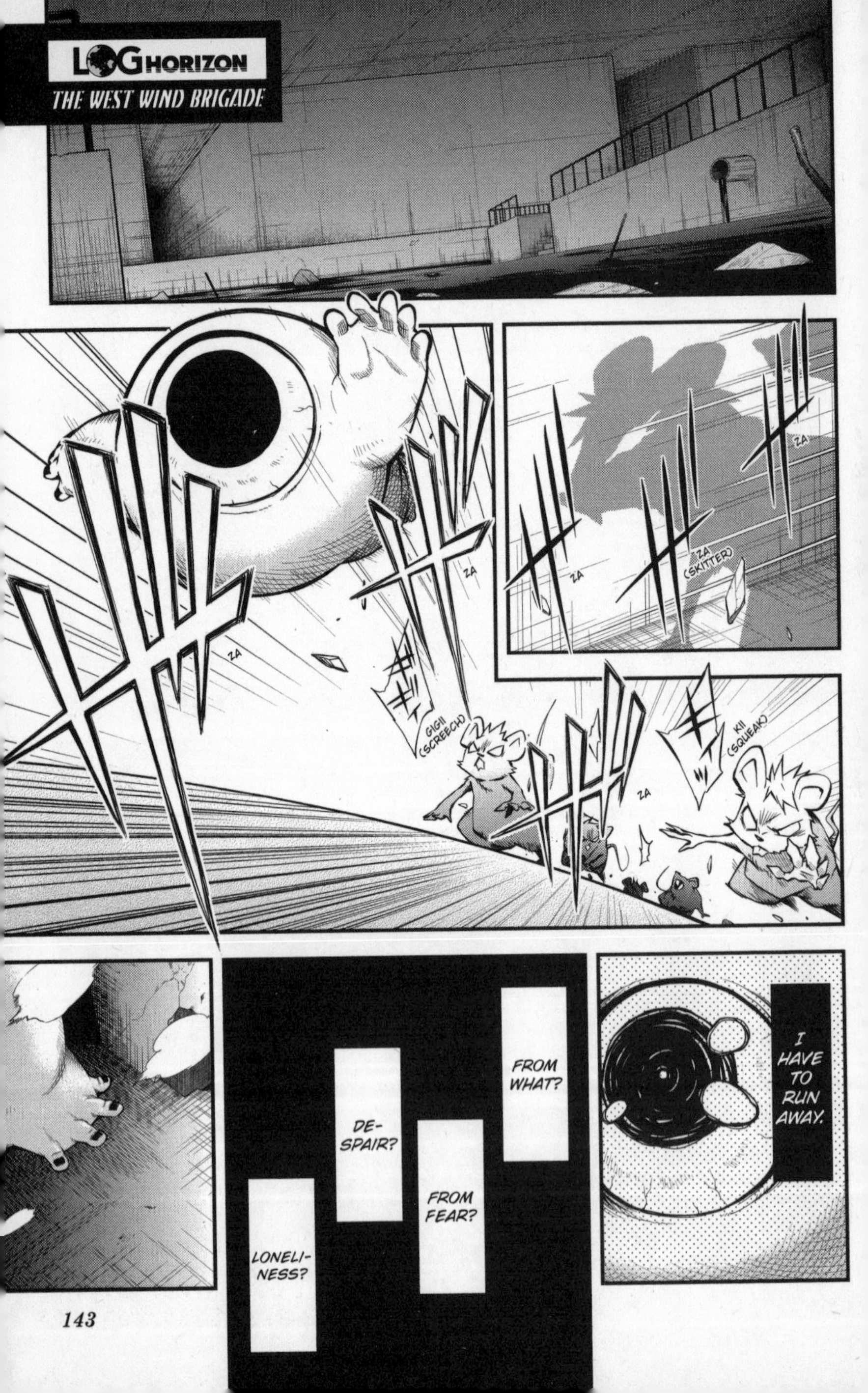
ZA
ZA
ZA
(SKITTER)
KII
(SQUEAK)
ZA
GIGII
(SCREECH)
ZA
ZA
I HAVE TO RUN AWAY.
FROM WHAT?
FROM FEAR?
DE-SPAIR?
LONELI-NESS?

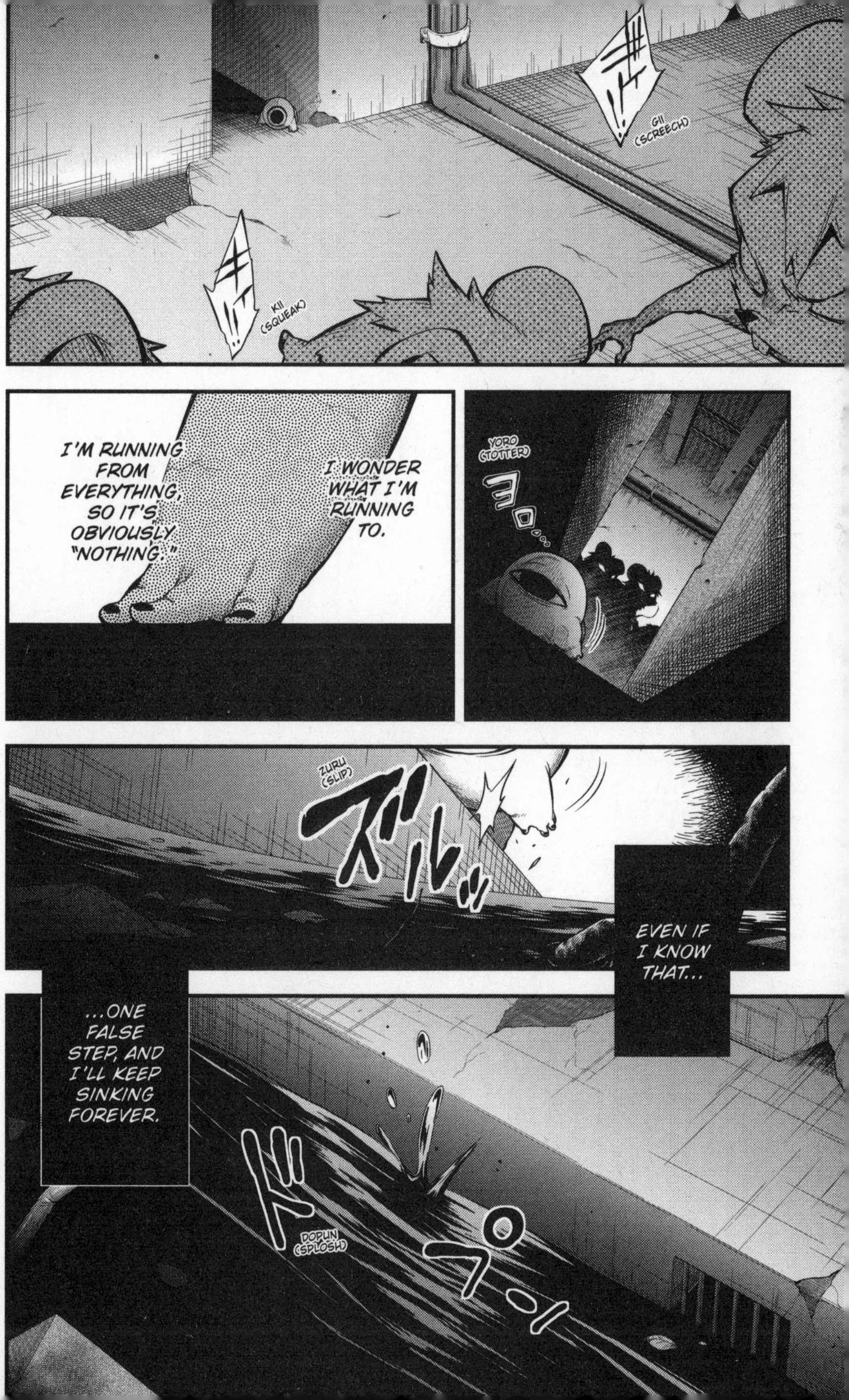
GII (SCREECH)
KII (SQUEAK)
YORO (TOTTER)
I WONDER WHAT I'M RUNNING TO.
I'M RUNNING FROM EVERYTHING, SO IT'S OBVIOUSLY "NOTHING."
ZURU (SLIP)
EVEN IF I KNOW THAT...
...ONE FALSE STEP, AND I'LL KEEP SINKING FOREVER.
DOPUN (SPLOSH)

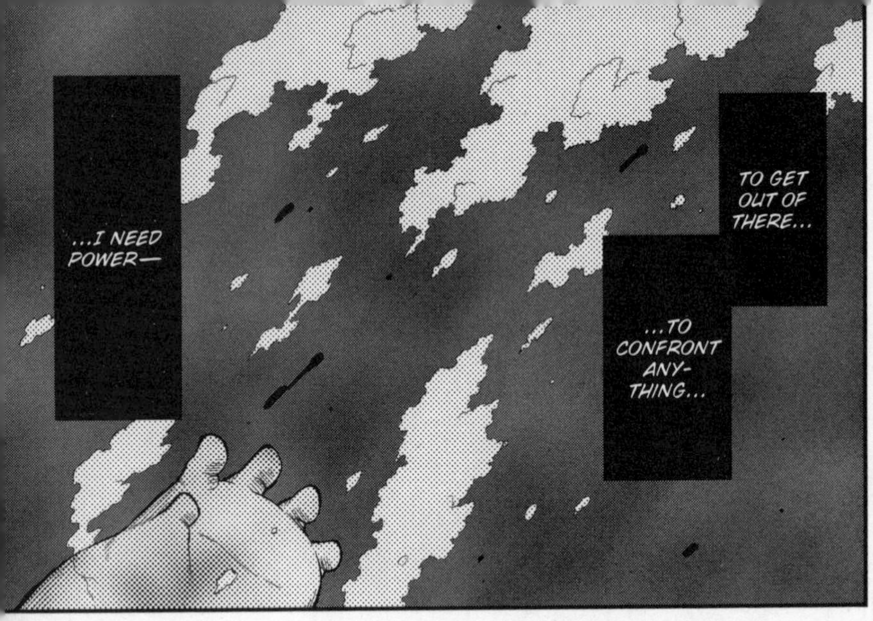
TO GET OUT OF THERE...
...TO CONFRONT ANY-THING...
...I NEED POWER—

CHAPTER : 53 Those Who Were One

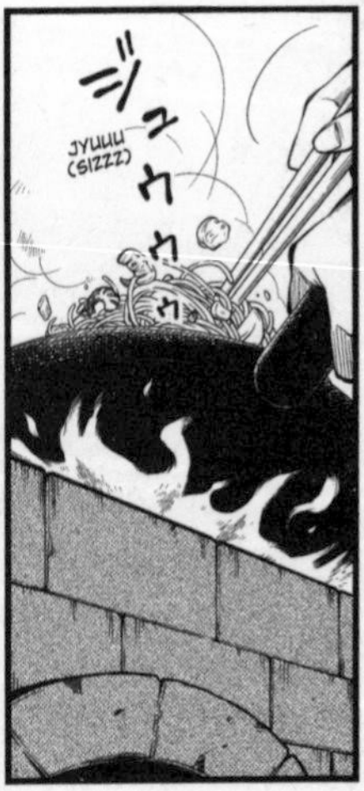
ジュウウウ
JYUUU (SIZZZ)

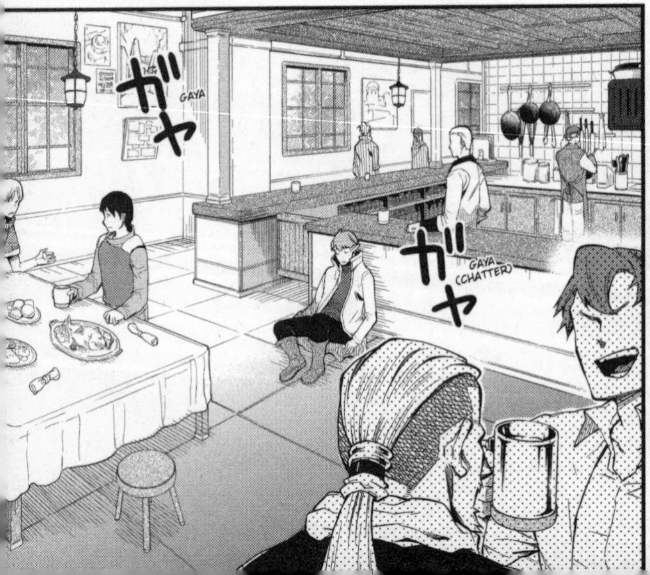
ガヤ
GAYA
ガヤ
GAYA (CHATTER)

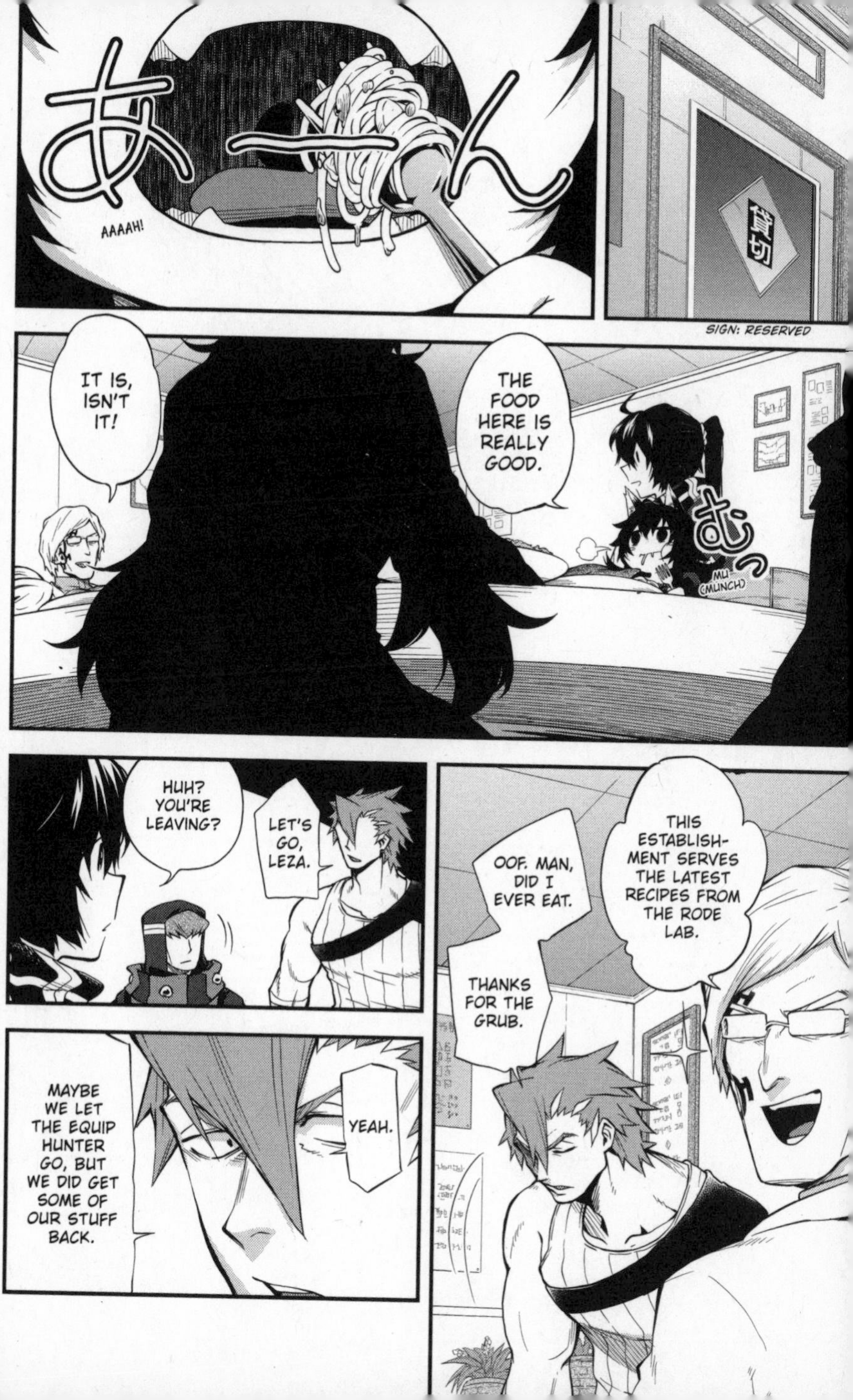
貸切
SIGN: RESERVED
あーん
AAAAH!
THE FOOD HERE IS REALLY GOOD.
むっ
MU- (MUNCH)
IT IS, ISN'T IT!
THIS ESTABLISHMENT SERVES THE LATEST RECIPES FROM THE RODE LAB.
OOF. MAN, DID I EVER EAT.
THANKS FOR THE GRUB.
LET'S GO, LEZA.
HUH? YOU'RE LEAVING?
YEAH.
MAYBE WE LET THE EQUIP HUNTER GO, BUT WE DID GET SOME OF OUR STUFF BACK.

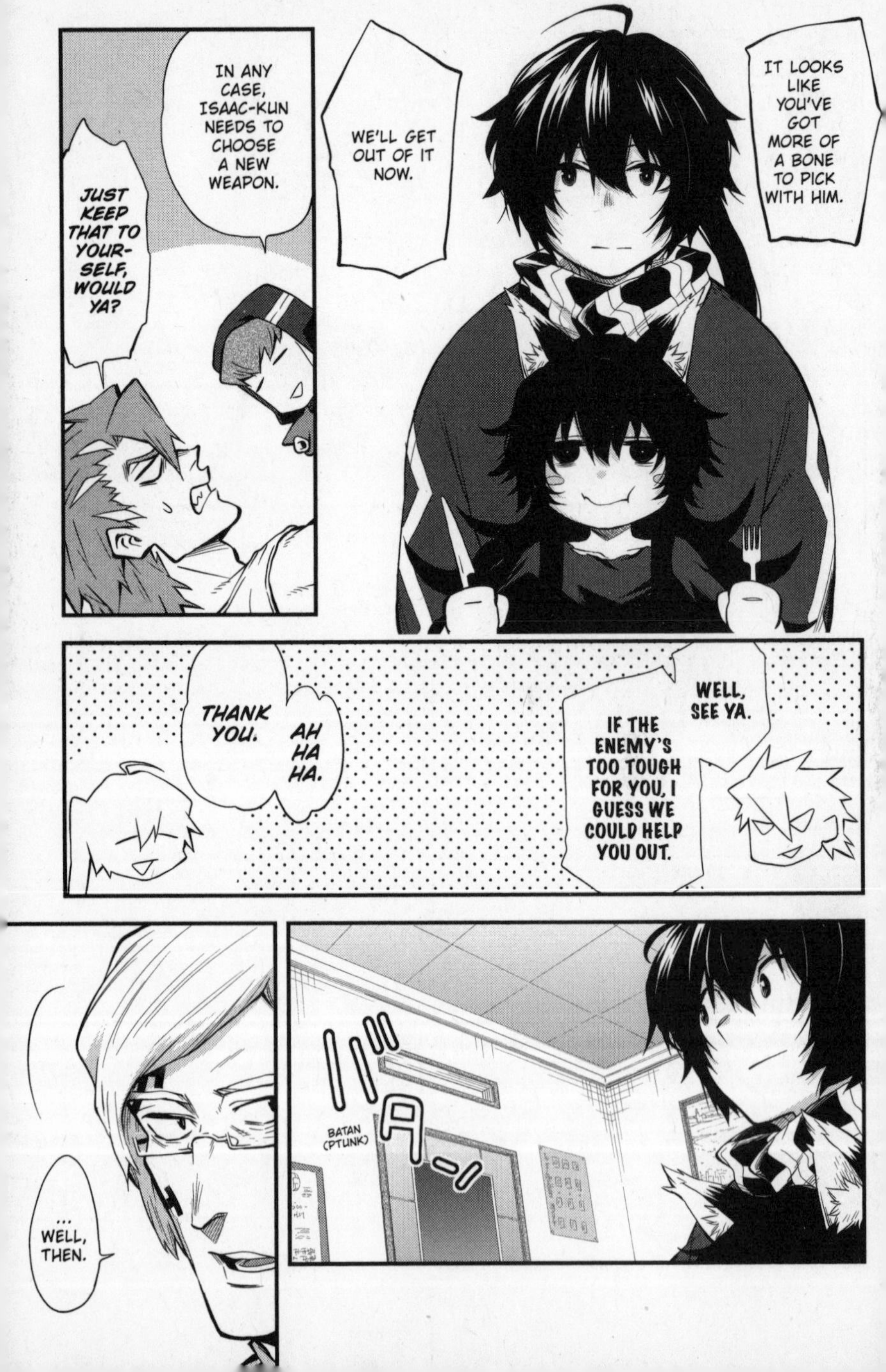

IT LOOKS LIKE YOU'VE GOT MORE OF A BONE TO PICK WITH HIM.
WE'LL GET OUT OF IT NOW.
IN ANY CASE, ISAAC-KUN NEEDS TO CHOOSE A NEW WEAPON.
JUST KEEP THAT TO YOUR-SELF, WOULD YA?
WELL, SEE YA.
IF THE ENEMY'S TOO TOUGH FOR YOU, I GUESS WE COULD HELP YOU OUT.
THANK YOU.
AH HA HA.
BATAN (PTUNK)
... WELL, THEN.

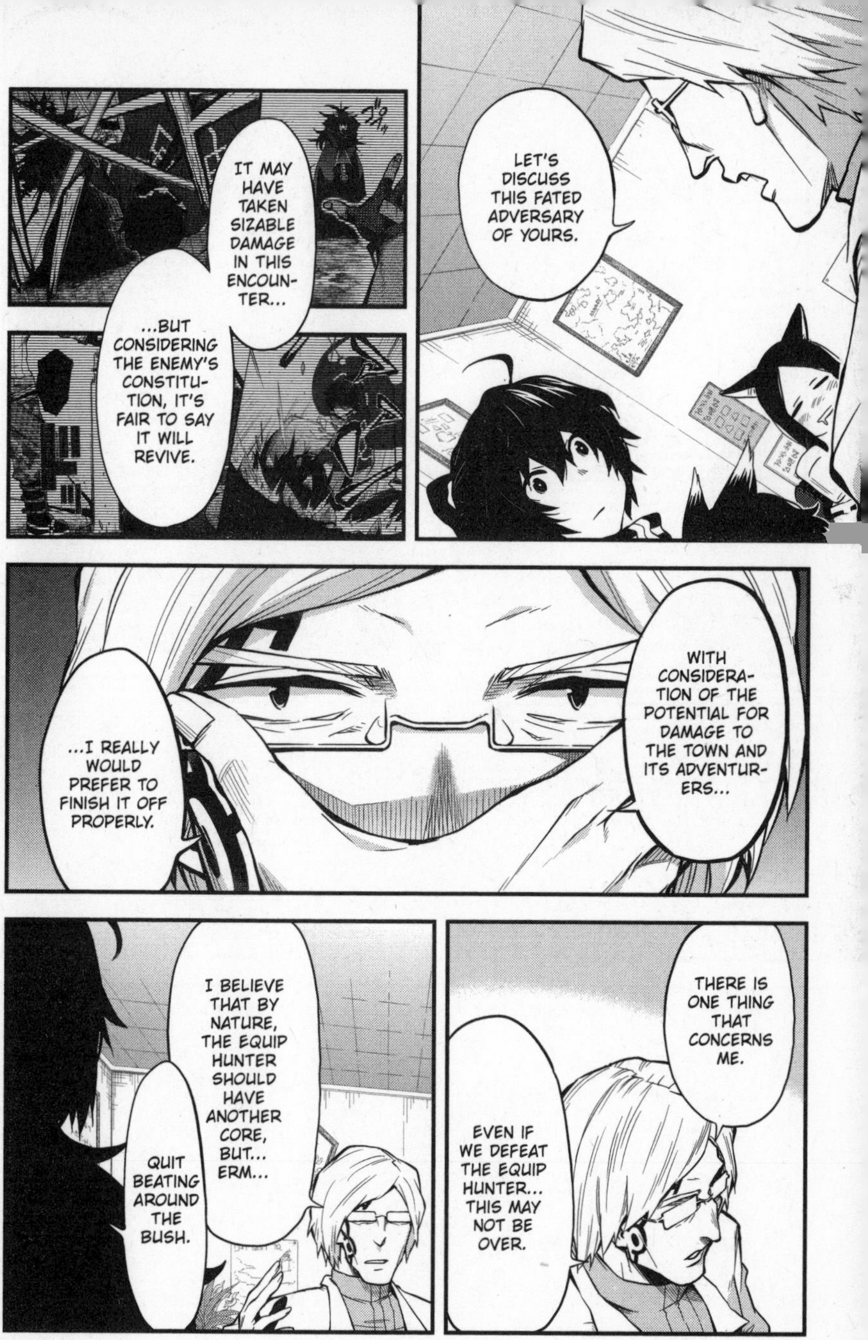
LET'S DISCUSS THIS FATED ADVERSARY OF YOURS.
IT MAY HAVE TAKEN SIZABLE DAMAGE IN THIS ENCOUNTER...
...BUT CONSIDERING THE ENEMY'S CONSTITUTION, IT'S FAIR TO SAY IT WILL REVIVE.
WITH CONSIDERATION OF THE POTENTIAL FOR DAMAGE TO THE TOWN AND ITS ADVENTURERS...
...I REALLY WOULD PREFER TO FINISH IT OFF PROPERLY.
THERE IS ONE THING THAT CONCERNS ME.
EVEN IF WE DEFEAT THE EQUIP HUNTER... THIS MAY NOT BE OVER.
I BELIEVE THAT BY NATURE, THE EQUIP HUNTER SHOULD HAVE ANOTHER CORE, BUT... ERM...
QUIT BEATING AROUND THE BUSH.

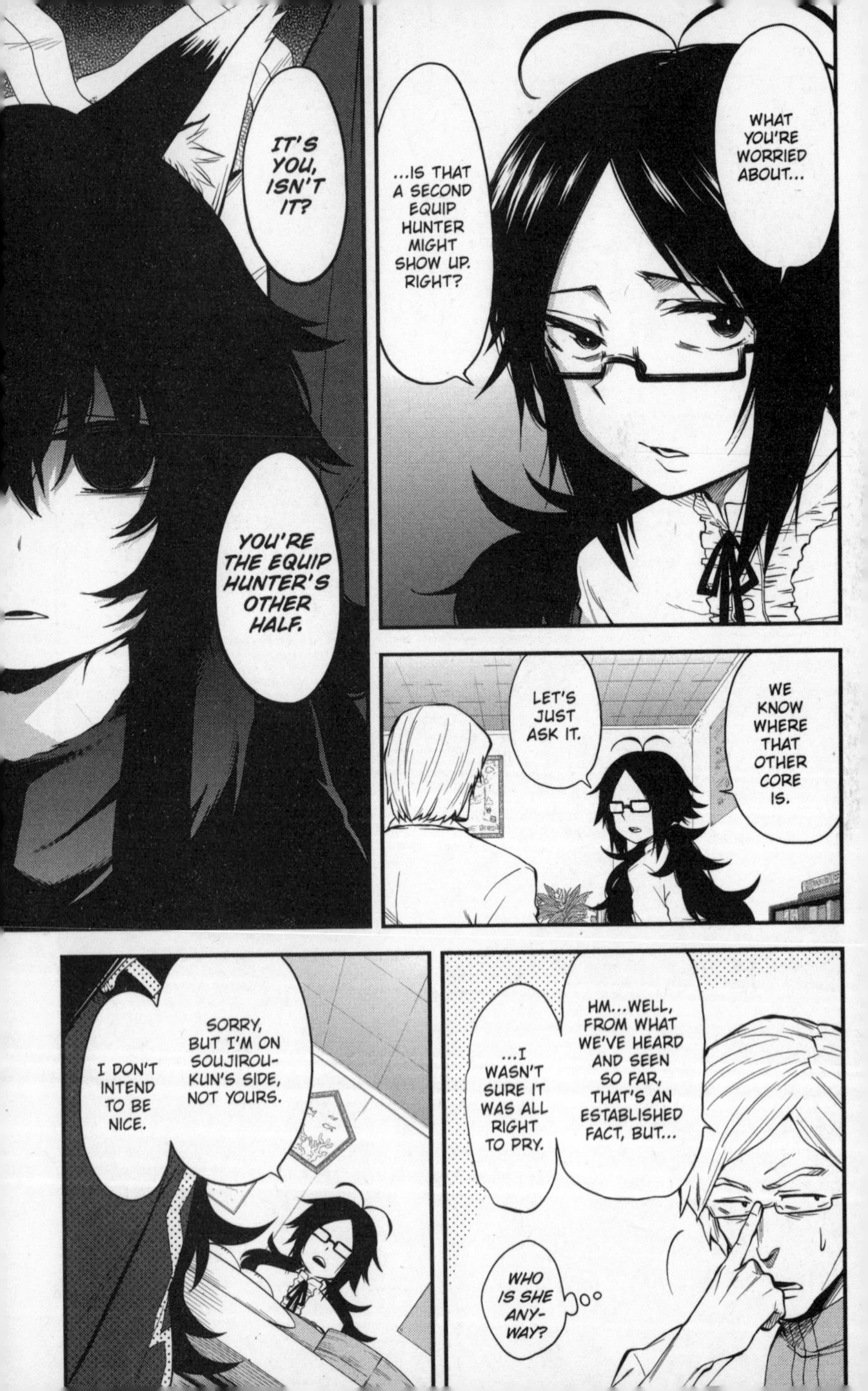
WHAT YOU'RE WORRIED ABOUT...
...IS THAT A SECOND EQUIP HUNTER MIGHT SHOW UP. RIGHT?
WE KNOW WHERE THAT OTHER CORE IS.
LET'S JUST ASK IT.
IT'S YOU, ISN'T IT?
YOU'RE THE EQUIP HUNTER'S OTHER HALF.
HM...WELL, FROM WHAT WE'VE HEARD AND SEEN SO FAR, THAT'S AN ESTABLISHED FACT, BUT...
...I WASN'T SURE IT WAS ALL RIGHT TO PRY.
WHO IS SHE ANY-WAY?
SORRY, BUT I'M ON SOUJIROU-KUN'S SIDE, NOT YOURS.
I DON'T INTEND TO BE NICE.

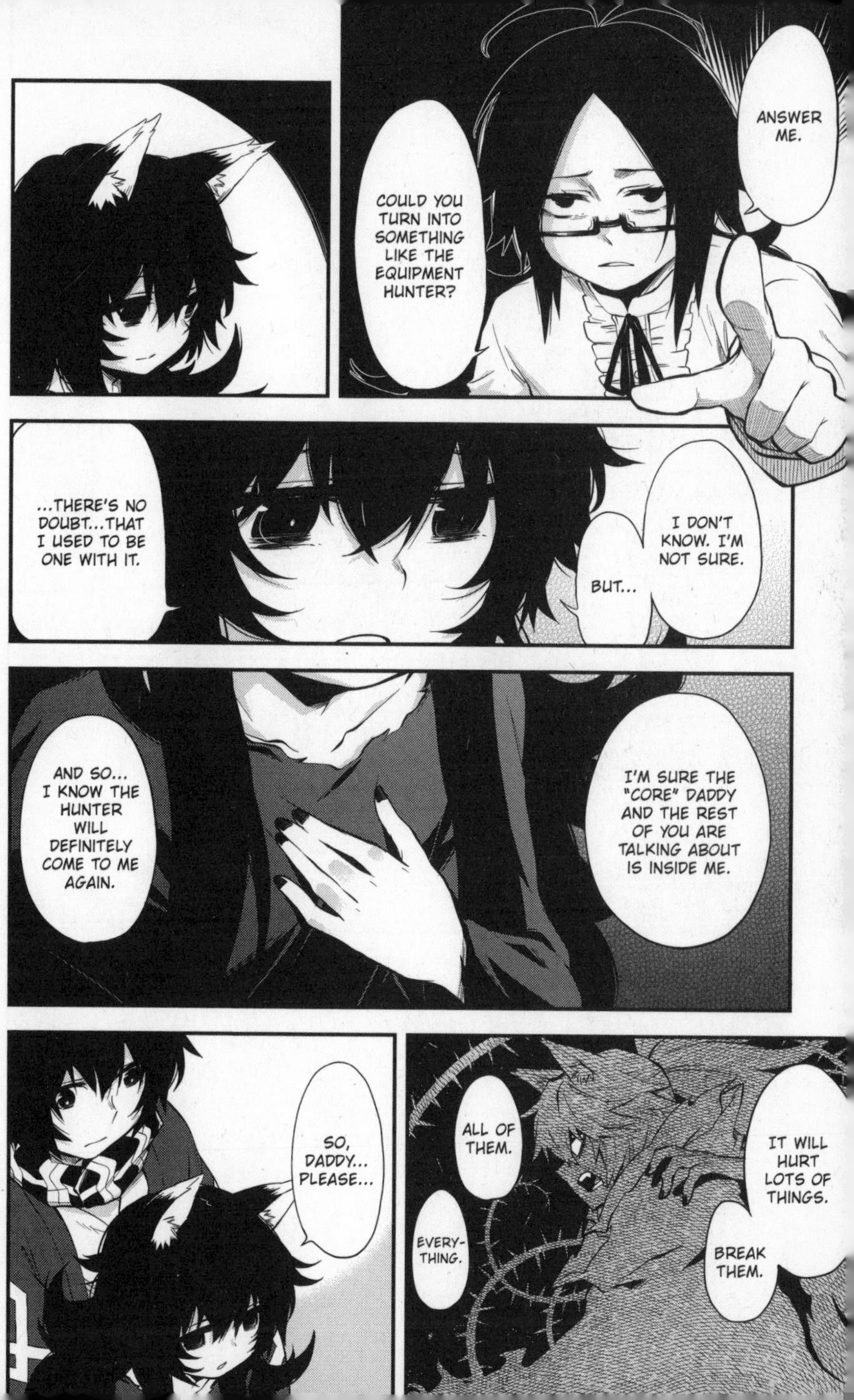
ANSWER ME.
COULD YOU TURN INTO SOMETHING LIKE THE EQUIPMENT HUNTER?
I DON'T KNOW. I'M NOT SURE.
BUT...
...THERE'S NO DOUBT...THAT I USED TO BE ONE WITH IT.
I'M SURE THE "CORE" DADDY AND THE REST OF YOU ARE TALKING ABOUT IS INSIDE ME.
AND SO... I KNOW THE HUNTER WILL DEFINITELY COME TO ME AGAIN.
IT WILL HURT LOTS OF THINGS.
BREAK THEM.
ALL OF THEM.
EVERY-THING.
SO, DADDY... PLEASE...

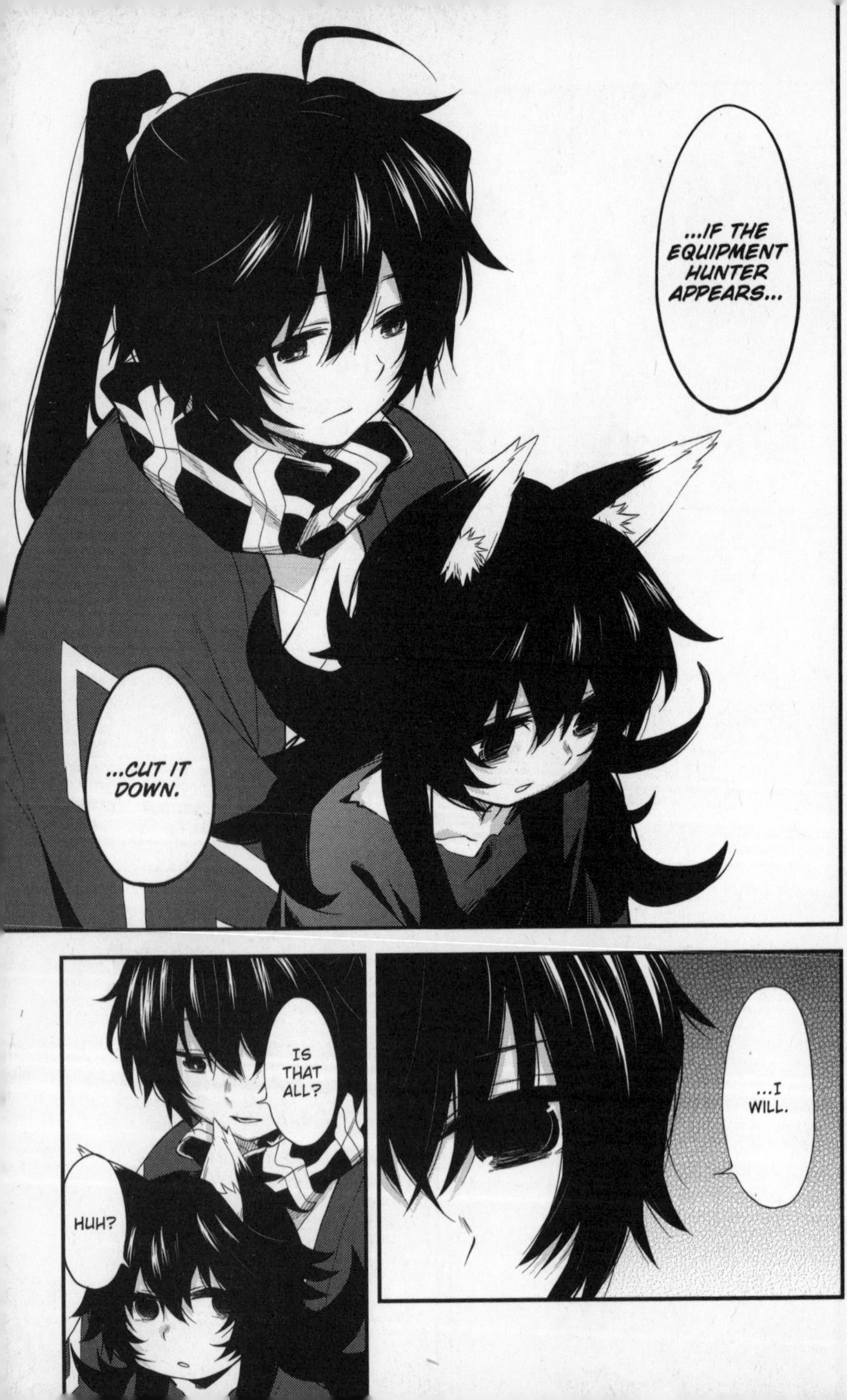
...IF THE EQUIPMENT HUNTER APPEARS...
...CUT IT DOWN.
...I WILL.
IS THAT ALL?
HUH?

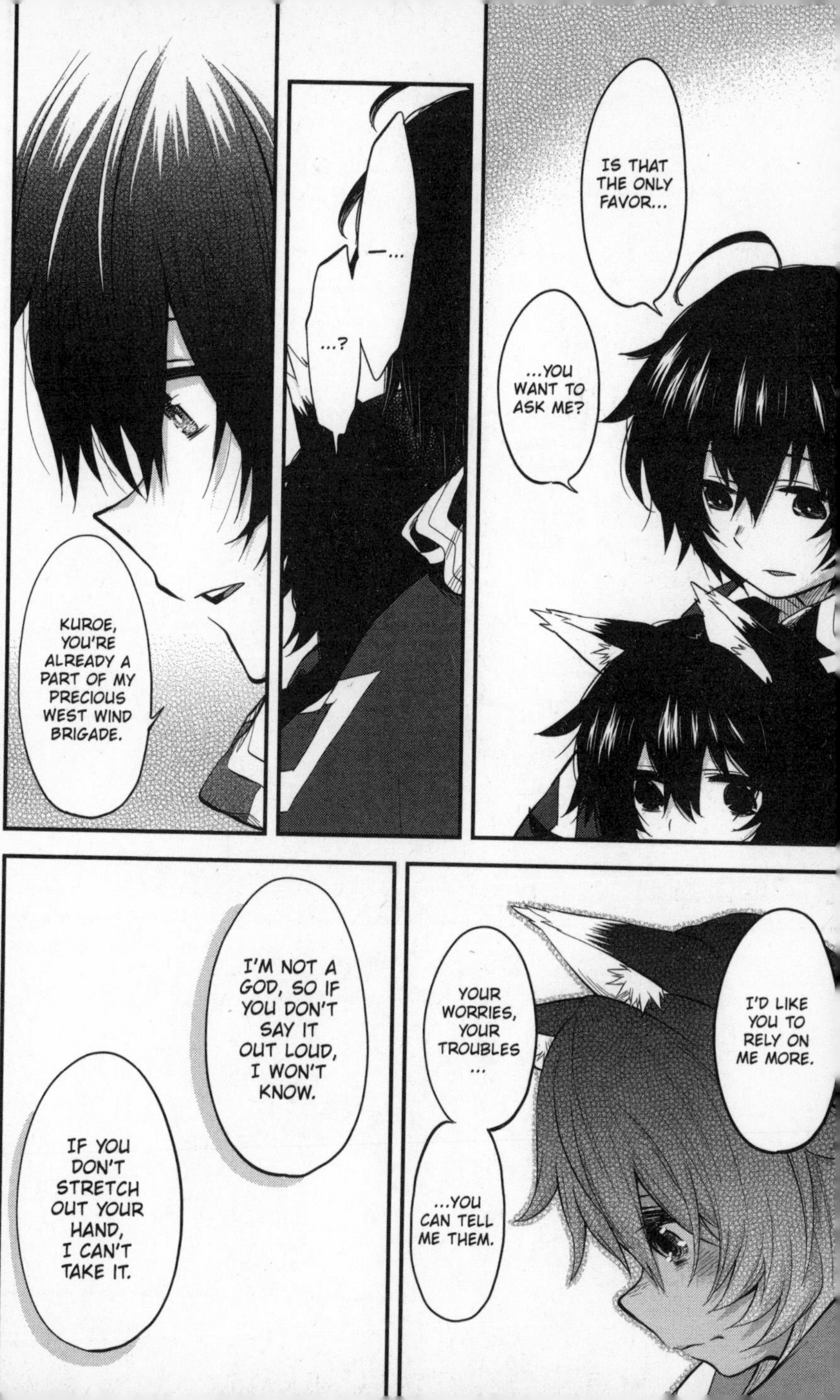
IS THAT THE ONLY FAVOR...
...YOU WANT TO ASK ME?
—...
...?
KUROE, YOU'RE ALREADY A PART OF MY PRECIOUS WEST WIND BRIGADE.
I'D LIKE YOU TO RELY ON ME MORE.
YOUR WORRIES, YOUR TROUBLES...
...YOU CAN TELL ME THEM.
I'M NOT A GOD, SO IF YOU DON'T SAY IT OUT LOUD, I WON'T KNOW.
IF YOU DON'T STRETCH OUT YOUR HAND, I CAN'T TAKE IT.

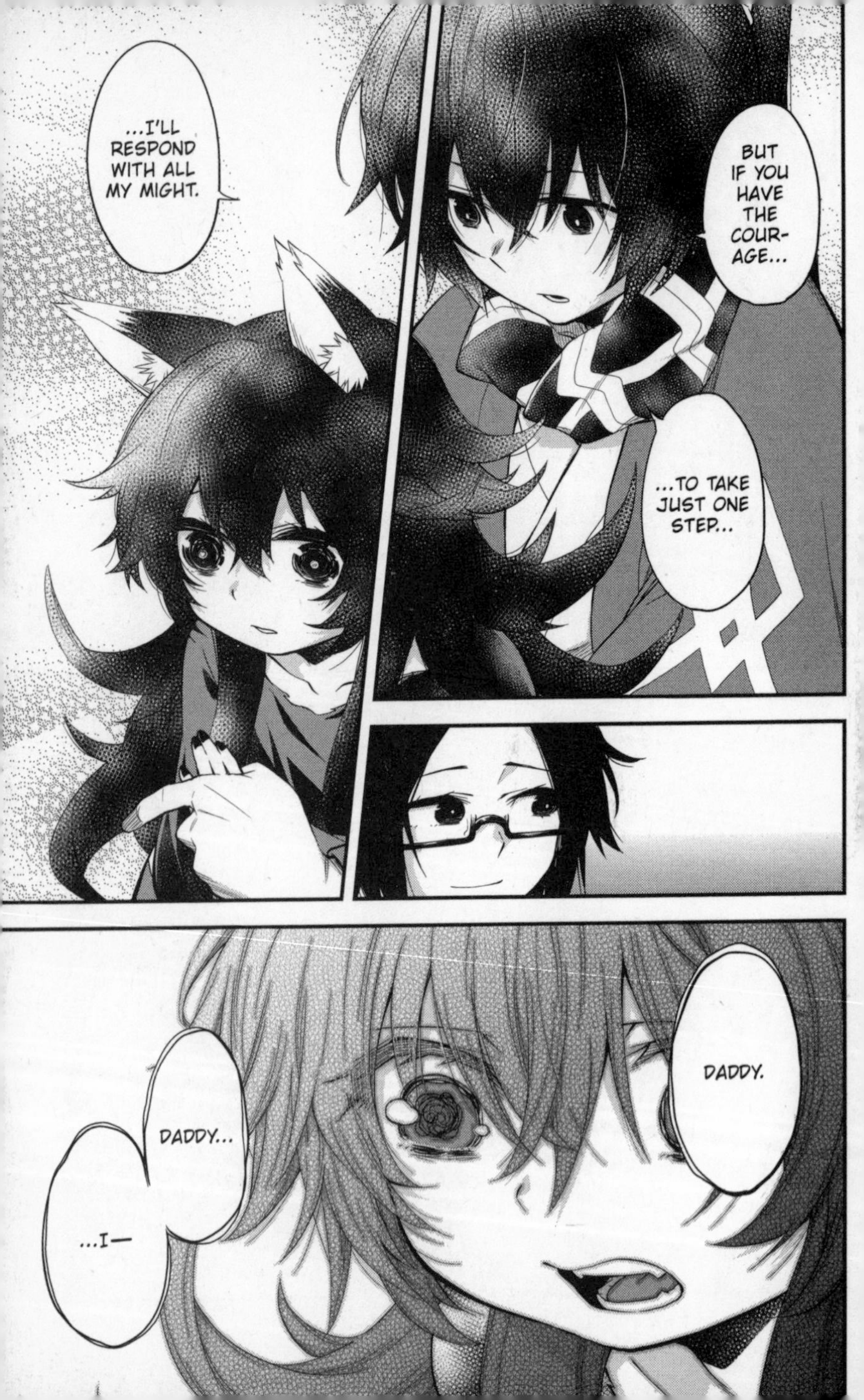
BUT IF YOU HAVE THE COURAGE...
...TO TAKE JUST ONE STEP...
...I'LL RESPOND WITH ALL MY MIGHT.
DADDY.
DADDY...
...I—

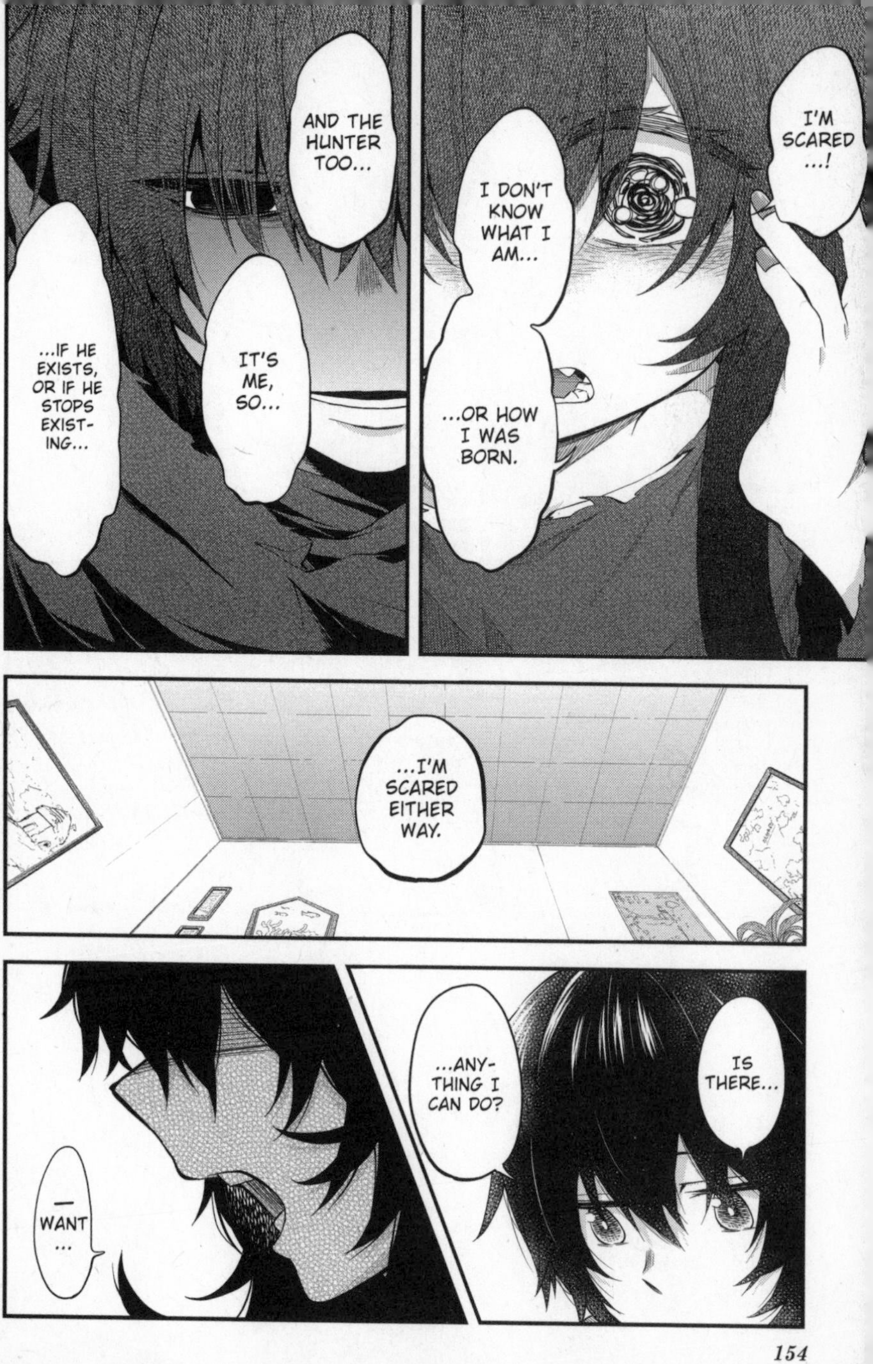
I'M SCARED ...!
I DON'T KNOW WHAT I AM...
...OR HOW I WAS BORN.
AND THE HUNTER TOO...
IT'S ME, SO...
...IF HE EXISTS, OR IF HE STOPS EXIST-ING...
...I'M SCARED EITHER WAY.
IS THERE...
...ANY-THING I CAN DO?
—WANT ...

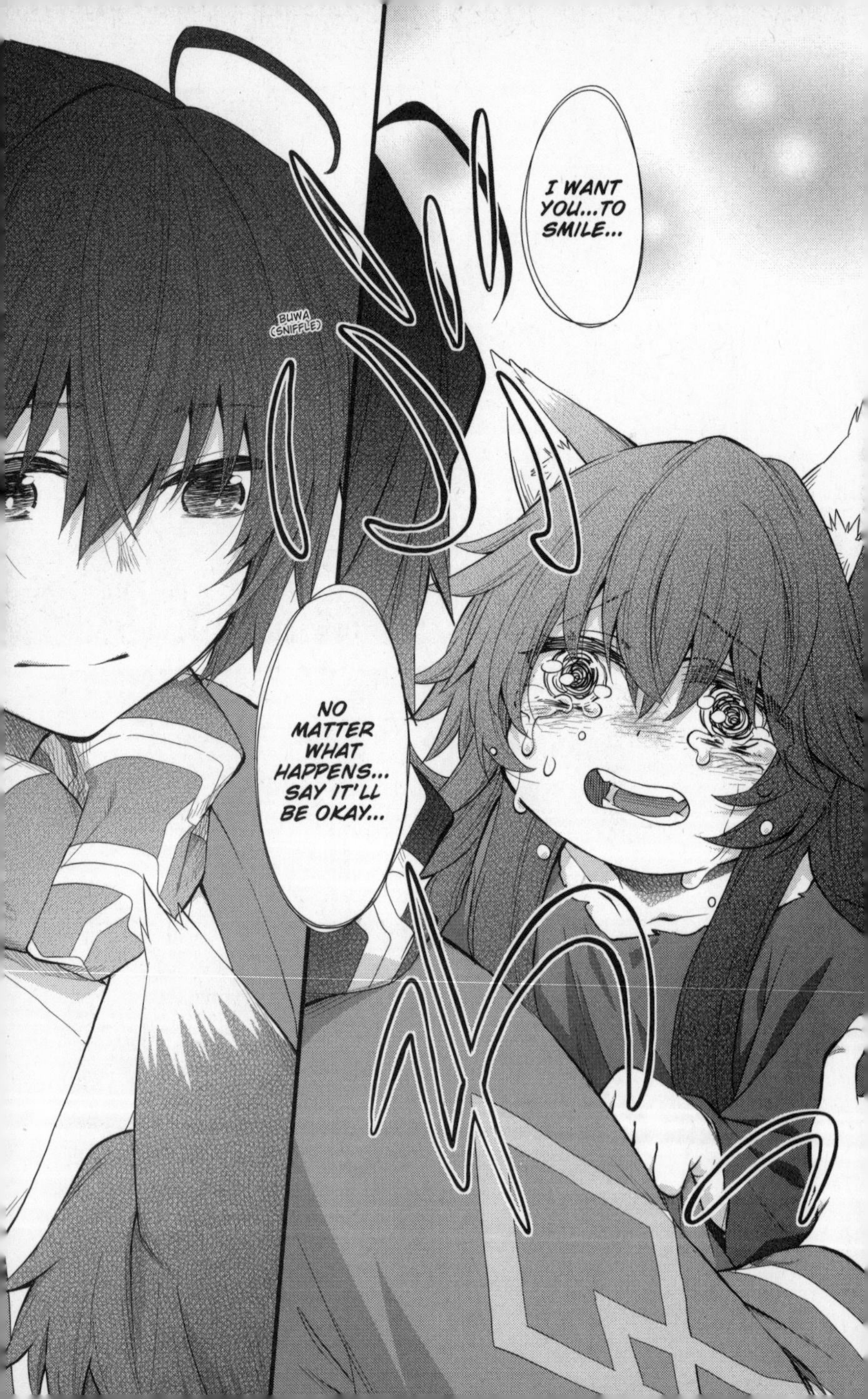
I WANT YOU...TO SMILE...
BUWA (SNIFFLE)
NO MATTER WHAT HAPPENS... SAY IT'LL BE OKAY...

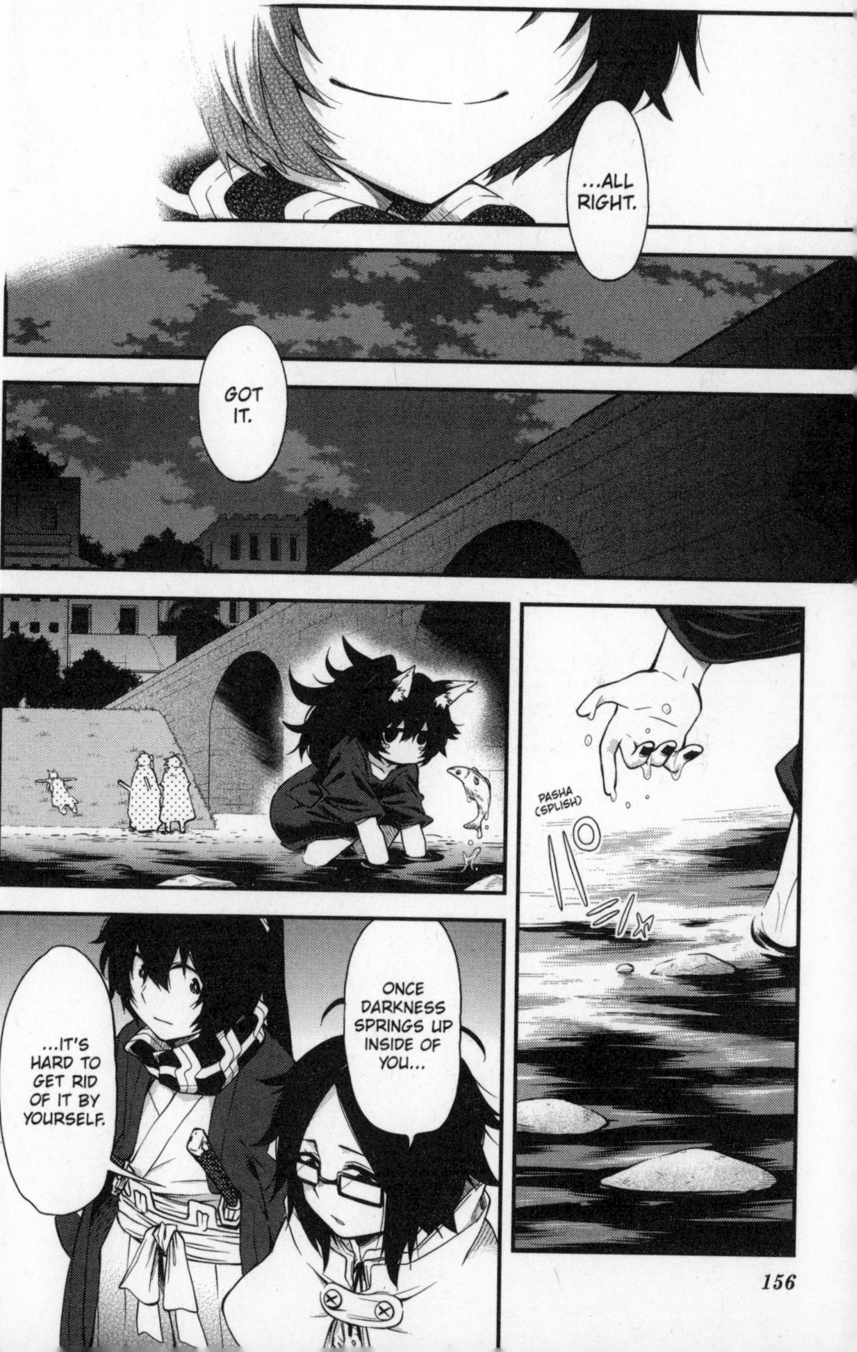
...ALL RIGHT.
GOT IT.
PASHA (SPLISH)
ONCE DARKNESS SPRINGS UP INSIDE OF YOU...
...IT'S HARD TO GET RID OF IT BY YOURSELF.

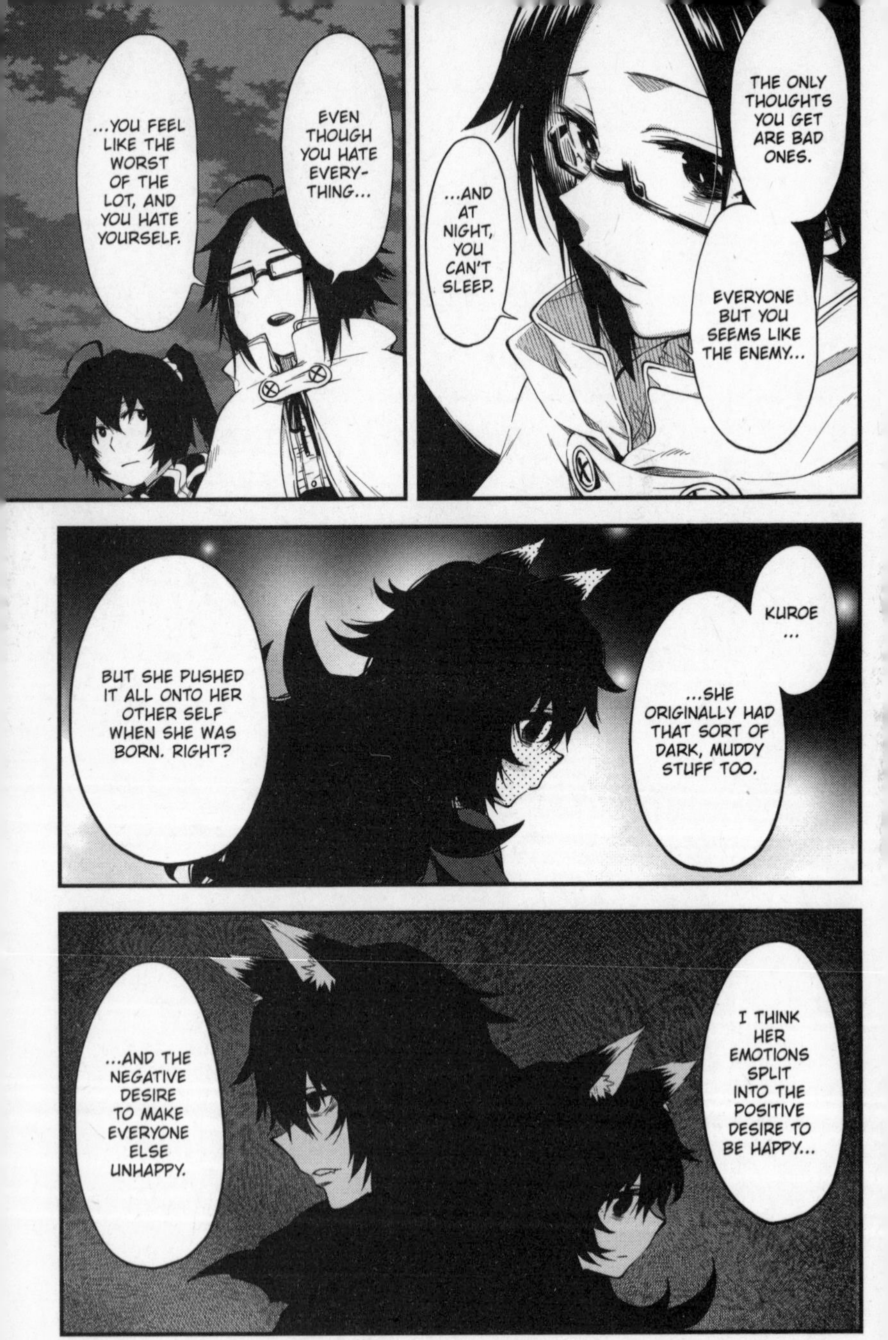
THE ONLY THOUGHTS YOU GET ARE BAD ONES.
EVERYONE BUT YOU SEEMS LIKE THE ENEMY...
...AND AT NIGHT, YOU CAN'T SLEEP.
EVEN THOUGH YOU HATE EVERY-THING...
...YOU FEEL LIKE THE WORST OF THE LOT, AND YOU HATE YOURSELF.
KUROE ...
...SHE ORIGINALLY HAD THAT SORT OF DARK, MUDDY STUFF TOO.
BUT SHE PUSHED IT ALL ONTO HER OTHER SELF WHEN SHE WAS BORN. RIGHT?
I THINK HER EMOTIONS SPLIT INTO THE POSITIVE DESIRE TO BE HAPPY...
...AND THE NEGATIVE DESIRE TO MAKE EVERYONE ELSE UNHAPPY.

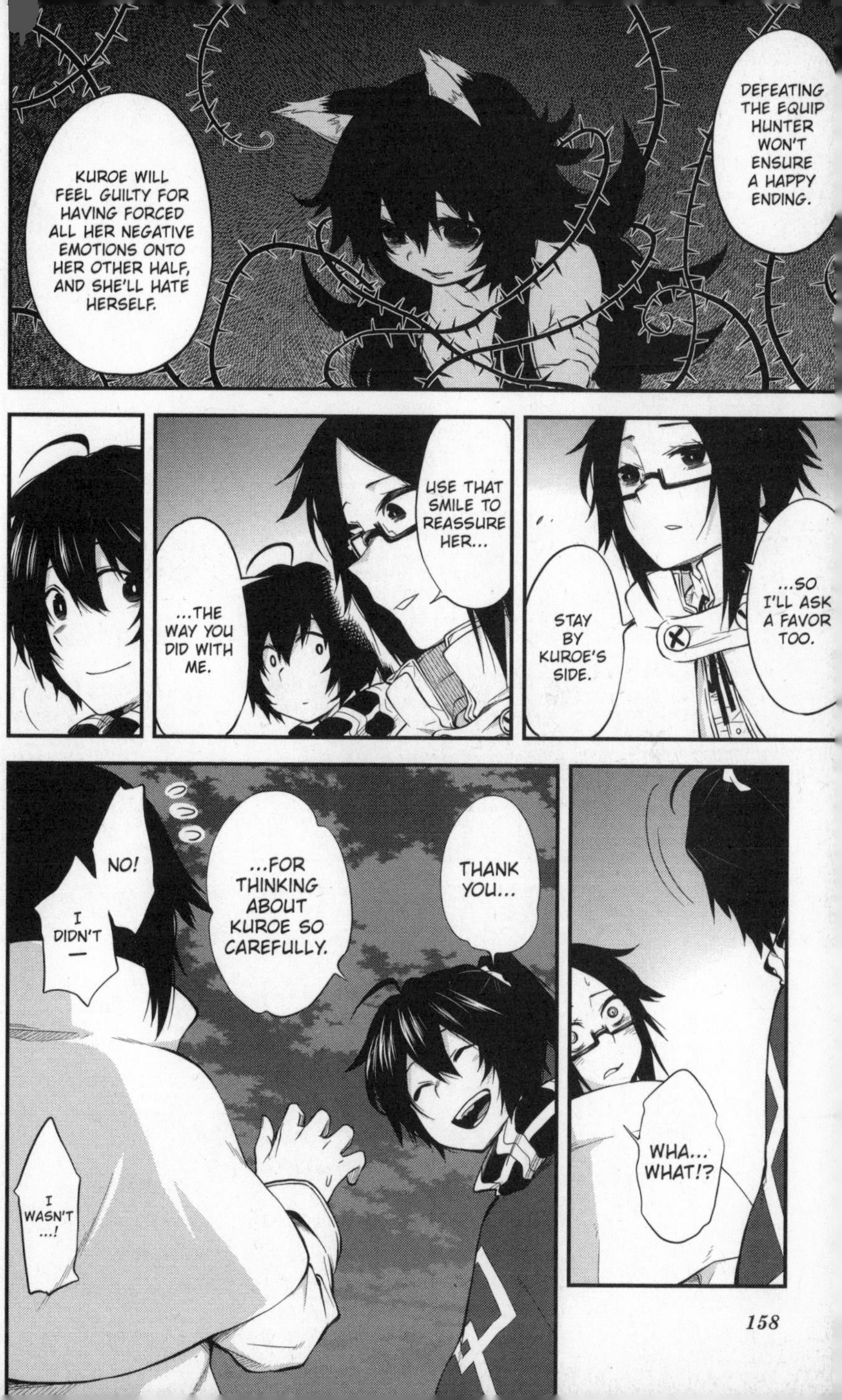
DEFEATING THE EQUIP HUNTER WON'T ENSURE A HAPPY ENDING.
KUROE WILL FEEL GUILTY FOR HAVING FORCED ALL HER NEGATIVE EMOTIONS ONTO HER OTHER HALF, AND SHE'LL HATE HERSELF.
...SO I'LL ASK A FAVOR TOO.
STAY BY KUROE'S SIDE.
USE THAT SMILE TO REASSURE HER...
...THE WAY YOU DID WITH ME.
WHA... WHAT!?
THANK YOU...
...FOR THINKING ABOUT KUROE SO CAREFULLY.
NO!
I DIDN'T —
I WASN'T ...!

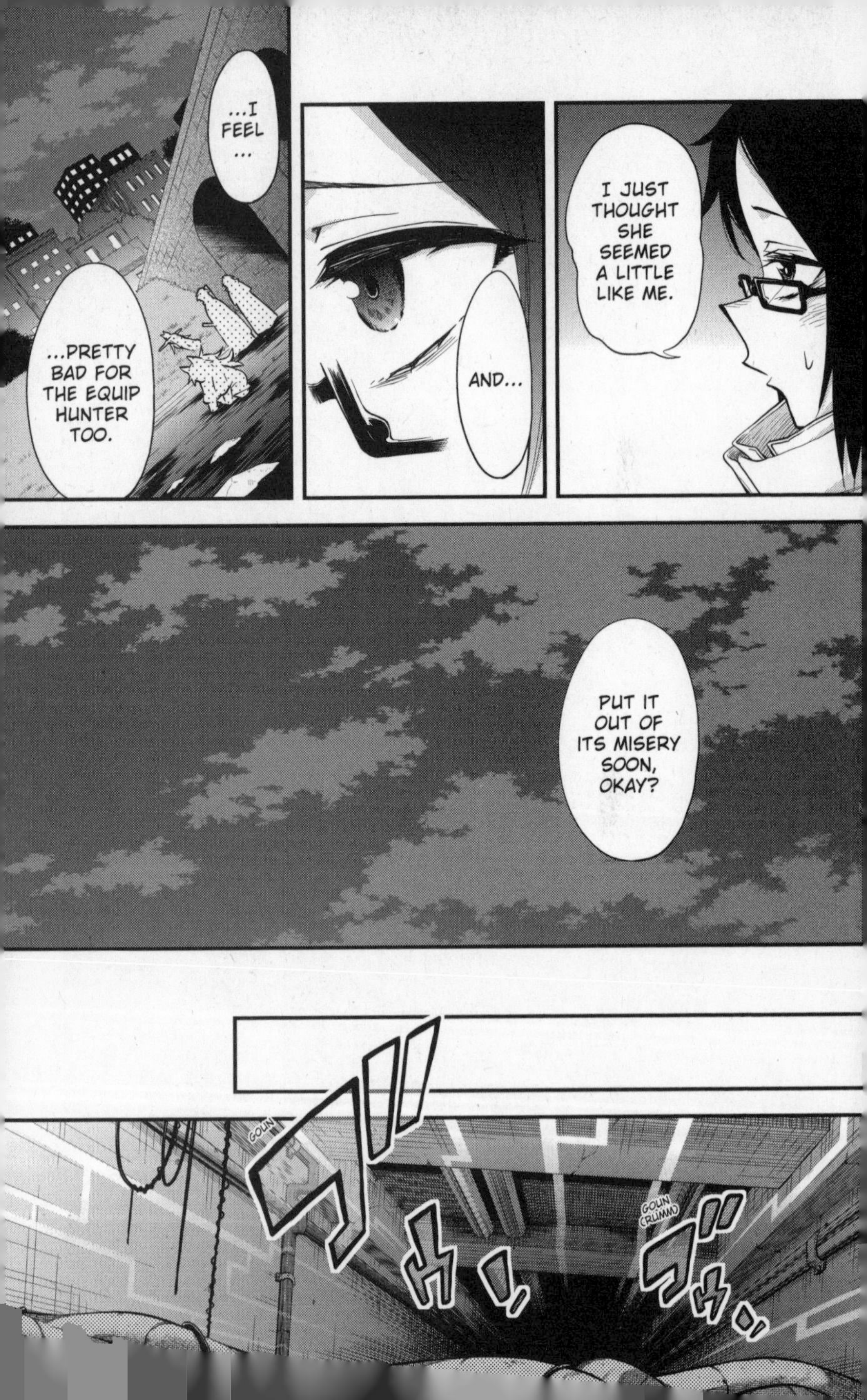
I JUST THOUGHT SHE SEEMED A LITTLE LIKE ME.
AND...
...I FEEL...
...PRETTY BAD FOR THE EQUIP HUNTER TOO.
PUT IT OUT OF ITS MISERY SOON, OKAY?
GOUN
GOUN (RUMM)

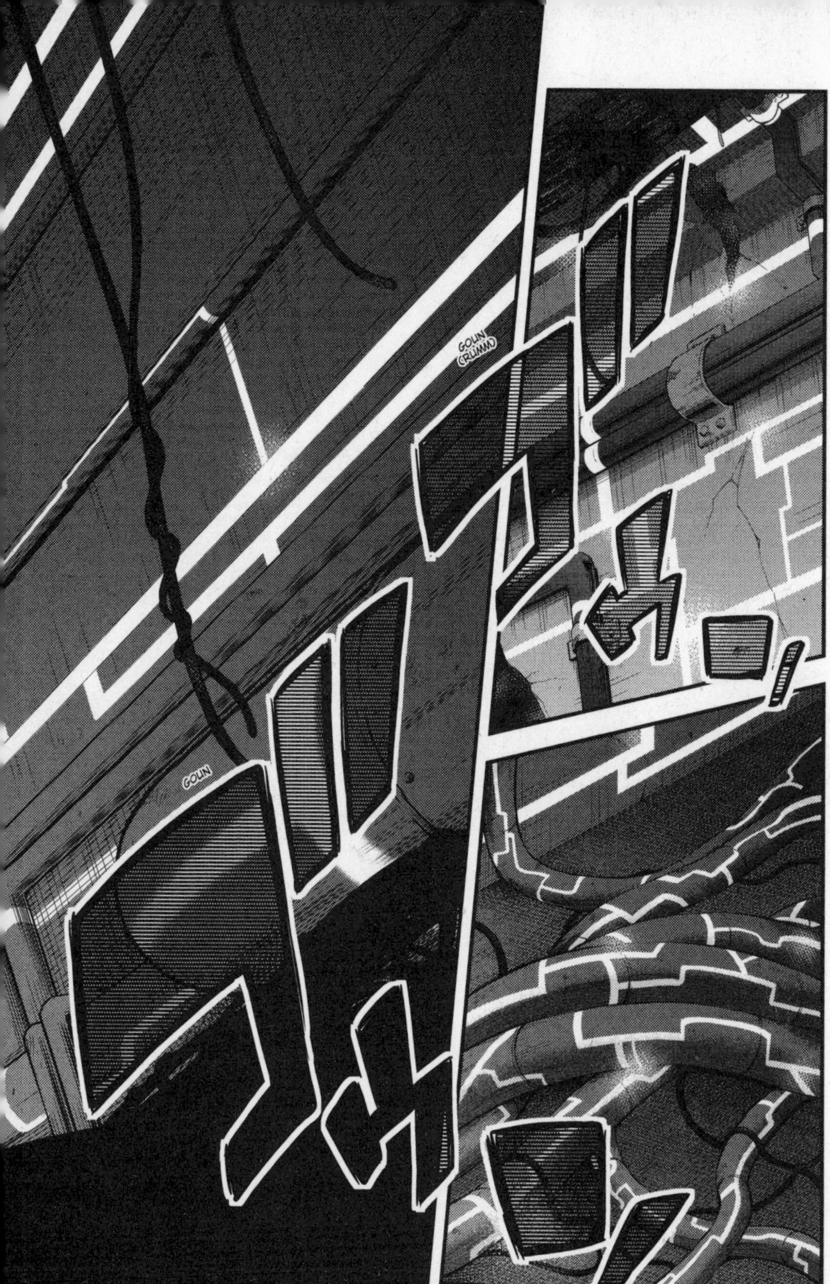
GOUN (RUMM)
GOUN

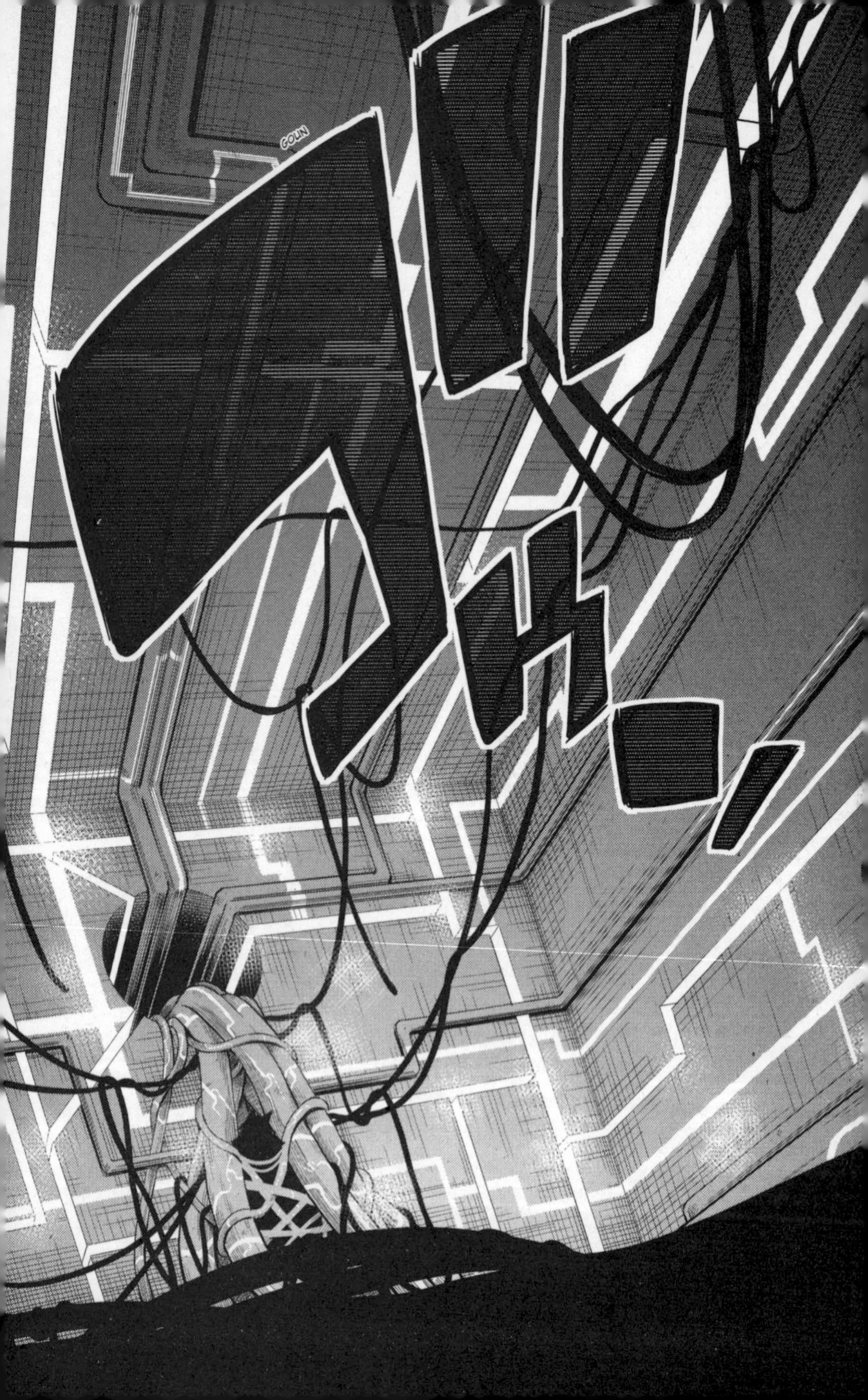
GOUN

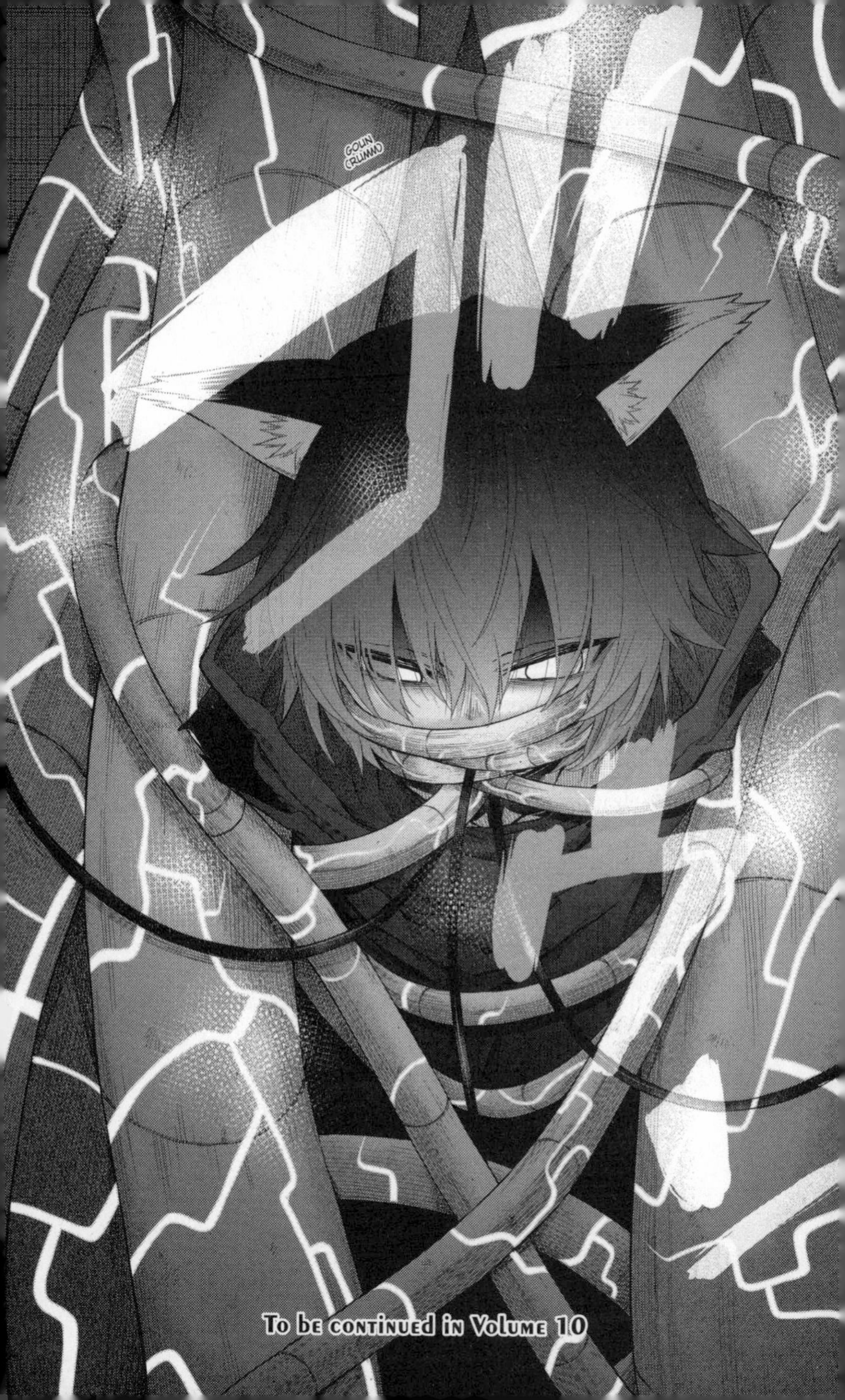
GOUN (CRUMM)
To be continued in Volume 10

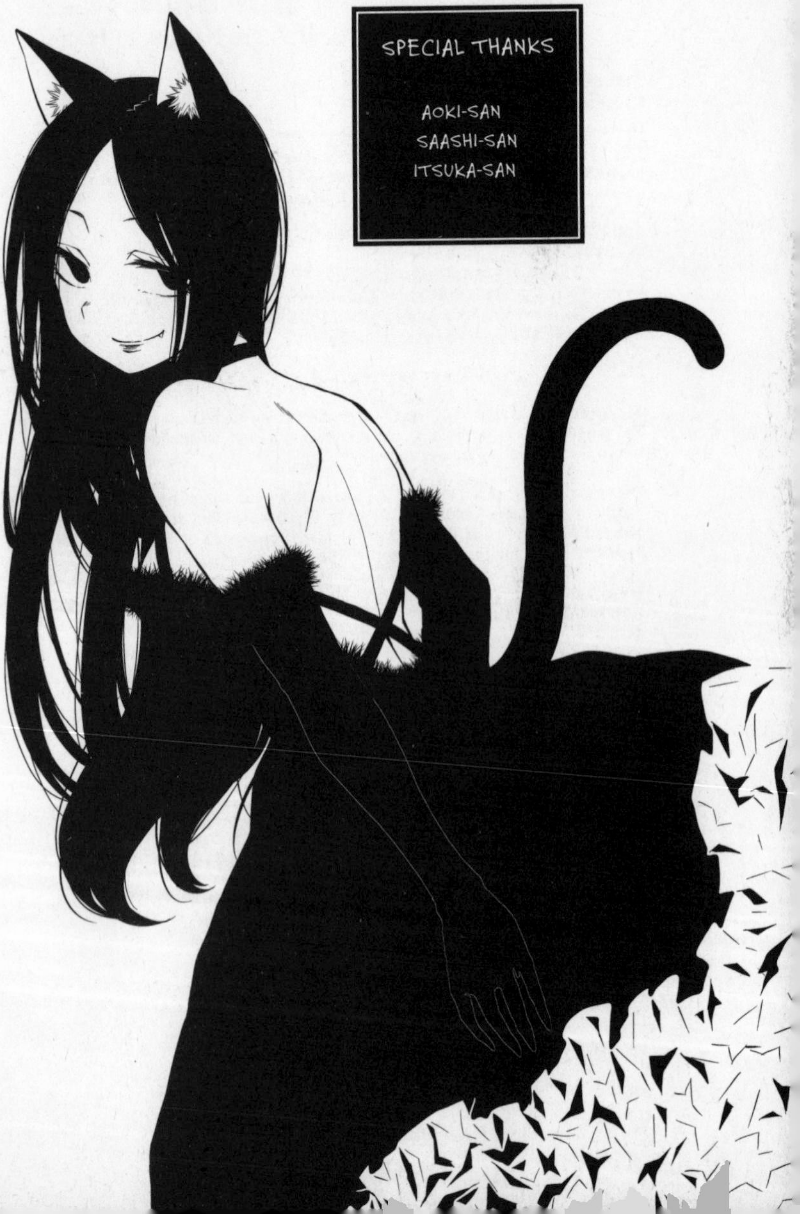
SPECIAL THANKS
AOKI-SAN
SAASHI-SAN
ITSUKA-SAN

LOG HORIZON
THE WEST WIND BRIGADE ❾

ART: Koyuki
ORIGINAL STORY: Mamare Touno
CHARACTER DESIGN: Kazuhiro Hara

Translation: Taylor Engel
Lettering: Brndn Blakeslee

LOG HORIZON NISHIKAZE NO RYODAN volume 9
© KOYUKI 2017
© TOUNO MAMARE, KAZUHIRO HARA 2017
First published in Japan in 2017 by KADOKAWA CORPORATION, Tokyo.
English translation rights arranged with KADOKAWA CORPORATION, Tokyo, through Tuttle-Mori Agency, Inc., Tokyo.

English translation © 2018 by Yen Press, LLC

Yen Press
1290 Avenue of the Americas
New York, NY 10104

Visit us at yenpress.com
facebook.com/yenpress
twitter.com/yenpress
yenpress.tumblr.com
instagram.com/yenpress

First Yen Press Edition: July 2018

Yen Press is an imprint of Yen Press, LLC.
The Yen Press name and logo are trademarks of Yen Press, LLC.

The publisher is not responsible for websites (or their content) that are not owned by the publisher.

Library of Congress Control Number: 2015952586

ISBNs: 978-1-9753-5332-2 (paperback)
         978-1-9753-0132-3 (ebook)

10 9 8 7 6 5 4 3 2 1

WOR

Printed in the United States of America